Study Guide

to accompany

Microeconomics

Third Edition

Michael L. Katz
University of California at Berkeley

Harvey S. Rosen
Princeton University

Prepared by
Robert Rosenman
Washington State University

Boston, Massachusetts   Burr Ridge, Illinois   Dubuque, Iowa
Madison, Wisconsin   New York, New York   San Francisco, California   St. Louis, Missouri

Irwin/McGraw-Hill

A Division of The McGraw-Hill Companies

Study Guide to accompany
MICROECONOMICS

2 3 4 5 7 8 9 0 BBC/BBC 9 0 9 8

ISBN 0-256-17177-7

http://www.mhhe.com

TABLE OF CONTENTS

PREFACE: HOW TO USE THIS BOOK

This study guide is intended to supplement your textbook, not replace it. It can be a valuable resource to help you understand what is important in the text, and to test yourself to see if you have understood the material Professors Katz and Rosen present. If you think that you can get what you need by just using the study guide, you are wrong. You may learn the definitions and acquire a rudimentary understanding of microeconomics, but you will lose the richness and comprehension that will accompany a careful reading of the entire text. Instead, try to coordinate the study guide with the textbook and the lectures.

- Start with the textbook *before the lectures*. Note the chapter outline given in the book's Table of Contents. These broad section titles should give you an idea of the topics you'll be studying.

- Next, read the chapter opening in the text, *and* the chapter introduction from the study guide. Together, they will put the topic in context.

- Now go back to the textbook, and read the chapter in its entirety. Try not to let this reading extend over several days. There are coordinated ideas in each chapter, and you will gain more from the later sections if the earlier sections are fresh in your mind. But make sure you understand the material as you go along. Read to understand, not just to read. Underlining will help bring you back to important points, but your own notes will help reinforce the material better. Take notes as you go along, preferably in the margins of the book.

- As you read each chapter, use the progress checks to test your understanding, and take extra time with graphs and equations. Also, use the margin definitions to start your own glossary of terms.

- You are now ready to listen to your instructor. Go in and take notes, but make sure you listen too. If the lectures are coordinated with the textbook (as they should be) you will be well prepared. Note the highlights of the lecture, and do not try to get down every word. You can fill in the lecture with your understanding of the textbook. Ask the instructor to clarify those parts of the book you found confusing.

- It is finally time for the study guide. Each chapter of this guide is divided into 5 sections.

    i. A chapter introduction. This explains the purpose of the chapter with respect to the big picture of microeconomics.

    ii. An outline of the chapter, which highlights of the important concepts covered in the textbook. This is where you can see if you know what you should know after having read the textbook and listened to the lectures. The **boldface** terms belong in your glossary.

    iii. An application or case. True understanding requires that you apply the tools and concepts, and here is that opportunity. These focus on fundamental chapter concepts, often using real examples. You should think about this part of the study guide as a learning tool, not as an evaluation of what you know.

iv. Multiple choice questions. You have reached the point where you think you have learned the materials. Now you need a way to evaluate yourself. Twenty multiple choice questions are the first step. Make sure you know not just the correct answer, but *why* it is the correct answer. These multiple choice questions are useful for testing your basic understanding.

v. Problems, which test your ability to apply microeconomics. Identify the problem, then decide how to address the problem (for example, choose a graph or equation), develop the tool (draw the graph or state the equation), and analyze the situation (explain what your graph or equation says). Answers to all questions and problems are in the back of the Study Guide.

- Finally, review and ask the instructor to clear up any material you did not understand. Use your instructor's office hours!

I've outlined a fairly rigorous regimen. But the reality is, like anything else, learning takes persistence and hard work. Athletes can't goof off, cram all their practice into a few days before the big meet, and expect to do well. Neither can scholars. The payoff comes at exam time. If you work hard (and long) now, you won't need to cram for exams, and you won't really have to study. Just a quick review, and it's off to Star Trek!

CHAPTER 1. THE MARKET ECONOMY

Chapter Introduction

From post-World War II to the late 1980s, world politics centered on the tensions between Western countries with market economies and the centrally planned economies of eastern Europe dominated by the Soviet Union.. While much of the tension arose from differing beliefs about political and social freedom, the dominant productive power of the market economies led to the demise of the centrally planned economies in the late 1980s. As the former Soviet block countries developed into fledgling market economies, even the Peoples Republic of China recognized the value of markets even while suppressing political freedom,. Under Deng Xiaping's leadership, markets became China's accepted form of economic organization, and capitalism became the path to greater productivity.

This chapter sets the stage for us to study market-based microeconomics. Although not technical or detailed, this chapter provides a basis for future analyses used in the text. The market economy is the stage, and here we introduce the characters - households and firms - and the basic premise for interaction - supply and demand. Later in the book households and firms are developed in detail, and then we explore the various ways - market types - in which they interact. But here, in chapter 1, the basic plot of economic motivation and market roles first appears.

Chapter Outline

This chapter explains the basic foundation that drives economic behavior, discusses how economists use model as representations, and introduces how markets work. Economic behavior, or economic decision making, derives from **scarcity**, which means that **productive resources** are insufficient to meet the wants and desires of all the people in a society. Productive resources include **natural resources**, **human resources and capital resources:** all the things used as inputs in production. **Economics** is the study of how people and institutions allocate the scarce resources among competing uses. **Microeconomics** focuses on how households (or individuals) and firms make decisions and interact. **Macroeconomics** focuses on problems and issues facing the economy as a whole, such as growth, inflation and unemployment..

We can summarize economic issues in three questions:

1. **What** is to be produced?

2. **How** is it to be produced?

3. **Who** get the output?

The answers come by considering the **opportunity cost** of using resources in particular ways. Every time we produce and distribute something, the resources used to produce that something can never be used to produce something else; this **foregone** use defines opportunity cost. The outcome determines the **allocation of resources** across competing uses. Although these questions arise in every society, they can be answered by various structures. A **market system** uses independent actions by **consumers** and **producers** to determine resource allocation.

Market systems are complex, so instead of struggling to explain all the nuances and intricacies of the millions of participants, we use simpler representations called **models**. Models use **descriptive prose**, **algebraic equations or graphs** to represent actions and constraints, and from them we can derive basic rules of behavior. One of the most basic rules of economics is the **equimarginal rule** which states that the sensible decision making requires that the **marginal benefit** should equal the **marginal cost**.

Models are tools by which we do economic analysis, but we also must decide upon our purpose. We can simply try to describe what is happening, or we can try to evaluate and judge it. These two types of analysis are called **positive analysis** and **normative analysis**.

A simple model of a market economy consists of two sectors: **households** and **firms (businesses)**. Households own the productive resources in an economy. Businesses buy these productive resources from the households in **factor markets** to use as **inputs** or **factors** to produce **goods** and **services**, and then sell the goods and services back to the households in **product markets**. Households receive income by selling the inputs to the businesses. Businesses get the money to buy the inputs by selling goods and services to the households. The **circular flow model** of the economy represents the linkages between households and businesses.

Supply and demand models explain how activities are coordinated within each market. This model is relevant whether it is a market for factors or goods and services. Every market has two types of decision makers, **buyers** and **sellers**. In the factor markets, businesses are the buyers (who **demand** the factors) and households are the sellers (who **supply** the factors). In Markets for goods and services, businesses and households trade roles. Households are the buyers and businesses are the sellers.

Prices guide seller and buyer behavior in each market by conveying information about whether there is too much of a supply (in which case the price will fall) or too little of a supply (in which case the price goes up) to meet the demand.

How much demand there is for a good depends on four major factors:

1. The price of the good determines the exact quantity of the good that will be sought by consumers. The **Law of Demand** says that normally the **quantity demanded** and price are inversely related. If price goes up, the quantity demanded goes down. This holds for all goods.

2. Income effects peoples' demand by constraining opportunities. Larger incomes allow more choices for consumption. Goods may be **normal goods** with demand that increases with income, or **inferior goods** with demand that decreases as income goes up. Most goods, for example housing, are normal goods. Inferior goods are harder to come by, but boxed macaroni and cheese is often used as an example.

3. Prices of related goods effect demand by being **complements** or **substitutes**. Coffee and doughnuts are complements. Coffee and tea are substitutes.

4. Tastes determine how much people like a good, which affects how much other opportunities they are willing to forego to get the good in question.

The **demand schedule** (or **demand curve**) shows the relationship between the price and the quantity demanded, *ceteris paribus*. *Ceteris Paribus* means "all else equal." For the demand curve, we assume nothing but price has changed. A price changes causes a movement on the demand curve, and is termed **a change in the quantity demand**. If the whole curve moves it is termed **a change or shift in demand**.

Three things determine the supply of a good:

1. The price of the good determines the exact quantity of the good that will be offered for sale in the market. Generally the **quantity supplied** increases as price goes up.

2. Prices of inputs effect the costs of production. If input prices go up, supply usually decreases.

3. The state of technology and other **conditions of production** help to determine the supply.

As with demand, changes in price are modeled differently than changes in the other factors that determine the supply of a good. The **supply schedule** (or **supply curve**) shows the relationship between the price and the quantity supplied , *ceteris paribus*. A price changes causes a movement on the supply curve, and is termed **a change in the quantity supplied**. If the whole curve moves it is termed **a change or shift in supply**.

Equilibrium occurs when no market participants have any incentive to change their behavior. In the market model, equilibrium is characterized by a situation that the quantity supplied equals the quantity demanded at a given price. If there is a larger quantity of a good being supplied than buyer demand, the price will fall. If there is too little supply to meet demand, the price of a good will increase. Within this context, prices play three roles:

1. Prices, and their movements, convey information about the relative quantities supplied and demanded, and how valuable a good is.

2. By imposing an opportunity cost, prices ration scarce resources. Only those willing to pay the going price are able to consume the good.

3. Prices determine incomes by rewarding best those people who supply the most scarce resources to the market.

An Application of Scarcity and Supply and Demand

You would think that bees would be free. After all, most people don't miss bees if they are not around: we normal citizens do not recognize any scarcity. In fact, when bees disrupt a picnic or other outdoor activities, most of us might wonder why such things were "invented" in the first place. But an article in *The Wall Street Journal* ("Wet Muddy Roads Make the Going Slow for These Itinerants," February 13, 1997, A1, Column 4) explains not only why bees are a scarce resource, but why the market mechanism is making the price of bees increase.

Bees are valuable because they are needed to produce the nations' crops. In the past, the supply of wild bees more than met farmers' needs for pollinating flowers. However, disease and habitat destruction have almost eliminated wild bees. Suddenly the fertilizing service that bees provide became scarce.

Question 1: Assume housing developments were responsible for the habitat destruction that killed wild bees. Explain the opportunity costs of maintaining wild bee habitats.

Question 2: Before wild bees disappeared, they were not a scarce resource. Explain what that means about the price of the service they provided.

Question 3: When nature provides a good, like wild bees, the quantity supplied hardly responds to price, so the supply curve for wild bees is vertical. Since the equilibrium price was zero, did the demand curve cross the supply curve? Graph this picture.

The scarcity of wild bees changed the way crops were pollinated. Instead of relying on wild bees, farmers needed to find a new way. Suddenly a demand for domestic bees arose.

Question 4: When wild bees disappeared, farmers were forced into a market for domestic bee service suppliers. Show graphically what happened to the demand for domestic beekeepers.

Rental rates for hives soared. Beekeepers responded by becoming migrants, loading their hives on trucks and, for a fee, transported them from farm to farm to help pollinate crops. "California's almond-growers alone will bring in close to one million hives this year, half of them from out of state." (WSJ, A4) Beekeepers from as far away as South Dakota brought bees to California for the almond season.

Question 5: When out-of-state beekeepers brought their bees to California because of the high rental rates they could charge, was that a change in supply or a change in quantity supplied? Graphically explain the difference.

Beekeepers have two major enemies; mites, which can destroy bees and the hives, and weather. About 20,000 hives were washed away in California last year, and thousands more were buried in snow in the Plains states. Wet weather in California made trucking the hives more difficult.

Question 6: Fighting mites and weather both increase the cost of producing and transporting bee hives. Graphically show what will happen to the supply of bees? Is this a move along the supply curve or a shift of the curve?

Question 7: Show graphically how increased demand and costs for domestic bees will affect the equilibrium price?

4

In fact, rental prices for hives in the California almond growing area went up to $42 this year from $26 last year.

Multiple Choice Questions

1. Michelle has been offered two jobs. The first job requires her to work 20 hours a week and pays $10 per hour. The second job also pays $10 per hour, but requires 30 hours per week. The opportunity cost of taking the second job is
    A. $100 per week
    B.   10 hours per week
    C. $200 per week
    D. $200 per week plus 10 hours per week.

2. The marginal benefit to Michelle from taking the second job instead of the first job is
    A. $100 per week
    B. $200 per week
    C. $300 per week
    D.   none of the above

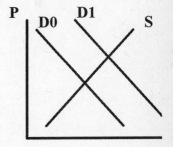

3. In the short run if, as shown, the demand curve shifts from D0 to D1
    A.   businesses would expand production, shifting out the supply
    B.   businesses would increase the quantity supplied.
    C.   we would expect the equilibrium quantity to fall.
    D.   we would expect the equilibrium price to fall as supply increased.

4. Your dentist probably tells you to floss every day. This is an example of
    A.   positive analysis
    B.   normative analysis
    C.   marginal benefit
    D.   marginal cost

5.   An equilibrium price in a market occurs when:
        A.   supply equals demand.
        B.   quantity supplied exceeds quantity demanded.
        C.   quantity demanded exceeds quantity supplied.
        D.   quantity demanded and quantity supplied are equal.

6.   Which of the following would cause the demand curve for an inferior good to shift to the right?
        A.   A drop in the price of the good.
        B.   A decrease in the price of a substitute good.
        C.   An increase in consumer income.
        D.   A decrease in consumer income.

7.   In a market economy, resource allocation is done predominantly by:
        A.   government economists.
        B.   individuals buying and selling goods.
        C.   private economists.
        D.   politicians.

8.   Which of the following is *not* a normative statement?
        A.   The homeless should get government provided housing.
        B.   Everyone should learn calculus.
        C.   If mortgage interest rates fall, new home sales should increase.
        D.   Interest on home mortgages should be tax deductible.

9.   In the simple circular flow model of an economy
        A.   the government sets who sells what goods.
        B.   individuals buy inputs from firms.
        C.   firms are the owners of capital.
        D.   individuals sell inputs to firms to use in production.

Questions 10-13 refer to the following graph about Bert's marginal benefits and costs of education:

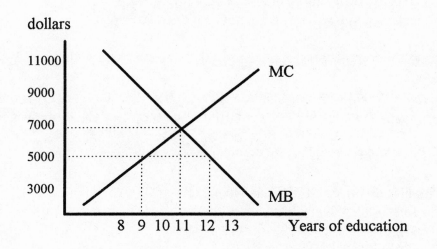

10. Given MB and MC how many years will Bert go to school?
     A.   9
     B.   10
     C.   11
     D.   12

11. Given MB if the MC of education were $5000 for every year of education, how many years would Bert go to school?
     A.   9
     B.   10
     C.   11
     D.   12

12. An increase in the wage rates paid to more highly educated people would likely
     A.   shift the MB curve to the left.
     B.   shift the MB curve to the right.
     C.   shift the MC curve to the left.
     D.   shift the MC curve to the right.

13. An increase in the wage that Bert could earn now would likely
     A.   shift the MB curve to the left.
     B.   shift the MB curve to the right.
     C.   shift the MC curve to the left.
     D.   shift the MC curve to the right.

14. Which of the following cause a demand curve to shift:
    A. a change in input prices.
    B. a change in tastes.
    C. a change of the price of the good in question.
    D. a change in technology.

Questions 15-16 refers to the following:

The demand for California wine is given by: $Q^D = 20,000 - 500P$ where Q^D is the quantity demanded per month and P is the price per bottle. The supply of California wines is given by:
$Q^S = 8,000 + 1500P$ where Q^S is the quantity supplied per month.

15. The equilibrium price of California wine is:
    A. $6
    B. $12
    C. $14
    D. $28

16. If sellers set the price at $12 per bottle:
    A. The quantity demanded will exceed the quantity supplied.
    B. The quantity supplied will exceed the quantity demanded.
    C. The market will be in equilibrium.
    D. The demand curve will shift to the right.

17. If one year, because of a wonderful grape crop, Washington State wines are seen as better than California wines
    A. California wines should increase in price, and the number of bottles sold should decrease.
    B. California wines should decrease in price, and the number of bottles sold should increase.
    C. California wines should decrease in price, and the number of bottles sold should decrease.
    D. California wines should increase in price, and the number of bottles sold should increase.

18. Due to a large crop, if the price of grapes falls in California
    A. California wines should increase in price, and the number of bottles sold should decrease.
    B. California wines should decrease in price, and the number of bottles sold should increase.
    C. California wines should decrease in price, and the number of bottles sold should decrease.
    D. California wines should increase in price, and the number of bottles sold should increase.

19. Suppose the supply curve for oats slopes up and the demand curve slopes down. If medical researchers announce that eating oats reduces the risk of cancer at the same time that frost destroys a major portion of the oat crop, then we know for sure that:
    A. the price of oats decreases.
    B. the price of oats increases.
    C. the quantity of oats sold decreases.
    D. the quantity of oats sold increases.

20. Most people don't floss every day because
    A. they disagree with their dentist about the marginal benefit of flossing.
    B. they believe dentists should not make normative statements.
    C. to them, the marginal benefit of healthier teeth is not as large as the marginal cost of the time it takes.
    D. the dentist does not understand the opportunity cost of flossing.

Problems

1. Suppose the demand curve for bees is very steep. If a mite infestation destroyed one-half of commercial bee hives in an area, would it have a greater effect on the rental rates for hives than if the demand curve was flat?

2. Strategic minerals, like chromium and manganese, have important functions for defense and national security purposes, but are difficult to mine and have very steep supply curves. If a new technology allows plastic to replace chromium for lots of uses, what should happen to the price of chromium?

3. Once again the news is reporting controversy among medical providers about the value of mammograms to women in their 40s. One primary issue is the lack of conclusive evidence that mammograms for women in this age group really have much value. Explain why economics would argue that until such evidence exists, general mammogram screening for women in their 40s is probably a poor use of scarce resources.

4. The controversy about mammograms is whether they should be recommended, but ignores whether women will actually seek mammograms. Explain the difference between studying the two types of problems.

5. During the 1970s the United States twice faced oil embargoes by middle-eastern oil producing nations. During the first embargo, federal law kept gasoline prices from increasing above a certain level. The result was long lines at gasoline stations, and rationing. When the second embargo came in the late 1970s, there was no restriction on the price of gasoline, but nor were there lines at stations or a need for rationing. Using the supply and demand graphs, show how the two periods differed.

6. By the early 1980s women found increasing opportunities in fields that were previously closed to them. As a result, fewer women trained as nurses, and hospitals found that they needed to increase the wage rates offered. By the late 1980s wages

rates for nurses had recovered to such a degree that men as well as women began entering that field. One of these situations was a structural change in the market, while the other was an example of a market moving towards equilibrium. Explain which is which.

CHAPTER 2. CONSUMER CHOICE

Chapter Introduction

Market economies are driven by the behavior of individual households and businesses. Behind the supply and demand curves of the market are households and businesses striving to make decisions that yield them the best outcomes. When they choose one alternative, they forego others, which gives rise to opportunity costs. For example, when a family decides to buy a new car, it may be giving up a luxury vacation for a couple of years. The equimarginal rule from chapter 1 provides a rationale for how people make choices. But economists' theory of how households make choices is much richer, and much more complicated.

Households face an almost limitless choice of goods and services that can be purchased, but a limited amount of money with which those purchases can be made. Money becomes the scarce resource that households must allocate over different uses. This chapter explains how consumers make choices to achieve the highest level of satisfaction possible, given that they must pay the going prices for various goods and services and that their incomes are limited. The theory of consumer choice is vitally important in three respects. First, it explains important aspects of human behavior in making consumption choices. Second, we will use this theory to derive household demand curves for goods and services and household supply curves of factors of production. Finally, it provides a tool to measure the consequences, both positive and normative, of various interventions in the market economy.

Chapter Outline

This chapter discusses how people make decisions about what to buy and how much of it to buy, given their incomes and the prices of various **goods**. Typical consumers do not have enough time or income to consume everything they might want. We represent consumers' choice by comparing what they want to do **(tastes)**, with what they can do, given limited budgets called **budget constraints**.

A simple model explains tastes by using assumptions that make the analysis manageable. We use this model to explain a consumer's choice among different **bundles of goods**. The model of tastes assumes three principles that help characterize the consumer as **rational.** That is, individuals must act logically for the model to accurately predict behavior. These assumptions about tastes are:

1. *Completeness*; Individuals are able to identify which of two bundles of goods they prefer, or if they are **indifferent** between them. Individuals can rank bundles by preference.

2. *Transitivity*; Individuals' preferences are consistent, so the ranking of bundles carries over between different sets of bundles.

3. *Nonsatiation*; Individuals never have all their wants met. There is always something she would like more of. Thus, "more is better."

An **indifference curve** represents tastes graphically. It shows all the different bundles of goods that make the individual equally happy - thus she would be indifferent between them. All bundles on the indifference yield the same level of satisfaction. Normally, the nonsatiation principle implies that indifference curves have negative slopes and do not cross. Otherwise, more would not always be better. "More is better" also implies that indifference curves lying to the northeast represent higher levels of satisfaction than those lying more towards the southwest. Consumers want to be as far to the northeast as possible. The negative of the slope of the indifference curve is called the **marginal rate of substitution (MRS)**. The MRS tells how many units of one good the individual will give up for one more unit of the other good. For example, if the $MRS_{mj}=2.5$ then the individual would give up 2.5 units of milk (m) if given one more unit of juice (j). The implication is that the individual is equally happy with 2.5 fewer units of milk if he has 1 more unit of juice. Normal indifference curves demonstrates **diminishing MRS**. Such indifference curves are convex (curved) to the origin.

Tastes that violate one or more of the three assumptions will have indifference curves that differ from the norm. **Perfect substitutes** have constant MRS, and linear indifference curves. **Perfect complements** violate the assumption of nonsatiation. When goods are perfect complements, they are consumed in fixed proportions, and have L-shaped indifference curves. Indifference curves that deal with economic "**bads**," slope upward, and violate nonsatiation. Pollution and investment risk are two examples of economic bads.

Economists often assign values to different bundles. We call these scores **total utility** and use **utility functions** to relate a value to a particular bundles of consumption. Most utility functions are **ordinal**. We cannot make **interpersonal comparisons** of utility, which would be possible if we used **cardinal** utility functions. Since it is impossible to determine if one person's utility is greater or smaller than another person's, cardinal utility functions are untestable.

Budget constraints represent the scarcity that forces consumers to make choices. A **price taking** consumer faces a linear budget constraint of the form $I=P_xX + P_yY$, where I is the person's budget, X and Y are goods, and the P's are the respective prices. The budget constraint separates the **feasible** consumption sets - what the consumer *can* do - from the infeasible set - what is beyond the consumer's purchasing ability. The slope of the budget constraint, the negative of the price ratio, shows the rate at which the *market* allows the individual to trade one good for the other. Changes in **relative prices** cause the budget constraint to pivot. Changes in income, holding prices constant, cause budget constraints to shift parallel . **Nonlinear budget constraints** occur when quantity rationing or quantity discounts exist, or individuals face multiple constraints, like both time and income constraints.

Individuals maximize satisfaction subject to their budget constraints. **Interior solutions** imply that **consumer equilibrium** meets two conditions. First, the indifference curve must be **tangent** to the budget constraint. Because tangent curves have the same slope, when there is an interior solution requires that the marginal rate of substitution equals the price ratio. (Recall that the MRS is the negative of the slope of the indifference curve, and the slope of the budget constraint is the negative of the slope of the budget constraint so if the two slopes are equal, so is the MRS and the price ratio.) The second condition requires that individuals spend all of their income. In this case, the individual consumes some of each good. Tastes are reflected by the slope of the indifference curve. Thus, different people facing the same budget constraint may rationally choose different bundles to maximize their satisfaction.

Corner solutions result when the MRS exceeds the price ratio everywhere, or the price ratio exceeds the MRS everywhere, except at a corner when they may be equal. When this happens, the individual consumes only one type of good.

Economists often use **composite goods**, a representation of all goods but one, on one of the axes. Usually the units of the composite good are adjusted so the price equals one. Using a composite good allows us to use these two-dimensional diagrams to analyze an individual's entire budget.

The MRS may be represented using **marginal utility (MU)**. In fact, the $MRS_{yx}=MU_x/MU_y$. Thus consumer equilibrium is reached when $MU_x/P_x=MU_y/P_y$ which means that total utility is maximized when the marginal utility of the last dollar spent on each good is equal and all income is spent.

An Application of Consumer Choice

Most workers receive compensation as a combination of wages and fringe benefits. Traditionally, employers have set up what are termed fixed benefit plans, which specify exact amounts of certain benefits like health insurance, vacation time and subsidized child care. Employees have little or no choice as to what combination of benefits they can consume. They often receive benefits that have little or no value to them personally. For example, a young, healthy, single individual without children would get no value out of subsidized child care and probably little from comprehensive health insurance. However, one of the newer ideas in employee compensation, flexible benefits plans, allow workers to get more value out of their compensation.

Question 1:   If a worker has no children, what is his marginal utility from employer subsidized child care? What would his indifference curve look like?

The graph to the right illustrates how traditional fixed benefits plans cost workers in total utility. On the vertical axis we put wages, which works perfectly as a composite good (since cash can be used to buy all sorts of things) with a unit price of $1. On the horizontal axis is health insurance, which for simplicity we will assume is the only fringe benefit.

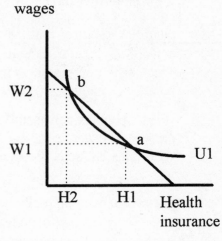

Under the traditional plan, all employees are given H1 units of health insurance, which cost the employer a total of $P_H H1$ dollars per employee. The total compensation to the worker is $I=W1+P_H H1$ where W1 is the worker's cash wages. For a little practice, suppose W1=$20,000, P_H=100 and H1=15. Then the workers total compensation equals $21,500.

Question 2:   Write the general equation for the workers budget constraint as if he could choose any mix of health insurance and wages.

Question 3:   What are the intercepts on the two axes?

Question 4:   What is the slope of the budget constraint?

Only by luck would the amount of health insurance given by the employer exactly match the amount the worker would choose if he made the decision himself. Fixed amounts of fringe benefits do not normally maximize an individual's satisfaction. As illustrated, the indifference curve through the point a at (H1, W1) is not tangent to the budget constraint that matches the total compensation I.

Question 5:   What is the relationship between the MRS_{WH} and the price ratio at point a (where the indifference curve and the budget constraint intercept)?

Question 6:   At point a, which has a larger marginal utility per last dollar spent, wages or health insurance?

Flexible benefits plans give workers choices to let them maximize their total utility. Under a flexible benefit plan, workers are given a budget equal to their total compensation, (I in the discussion above,) and are allowed to allocate that budget among wages and different benefits. If the plan is completely flexible, it is equivalent to receiving the total budget as wages, so W=I, and workers purchase benefits, sometimes through employers, just as they make any other consumption choices.

Question 7:   If the employer changed to a flexible benefits plan, what would happen to this workers consumption of health insurance and other goods (wages)?

Question 8:   Would the MRS_{WH} increase or decrease? What would happen to total utility?

Workers are not always hurt by fixed benefit plans. If a fixed benefits plan offers less of a benefit than an individual would like to consume, he can usually supplement it with an outside purchase.

Question 9:   What is the relationship between MRS_{WH} and the price ratio at point b?

Question 10:   Show how much of his wages a worker who receives a fixed benefit plan at point b (H2, W2) would spend on additional health insurance. HINT: Draw in the utility maximizing consumption.

Sometimes an individual who gets less of a benefit than he would desire would be better off if the employer offered it *if* the employer can get the benefit cheaper - like group health insurance which is cheaper than individual health insurance. On the same principle, employees might pay more to buy additional units of group life insurance.

Question 11:   Suppose the employee at point b could purchase additional health insurance, but at a rate that exceeded P_H. What would his budget constraint look like?

You can see that this employee would be better off if his employer would buy the additional health insurance for him, and reduce his wages.

Multiple Choice Questions

1.   The economic theory of choice assumes that a consumer's preferences are:
   A.   transitive but not complete.
   B.   complete but not transitive.
   C.   neither transitive nor complete.
   D.   both transitive and complete.

2.   When a person's preferences are transitive it means:
   A.   her indifference curves are straight lines.
   B.   her budget constraint has a negative slope.
   C.   her indifference curves do not intersect one another.
   D.   her budget constraint is tangent to her indifference curve.

3.   Perfect complements have:
   A.   constant MRS and L-shaped indifference curves.
   B.   constant MRS and linear indifference curves.
   C.   diminishing MRS and L-shaped indifference curves.
   D.   diminishing MRS and linear indifference curves.

4. To measure the marginal rate of substitution we can do all of the following except:
    A. find the rate at which a person will trade one good for another.
    B. find the ratio of the marginal utilities.
    C. find the negative of the slope of an indifference curve.
    D. find the negative of the slope of the budget constraint.

5. If the marginal rate of substitution is decreasing then:
    A. both goods are perfect substitutes.
    B. both goods are perfect complements.
    C. there is diminishing marginal utility.
    D. the price of one of the goods is increasing.

6. If income falls and all prices remain the same the budget constraint will:
    A. shift away from the origin.
    B. shift toward the origin.
    C. get steeper.
    D. get flatter.

7. Look at the budget constraint to the right. If the price of X goes up the budget constraint will
    A. shift away from the origin.
    B. shift toward the origin.
    C. get steeper.
    D.   get flatter.

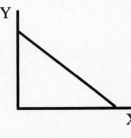

8. Ordinal utility functions mean:
    A. it is possible to make interpersonal comparisons of utility between people.
    B. a bundle that has a utility value of 50 is exactly 5 times better than a bundle that has a utility value of 5.
    C. the larger the value of the function, the more preferred the bundle is.
    D. there will be diminishing marginal rates of substitution.

9. Nonlinear budget constraints can result from:
    A. both goods being complements.
    B. both goods being substitutes.
    C. discounts on the purchase of large quantities of one of the goods.
    D. diminishing marginal rate of substitution.

10. Rational individuals make consumption choices based on
    A. relative prices and relative income.
    B. absolute prices and relative income.
    C. relative prices and absolute income.
    D. absolute prices and absolute income.

11.   In a graph with $5 bills on the horizontal axis and $20 on the vertical axis:
  A.   the MRS will be 4 and the slope of the budget constraint will be - ¼.
  B.   the MRS will be ¼ and the slope of the budget constraint will be -4.
  C.   the MRS will be ¼ and the slope of the budget constraint will be - ¼.
  D.   the MRS will be 4 and the slope of the budget constraint will be -4.

Questions 12-14 refer to the following:

The price of grapes is $1 per bunch and the price of deli sandwiches is $2 each. Both Sally and Harry have $5 to spend on lunch.

12.   Suppose that, in equilibrium, Harry eats both deli sandwiches and grapes. At his optimal consumption bundle, Harry's marginal rate of substitution between deli sandwiches and grapes must be:
  A.   less than two.
  B.   equal to two.
  C.   greater than two.
  D.   equal to one-half.

13.   Suppose that Sally eats more deli sandwiches than Harry. Then Sally's marginal rate of substitution must be:
  A.   less than two.
  B.   equal to two.
  C.   greater than two.
  D.   equal to one-half.

14.   Now suppose that Harry gets $7 for lunch instead of $5, while Sally still has $5. Then if Harry now eats more deli sandwiches than Sally we can conclude that:
  A.   his marginal rate of substitution is less than Sally's
  B.   he likes deli sandwiches more than Sally does.
  C.   he has decreased the number of grapes sandwiches he eats.
  D.   his marginal rate of substitution has stayed the same.

15.   If a person satisfies the nonsatiation assumption, then a bundle consisting of one glass of orange juice and 3 bagels must be preferred to which of the following bundles?
  A.   two glasses of orange juice and 2 bagels.
  B.   no orange juice and 4 bagels.
  C.   one glass of orange juice and 2 bagels.
  D.   two glasses of orange juice and 3 bagels.

Questions 16-18 refer to the following graph of Diane's decision about lunch..

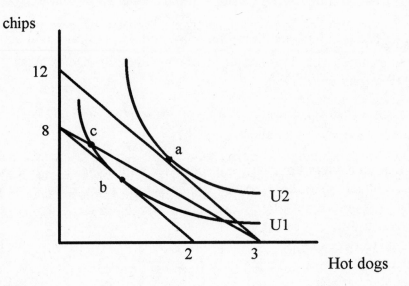

16. If chips cost 25 cents per bag and hot dogs cost $1 and Diane has $2 to spend on lunch:
    A.   her best consumption, given her budget, is at point a.
    B.   her best consumption, given her budget, is at point b.
    C.   her best consumption, given her budget, is at point c.
    D.   her best consumption, given her budget, is not shown

17. If Diane's budget constraint shifts from the line connecting 8 bags of chips to 2 hot dogs to the line connecting 12 bags of chips to 3 hot dogs then, *ceteris paribus*:
    A.   Diane's income increased by 50 percent.
    B.   the prices of both goods fell by 33%.
    C.   either a or b is correct.
    D.   neither a nor b is correct.

18. If Diane's budget constraint shifts from the line connecting 8 bags of chips to 2 hot dogs to the line connecting 8 bags of chips to 3 hot dogs then, *ceteris paribus*:
    A.   the price of hot dogs fell relative to the price of chips.
    B.   the price of hot dogs rose relative to the price of chips.
    C.   her income rose relative to the price of hot dogs.
    D.   the income rose relative to the price of hot dogs.

19. Suppose for Ben hot dogs and hamburgers are perfect substitutes with an MRS = 1. Hot dogs cost $1 each, while hamburgers cost $2 each. Then we would find that:
    A. Ben eats both hot dogs and hamburgers, but eats twice as many hot dogs as hamburgers.
    B. Ben eats both hot dogs and hamburgers, but eats twice as many hamburgers as hot dogs.
    C. Ben eats only hot dogs.
    D. Ben eats only hamburgers.

20. Tom divides his consumption between bagels and milk. Milk costs $1 per glass and bagels cost $2 each. In equilibrium Tom consumes both goods. Suppose he has chosen a bundle in which the marginal utility of his last bagel was 25 utils, and the marginal utility of his last glass of milk was 10 utils. The total cost of this bundle matches his income. Then:
    A. Tom is in equilibrium.
    B. Tom can increase his utility by consuming more milk and fewer bagels.
    C. Tom can increase his utility by consuming more bagels and less milk.
    D. none of the above is correct.

Problems

1. A college student prefers hamburgers to hot dogs, hot dogs to chicken, and chicken to hamburgers. Can a model of rational economic behavior explain these preferences?

2. Pullman, Washington is a college town. Over the past few years, the typical professor's salary increased 4 percent. During the same time, the price of housing increased about 20 percent while the prices of other goods, on average, went up about 10%. Show what happened to the budget constraint of the typical professor.

3. Time can be a constraint, just like money. At an amusement park, patrons often face this dual constraint. Suppose there are 2 types of rides, X and Y. X rides cost $2 per turn, and take 30 minutes per turn. Y rides cost $1 per turn, and take 15 minutes per turn. If an individual has $20 and 4 hours, graph her feasible consumption set.

4. Now suppose X rides cost $2 per turn, but take 15 minutes, and Y rides cost $1 per turn and take 20 minutes. Graph the new feasible consumption set. Can you tell how many of each type of ride this person will take?

5. Two sisters at a movie each have $5 to spend on candy and popcorn. The older sister buys 1 small popcorn for $2.00 and three candy bars for $1 each. The younger sister buys a large popcorn (equal to 2 small popcorns) for $4.00 and 1 candy bar for $1. Which sister has the larger MRS_{CP} and which has the larger marginal utility of popcorn?

6. A third sister spends all her money on candy. Compare her MRS to the price ratio of candy to popcorn.

7. Almost all workers are covered by Old Age and Survivors Insurance, better known as Social Security, which requires that they and their employers must pay a tax that provides some disability insurance and future retirement benefits. Many economists argue that workers could get a better return by saving on their own. But government policy makers are afraid that workers won't save enough, that instead workers would spend their wages on current consumption. Using a graph, explain what policy makers must think is the relationship between the price ratio of wages and Social Security and the MRS_{WS}.

CHAPTER 3. COMPARATIVE STATICS AND DEMAND

Chapter Introduction

We all continually make consumption choices from among a seemingly limitless set of goods and services. Every time we go to the store, we must decide if we will have chicken or fish for dinner, whether that expensive new shirt is worth the cost, or if we would rather go bowling or to a movie on Saturday night, or just stay home and "veg out." And we do it almost seamlessly. Prices change, so does our budget, and although we may hesitate sometimes and splurge at other times, our consumption decisions incorporate these seemingly endless changes.

We repeat this process time and time again. We also get quite good at it. One day we go to the supermarket and steak is $4 a pound while ground beef is $1.50. Other times, steak is on sale for $2 per pound, and we make the decision to have the good stuff for once. Prices have changed, and we adjust our buying to reflect the changes. Similarly, we face changes in our budget constraints. Our Great-Aunt Martha, who always smells of rose water, visits and slips us $50 - an almost unbelievable increase in this month's budget. It goes towards some of those luxuries - a better brand of beer, or steak when it isn't on sale, or an extra movie or two. Again, we adapt to a change in our situation -- this time our budget -- with alacrity, knowledge and confidence.

In the previous chapter, we saw how households make choices that give them the highest level of satisfaction possible. Now, using a process called comparative statics, we see how households adjust their consumption to changes in relative prices and income. It is a natural process where we make liberal use of the *ceteris paribus* rule to focus on one change at a time. Comparative statics also provides the basis for consumer demand: the buyers side of the market that we looked at in chapter 1. We use it here to derive individual and market demand curves for a particular good, and learn about some measures that summarize the effects we can expect as prices and incomes change.

Chapter Outline

This chapter explains how we use consumer choice theory to predict how people and households adjust their consumption behavior to changes in incomes and relative prices. This process, called **comparative statics**, follows a three-step strategy:

1. Find the equilibrium bundle for the initial set of income and prices.

2. Find the equilibrium bundle after some change in income or prices.

3. Compare the two bundles.

Comparative statics is important because it gives us testable predictions about how people will react if their incomes change or if the relative prices of goods change. It is most useful to explore three types of changes: when the **own-price** of a good changes; when the **price of a related good** changes, and when the **budget**, which we usually refer to as **income**, changes.

Own-price changes means there has been a change in the price of the good we are interested in. Nothing else has changed, so except for the difference in own-price, it is a *ceteris paribus* situation. We learned last chapter that when the price of a good changes the budget constraint pivots out if the price has fallen, and in if the price has increased. By finding the tangency between the budget constraint and the highest possible indifference curve we can see how each person's consumption has adjusted to the price change. Although the consumption bundle has changed, tastes have not: the individual can now just achieve a higher level of utility than was previously possible.. After the reoptimization, the consumption of either good can increase or decrease. The **price-consumption curve** shows what bundles of goods the individual will consume as the price of one good changes. The shape of the price-consumption curve depends on the person's tastes.

To derive an **individual's demand curve** for the good in question, we simply note the quantity of the good she will consume before and after the price changes. The budget constraint implicitly expresses the change in price through its slope. By plotting the price change and concomitant change in quantity of the good in question on a new graph, with price on the vertical axis and quantity in the horizontal axis, we see the individual's demand curve for the good. Using comparative statics, we derive an individual's demand curve for a good from her indifference map.

Cross-price effects measure the impact of a change in the price of one good on the quantity demanded of another good. When two goods are **substitutes** an increase in the price of one of the goods leads to an increase in the quantity demanded of the other, *ceteris paribus*. This indicates that the goods satisfy similar wants or needs. **Complements** have the opposite effect. If the price of a good increases, the quantity demanded of a complement decreases, *ceteris paribus*. **Unrelated goods** are those for which a price change in one does not change the quantity demanded of the other.

Own-price changes move us *along* the demand curve, causing a change in the quantity demanded of a good. Cross-price effects tell us how one good's demand curve will shift if the price of another good changes. Thus, cross-price effects cause a change in demand - a shift in the entire demand schedule. When two goods are substitutes, an increase in the price of one will cause the demand curve of the other to shift out. If they are complements, the demand curve would instead shift inward. The shift of a demand curve is called a **change in demand**.

Income changes cause parallel shifts in the budget constraint. We use comparative statics to see how the bundle of goods has changed from this shift, again *ceteris paribus*. The **income-consumption curve** traces the equilibrium bundles of goods as income changes. If the consumption of a good goes up as income goes up it is termed a **normal good**. The consumption of **inferior goods** goes down as income goes up. When the budget constraint shifts, new quantities of each good are demanded. A graph of the relationship between income and the quantity demanded of *one* of the goods is called an **Engel curve**. Engel curves have quantity demanded on the horizontal axis and income on the vertical axis. Changes in income can change demand. If the good is a normal good, an increase in income causes the demand curve to shift to the right. Increases in income cause the demand curve for inferior goods to shift to the left.

When we use data on consumer demand we must be careful that we interpret it under the restrictions of *ceteris paribus*. When we compare the quantity demanded for a good from two different time periods, it is unlikely that incomes or the price of all other goods are unchanged. Thus, the quantities demanded we are trying to compare are probably not on the same demand curve.

Market demand shows the relationship between a commodity's price and the quantity demanded by all buyers in the market, *ceteris paribus*. We find it by the **horizontal summation** of individual demand curves. Even if a few individuals have erratic consumption, if most people follow the normal behavior implicit in the theory of choice, market demand will slope downward.

Comparative statics is useful for understanding real-world policy issues such as government welfare programs. **In-kind transfers** end up being equal to changes in income. There is a parallel shift out of the budget constraint. However, comparative statics allows us to see that while some people may be indifferent between getting cash and goods in-kind, others would definitely prefer getting cash. By making charitable giving tax deductible, the price of charity has gone down. There is a pivot in the budget constraint.

Elasticities are simple numerical measures that explain how the quantity demanded responds to various changes. When an elasticity has a large value it means that the quantity demanded is *very* responsive to the change. If it has a small value, quantity demanded is unresponsive to the change. The **price elasticity of demand** measures how responsive quantity demanded is to own-price changes. It has the formula

$$o_p = -\%\Delta X/\%\Delta p = -(\Delta X/X) \div (\Delta p/p) = -(\Delta X/\Delta p) \div (p/X)$$

where $\%\Delta$ means percentage change, X is the quantity demanded of the good, and p is its price. Because demand slopes downward, the negative sign makes the price elasticity positive. As o_p increases in value, the quantity demanded is more responsive to price. Another formula for o_p is known as the **point elasticity of demand.** Since $\Delta X/\Delta p$ is the inverse of the slope of the demand curve it has the form

$$o_p = -(1/s) \div (p/X)$$

where s is the slope of the demand curve. The **arc elasticity of demand** uses the averages of the old and new price and quantity in the formula. Vertical demand curves have $o_p = 0$. Horizontal demand curves have $o_p = \infty$. When demand curves are linear, elasticity is zero. When price is zero, elasticity approaches infinity as price approaches the vertical intercept. At its midpoint, a linear demand curve has an elasticity equal to one.

Using the price elasticity of demand, we can predict how the **total expenditure** on a good changes when its price changes. When demand is price inelastic, $o_p < 1$, and a decrease in price will lower total expenditure. When $o_p > 1$ demand is elastic, total expenditure goes up when the good's price decreases. Unit elastic means $o_p = 1$, and changes in price leave total expenditure unchanged. Elasticity depends on; the presence or absence of close substitutes for a commodity, how large a share of a person's total budget the good takes, and what the time frame is.

Two other important elasticities are the **cross-price elasticity of demand** and the **income elasticity of demand**. The cross-price elasticity of demand for good X with respect to the price of good Y is given by

$$o_{xy} = \%\Delta X / \%\Delta p_y$$

where p_y is the price of Y. Goods that are complements have a negative cross-price elasticity. Substitutes have a positive cross-price elasticity. The income elasticity is given by

$$o_I = \%\Delta X / \%\Delta I$$

where I stands for income. **Luxury goods** have an income elasticity of demand that exceeds one.

The appendix to chapter 3 uses calculus and the **Lagrange method** to find the consumer's equilibrium. The **Lagrangian formula** is a statement of the utility function and the budget constraint all in one. We find the **first order necessary conditions** by taking the **derivatives** of the Lagrangian formula with respect to the goods and the **Lagrangian multiplier.** The Lagrangian multiplier is the **marginal utility of income**. You can find the demand curves by solving the **first order necessary conditions** for optimization.

An Application of Comparative Statics and Demand

Sometimes demand just doesn't make sense. That might be your first reaction to the news that caviar, along with martinis and cigars, is back.   An article in *The Wall Street Journal* ("The '80s are Gone, But Caviar is Back, September 6, 1996, B1, Column 3) explains why salty eggs of this prehistoric fish are enjoying increasing popularity at some of the nations top restaurants. Nightspots and boutiques in New York, Atlanta, Washington and Miami report surging demand even as the price goes up. Celebrities from Sharon Stone to Madonna to Larry King and Art Buchwald seem to be leading the way.

So why does caviar seem to go against the standard notion that demand curves slope downward? Well, it probably doesn't. For most of us, with limited incomes and rational behavior, if the price of caviar increases we'll consume less of it after the price goes up, assuming we every had consumed any.

Question 1:   Suppose you indulged in 2 ounces of caviar a year. If the price of top grade caviar increases to $45 from $30 for a 1 ounce jar, show graphically how your consumption of other goods would change if you moved to one jar per year.

Question 2:   Now suppose you decide to keep consuming 2 ounces of caviar, even though the price is higher. Graph your price-consumption line and your demand curve. What is the slope of the price-consumption line?

Question 3:   Suppose your personal demand for caviar is unit elastic. How much caviar would you consume per year after the price has changed? Assume you can buy parts of a jar.

The point of the article is that people are buying more and more caviar even as the price increases.

Question 4:   Graph the price-consumption line for a person who buys more caviar as the price goes up. What happens to the consumption of other goods. What is the slope of the price-consumption line?

One reason given for caviar's return is that the rich and nouveax riche have returned to exclusive, exotic and exorbitantly priced goods that reject the austerity of the early 1990s. Brooke Gilbert, a 25-year-old woman from New York claims to "...like it because it is expensive." Her brother Cary likes his caviar with brie and champagne.

Question 5:   Ms. Gilbert indicates a change in tastes is somewhat behind the resurgence of caviar. Graphically show how indifference curves must have moved, even if prices and incomes were the same.

Question 6:   Suppose the price of champagne goes down, and it is a normal good. Graphically show what would happen to the demand curve for caviar if most people are like Mr. Gilbert.

Question 7:   Vodka is the traditional drink to have while eating caviar. What is the sign of the cross-price elasticity of demand for caviar with respect to the price of vodka? Explain.

Another explanation for the surging demand for caviar is the booming economy, making people feel rich again. Clearly, the new demand may be due to changing incomes. But the demand for caviar has grown faster that incomes.

Question 8:   Graphically show how a change in income might lead to a change in the quantity demanded of caviar. According to the discussion in this case, can you say anything about the slope of the income-consumption line? Why or why not?

Question 9:   Would the slope of the Engel curve for caviar be positive or negative? Explain. What type of good is caviar? What is the lowest value the income elasticity of demand could have?

Reports from sellers and restaurants are that the quantity demanded of caviar has gone up 40% at the same time that the price has also gone up 50%.

Question 10: Does that mean the price elasticity of demand for caviar = -0.8? If not, why not? For this last question, you may want to think if *ceteris paribus* applies.

Finally, keep in mind that we have been talking only about the demand side of the market. It is possible that the supply curve has been shifting in at the same time the demand curve is shifting out. As we saw in chapter 1, one possible result is higher prices and larger equilibrium quantity.

Multiple Choice Questions

1.   If two goods are substitutes, the price-consumption line for the two goods slopes
    A.   upward
    B.   downward
    C.   is horizontal
    D.   is vertical

2.   For which of the following situations can we be confident that comparative statics yields valid predictions?
    A.   We compare the typical lunch purchase of students in 1994 to her lunch purchases in 1995.
    B.   We look at a student's lunch purchases on a day that she finds $2 on her way to school to the day before.
    C.   We look at a student's lunch purchases on a day that all the prices in the cafeteria are changed to the day before.
    D.   We compare the lunch purchases of two students, one who is from a wealthy family and one from a middle class family.

3.   The relationship between the _____ curve and the _____ curve is equivalent to the relationship between the _____ curve and the _____ curve.
    A.   price consumption / demand / income consumption / budget
    B.   price consumption / supply / income consumption / Engel
    C.   price consumption / demand / income consumption / supply
    D.   price consumption / demand / income consumption / Engel

4.   Market demand curves are the _____ individual demand curves.
        A.   vertical summation of
        B.   horizontal summation of
        C.   vertical difference between
        D.   horizontal difference between

5.   At any particular quantity demanded, the value of the price elasticity of demand
        A.   depends on the units of measure.
        B.   has the same value as the slope of the demand curve
        C.   determines how changes in quantity will change total expenditure.
        D.   determines how changes in price will change total expenditure.

6.   Suppose a bus ride costs $1. The transit authority raises the price of a ride by
        10%. The own-price elasticity of demand for bus service is 0.5. Then we would
        expect that:
        A.   the number of riders should increase by 50%.
        B.   the number of riders should increase by 5%.
        C.   the number of riders should decrease by 50%.
        D.   the number of riders should decrease by 5%.

7.   The price of bus service goes from $1 To $1.25 and the number of riders falls from
        5000 per day to 4000 per day. Then
        A.   the price elasticity of demand is elastic.
        B.   the price elasticity of demand is inelastic.
        C.   the income elasticity of demand is elastic.
        D.   the income elasticity of demand is inelastic.

8.   Coffee and tea are substitutes. That means the cross-price elasticity of demand for
        coffee with respect to the price of tea is
        A.   negative.
        B.   positive.
        C.   less than -1.
        D.   zero.

9.   Coffee and tea are substitutes. Milk and coffee are complements. Milk and tea are
        unrelated. *Ceteris paribus*, and increase in the price of milk should:
        A.   increase the quantity demanded of coffee and decrease the quantity
                demanded of tea.
        B.   decrease the quantity demanded of coffee and increase the quantity
                demanded of tea.
        C.   increase the quantity demanded of coffee and increase the quantity
                demanded of tea.
        D.   decrease the quantity demanded of coffee and decrease the quantity
                demanded of tea.

10.   Karen's consumption of Diet Coke increases from 26 six-packs per year to 52 six-packs per year when the price of Diet Coke falls from $1.50 a six-pack to $1 a six-pack, *ceteris paribus*. The value of Karen's arc elasticity of demand is:
    A.   1.675.
    B.   0.6.
    C.   3.
    D.   0.33.

11.   If a 5% increase in income leads to a 10% increase in the quantity demanded of orange juice, ceteris paribus, then the value of the income elasticity of demand for orange juice is:
    A.   0.5, and orange juice is an inferior good.
    B.   0.5, and orange juice is a normal good.
    C.   2 and orange juice is a normal good.
    D.   2 and orange juice is a luxury good.

Questions 12-15 refer to the following graph:

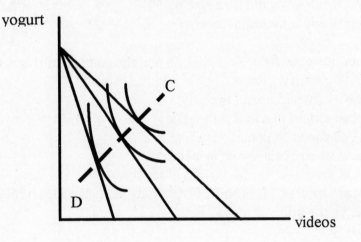

12. The line DC is:
    A.   an income-consumption line
    B.   an Engel curve
    C.   a price-consumption line
    D.   a demand curve

13. Videos and yogurt are
    A.   substitutes
    B.   complements
    C.   unrelated goods
    D.   luxury goods

14. The demand curve for videos is:
    A.   upward sloping.
    B.   downward sloping.
    C.   vertical.
    D.   horizontal.

15. The Engel curve for videos must be:
    A.   upward sloping.
    B.   downward sloping.
    C.   vertical.
    D.   horizontal.

Questions 16-17 refer to the following graph.

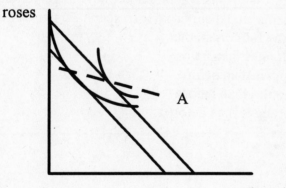

16. The Engel curve for roses must:
    A.   slope upward.
    B.   slope downward..
    C.   be horizontal.
    D.   be vertical.

17.	The income elasticity of demand for chocolates must be:
	A.	negative.
	B.	positive but less than 1.
	C.	positive and greater than 1.
	D.	zero.

18.	Food stamps can be used instead of money to buy food. Suppose Bill divides his income between food and all other goods. Food costs $2 per unit and is a normal good. Bill currently consumes over 50 units of food. If he starts receiving $100 a month in food stamps
	A.	his budget constraint will pivot outward by 50 units of food.
	B.	he will be equally satisfied as if he received $100 in cash.
	C.	he will be less satisfied than if he received $100 in cash.
	D.	will consume exactly 50 units of food more.

19.	At a zero price the demand for a good with a linear demand curve is 100 units. When the price is $10 per unit 45 units of the good are demanded. When the price is $10 the price elasticity of demand is:
	A.	inelastic
	B.	elastic
	C.	equal to 1.
	D.	equal to infinity.

20.	Tom's utility satisfies transitivity, completeness and nonsatiation. He views both apples and oranges as normal goods and treats them as substitutes. When apples and oranges both cost 50 cents Tom eats 2 apples and one orange per day. If the price of oranges falls to 25 cents, and Tom decides to spend $2 per day on fruit, then, *ceteris paribus*, we know for certain that:
	A.	Tom will eat more oranges than before.
	B.	Tom will eat more apples than before.
	C.	Tom will eat fewer apples than before
	D.	Tom will eat fewer oranges than before..

Problems

1.	If the cross-price elasticity of demand between hot dogs and the price of beer is -0.15, and the price of beer goes from $1 to $1.25, how much of a decrease in hot dog sales should be expected?

2.	An individual buys food and beer. Graphically show how the following three programs change an individual's budget constraint: a) a 10% decrease in the price of beer, b) a coupon which lowers the price of the first 4 bottles of beer by 50%, and c) a coupon good for 2 free beer.

3.	The adjacent states of Washington and Idaho both have sales taxes. In Washington the sales tax is 7.5%, but food is excluded. In Idaho, the sales tax is only 5%, but also applies to food. Is it possible to do a comparative statics analysis of the difference in the price of food using data from the two states? Support your argument.

4. Given a demand curve X = 1000 - 20P where X is the quantity demanded of the good and P is its price, find price elasticity of demand if a) P =10, b) P = 20, and c) P = 30.

5. A firm wishes to encourage its employees to get more education. It is considering two plans which would subsidize education. They are: a) $500 of free tuition per year, and b) 10% tuition subsidy for tuition costs. Assume education is a normal good. Evaluate both plans for effectiveness in encouraging more education.

6. The company chose the first plan of $500 of free education per year and found that on average the amount of education employees got went down. An economist suggested that maybe education was not an normal good for these employees. Explain how the economist came to that conclusion.

7. Suppose when Ann has an income of $100 per week, and she consumes 10 units of food and 10 units of clothing. After she gets a raise to $140 per week, she consumes 13 units of food and 11 units of clothing. Draw her Engel curve for food.

8. An individual's income goes up 10% but her spending on housing goes up 15%. Draw her income-consumption line and Engel curve for housing.

9. A public transit system charges $1 per ride and has 100,000 riders per day. It plans on increasing the price per ride to $1.20, and expects a 25% decrease in the number of riders. An economist suggests instead that they lower the price of a ride to increase revenues. Explain why.

10. A consumer has a utility function $U = 2X^{1/2}Y^{1/2}$, her income is 150, the price of X is 2 and the price of Y is 1. Find her consumption of X and Y. Derive her demand curve for X.

11. Find the change in her consumption if her income falls to 100.

12. Find the change in her consumption if her income is still 150, but the price of Y increases to 2.

CHAPTER 4. PRICE CHANGES AND CONSUMER WELFARE

Chapter Introduction

Government policies often effect prices dramatically. The textbook starts this chapter with the example of sugar. US and European governments restrict the import of sugar to protect domestic producers from foreign competition. Other goods also fall under similar protection. Almost no ice cream is imported into the United States because of import restrictions, and peanut farmers in Georgia and a few other select states are protected not only from foreign producers, but from farmers in other states, who are not allowed to sell peanuts to processors for peanut butter or candy. As a result, consumers pay higher prices for these goods.

Some other policies favor consumers. Federal and state subsidies for higher education reduce the tuition students must pay. Flood insurance, certain foods, and housing all can be had for lower prices because of government policies that encourage production or subsidize purchases. Even private business gets involved. Airlines reward frequent flyers with free trips and other benefits - essentially lowering the price of travel. And when car sales slow, manufacturers offer rebates to car buyers and dealers

But what do all these different prices mean for consumer welfare? In the previous chapter we learned how consumers react to price changes. Comparative static analysis determines demand curves. Generally as the price of a good fell, the quantity demanded goes up. Unfortunately, just knowing what happens to consumption does not tell us what happens to consumer satisfaction. In this chapter we address that question. We use the theory of demand and a deeper analysis of consumption choice to understand the welfare consequences of price changes.

Chapter Outline

This chapter uses consumer theory to explain the multiple effects a change in the price of one good has on all consumption. In chapters 2 and 3 we developed the **"Law of Demand"** - that demand curves slope downward. Another way of thinking about the "Law of Demand" is that when the price of a good goes up, the quantity demanded goes down, *ceteris paribus*. Although generally a good description, this "law" is not a theoretical certainty because price changes have *two* effects.

When the price of a good goes up, that good becomes more expensive relative to other goods. **Relative price** has increased. We show this by the pivot inward of the budget constraint. But also, a person's income is worth less. Additionally, when the price of a good increases, the feasible consumption set is smaller. People can buy less of everything. **Relative income** has decreased. The change in consumption that comes exclusively from the fact that the relative prices of goods has changed is called the **substitution effect**. The **income effect** is the change in consumption that is attributable to the effect that **real income** has changed.

32

   To examine the separate substitution and income effects we decompose the price change into two parts by the following method:

1. Determine the change in consumption that occurs from a price increase.

2. Restore sufficient income so that the original utility level is restored, albeit with a different mix of goods. This is what we mean by keeping real income constant.

3. The change in consumption holding utility constant is the substitution effect.

4. The change in consumption from the change in real income is the income effect.

Graphically, the substitution effect is found by locating the tangent to the *original* indifference curve that has the same slope as the new budget constraint. The income effect is the shift from that tangent to the new point of consumption on the new actual budget constraint. If the price of other goods (those not suffering a price change) is normalized to 1, the vertical distance is the amount of income needed.

   Since the substitution effect holds utility constant, we must be moving so the quantity demanded of the goods whose price has increased must fall. The substitution effect is always negative. The change in consumption holding utility constant is called the **compensated response**. The observed change in quantity is called the **uncompensated response**.

   The substitution and income effects together determine if the Law of Demand holds for any particular good. The substitution effect always has the quantity demanded of a good to decrease when the price goes up. For normal goods, the income effect is also negative. As the price goes up, the income effect indicates less will be demanded. Normal goods thus necessarily satisfy the Law of Demand.

   But inferior goods have an income effect that increases the quantity demanded when the price of the good goes up. If the income effect of an inferior good is larger than the substitution effect, the good is called a **Giffen good** and it violates the Law of Demand. All Giffen goods are inferior goods, but not all inferior goods are Giffen goods. If the substitution effect is strong than the (inferior) income effect, the good will still adhere to the Law of Demand.

   By decomposing the income and substitution effects we can thus show that when the price of a good changes

$$\text{Observed response} = \text{Substitution effect} + \text{Income effect.}$$

Algebraically, this can be written

$$\Delta x/\Delta p = (\Delta x/\Delta p)_{comp} - x_1 \times \Delta x/\Delta I$$

where $\Delta x/\Delta p$ is the observed response, $(\Delta x/\Delta p)_{comp}$ is the substitution effect (which must be negative), $-x_1$ is the original amount of the good consumed, and $\Delta x/\Delta I$ is the income response of the quantity demanded. Taken together, $-x_1 \times \Delta x/\Delta I$ is the income effect.

This equation is called the **Slutsky equation**. An important implication of the Slutsky equation is that when x_1 is small, the income effect is also small. When only a small amount of a good is consumed, there is not much difference between the compensated and observed (uncompensated) effects.

The **welfare effect** is the utility loss a person suffers when a price increases. Because utility is ordinal, not cardinal, it is difficult to measure welfare effects. We use the income effect to obtain a monetary measure of utility changes. Two measures are commonly used. The **compensating variation** (CV) is the amount of money an individual would need to be given to restore her initial utility after a price change. To calculate the substitution effect we necessarily must find the compensating variation. Thus, the CV is the amount of money we would need to give a person after a price change so that they don't lose any utility. It is based on the *new* price ratio. An alternative measure, the **equivalent variation** (EV) is the amount of income we must take from an individual if prices *don't* change to cause the same utility loss as the price increase. To find the EV, keep the *original* price ratio, but remove income until the person's utility falls to the level it would be at after a price increase.

CV and EV provide useful ways to analyze significant economic problems. Assuming normally shaped indifference curves, any subsidy that changes relative prices provides less value to the recipient, in terms of EV, than it costs the government to provide, because of the substitution effect. Similarly, taxes on specific goods have a larger burden than would a lump sum or general tax which does not change relative prices. Policies that tax a specific good, then rebates the tax revenue to the individual will not fully restore utility because the revenue collected is less than the CV.

Although the CV is a powerful tool for measuring changes in people's welfare it can be cumbersome to work through. Thus economists often choose to measure welfare effects using the demand curve. Each point on an individual's demand curve approximates the individual's marginal value of consuming that unit of the good. Thus, the demand curve may be thought of as a **marginal valuation schedule**. Each point on the demand curve shows the **willingness to pay** for that unit. The area under the demand curve between two levels of consumption represents the total value placed on consuming those units. The difference between what a person is willing to pay (the total value placed on consuming certain units) and what the individual must pay for those units is called the **(Marshallian) consumer surplus**. Graphically, it is the area under the demand curve and above the price. **Two-part tariffs** use a lump-sum access fee to attempt to extract some part of the consumer surplus. Price increases reduce the consumer surplus. This change in the consumer surplus is a monetary measure of the welfare loss associated with a price increase. Restrictions on the quantity of a good that can be imported, called a **trade quota**, cause a loss in consumer surplus. Part of the lost consumer surplus is transferred to producers in the form of higher prices, often referred to as **quota rents**. Deadweight loss is that part of the consumer surplus that is wasted as less quantity is sold.

The demand curve assumes money income is fixed, But since price increases lower the value of money income, the demand curve only approximates the marginal valuation curve. An **exact marginal valuation curve** must compensate for the income effects that come from price changes. **Compensated demand curves** adjust the quantity demanded of a good for the income effect that comes from price changes, by finding the quantity demanded at each price while holding utility constant. Compensated demand curves, which are exact marginal valuation curves, show only the substitution effect of price changes. **Ordinary demand curves** reflect both substitution and income effects. Consumer surplus measured from a compensated demand curve is exact.

For normal goods, the compensated demand curve is steeper than the ordinary demand curve. For inferior goods, the opposite is true. When the income effect is small, the compensated demand curve and the ordinary demand curve are close together, and the Marshallian consumer surplus closely approximates the exact consumer surplus. Since it is often (nearly) impossible to measure the compensated demand curve, economists regard Marshallian consumer surplus as a useful tool.

An Application of Price Changes and Consumer Welfare

Forensic economists work with attorneys to assess the economic consequences of torts, that is, when one person hurts another. One type of tort that forensic economists often work in is personal injury cases. Suppose one individual injures another in a car accident. The first person is liable for the welfare loss the second person suffers. Forensic economists estimate monetary values of the lost utility. Professors Fort and Rosenman ("Estimating the Value of Lost Health," *Journal of Legal Economics*, Vol. 5, 1995, pp. 63-74) proposed income-substitution analysis as the best way to attribute a monetary value on lost health.

Fort and Rosenman began by assuming that people who are injured can divide their consumption into two parts - goods that are affected by the injury and those that aren't. For example, a woman who enjoys gardening and reading might find that gardening is affected but reading is not. By assessing how much the gardening was hindered, analysts can adjust the "price" of gardening. Fort and Rosenman did their original analysis in terms of household expenditure, but a later extension does it in terms of time. If injuries force the women to work twice as long to achieve the same amount of gardening as she could prior to her injuries, the time price of gardening, relative to reading, had doubled. Thus, somehow we need to compensate this woman for the lost time.

Question 1: For the individual discussed, suppose she has 20 hours a week to spend on gardening or reading. Graphically show how her time budget constraint shifted after her injury. Draw in a pre-injury and post-injury indifference curves.

There are two possibilities for measuring her loss (in terms of time)- the equivalent variation (EV) and the compensating variation (CV).

Question 2: Look at the graph below. Which shift is her EV and which is her CV. Which is bigger?

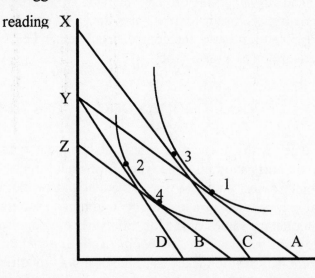

The purpose of liability awards is to "make the person whole again" by awarding monetary compensation that theoretically restores injured parties to the level of satisfaction they enjoyed prior to the accident.

Question 3: Would the EV or the CV be the proper compensating principle under this rule of law? Explain.

Because we cannot measure utility level, Fort and Rosenman recommend providing sufficient compensation so the injured person could, at least theoretically, consume her prior level of goods *at the new price level*. Although this would overcompensate the injured person, the law requires that when there is uncertainty in the level of compensation due, it favor the injured person.

Question 4: Graphically show how the compensation approach proposed by Fort and Rosenman will overcompensate rather than under-compensate the injured person.

Question 5: Contrast two injuries to the same person. The more severe injury makes it so it takes twice as long to do the same amount of gardening. The less severe injury makes it so it takes only one and one-half times as long. Which injury do you think will have a greater amount of excess compensation? Explain.

To find how much compensation was due, the compensation in terms of hours is turned into dollars by paying the injured person for her lost time at her market wage. By working less, she can achieve the same or higher level of satisfaction from leisure activities with the extra time.

Multiple Choice Questions

1. A Giffen good:
    A. must be an inferior good.
    B. must be a luxury good.
    C. must be a normal good.
    D. must have a zero income effect.

2. If Karen is willing to pay $35,000 in cash for a convertible BMW, her consumer surplus if she receives one free is:
    A. $0.
    B. -$35,000.
    C, 5,000.
    D. more than $35,000.

3. Slutsky equation separates the observed effect of a _____ change on _____ into a _____ effect and an _____ effect.
    A. quantity demanded / consumer surplus / price / income
    B. income / quantity demanded / substitution / income
    C. price / quantity demanded / substitution / income
    D. price / income / substitution / income

4. Consumer surplus calculated using the _____ demand curve is more exact than Marshallian consumer surplus which is calculated using the _____ demand curve.
    A. ordinary / compensated
    B. compensated / ordinary
    C. individual / market
    D. market / individual

5. The sign of the substitution effect of a price change:
    A. is always negative.
    B. is always positive.
    C. is always zero.
    D. may be negative or positive.

6. The equivalent variation of a price change is calculated using the _____ set of relative prices, while the compensating variation is calculated using the _____ set of prices.
    A.   new / original
    B.   absolute / nominal
    C.   nominal / absolute
    D.   original / new

7. Jones consumes 4 pounds of king crab legs per month when the price is $7 a pound and zero pounds per month after the price rises to $22 a pound as the result of an import restriction. The reduction in Marshallian consumer surplus that Jones suffers because of the quota on king crab legs is:
    A. $58.00.
    B. $44.00.
    C. $30.00.
    D. $0.

8. Monet is a member of the Los Angeles County Museum of Art. Monet's annual membership fee is $150 and he also pays $3 per visit to the museum. This type of pricing system is known as
    A.   a two-part tariff.
    B.   a compensated demand system.
    C.   a revealed preference system.
    D.   an equivalent variation.

The following graph applies to question 9.

All other goods

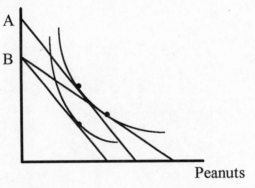

Peanuts

9.   Jimmy's change in consumption of peanuts and all other goods in response to a fall in the price of peanuts is illustrated above. The distance AB measures:
      A.   an equivalent variation.
      B.   a compensating variation.
      C.   a substitution effect.
      D.   an income effect.

The following graph is used for question 10

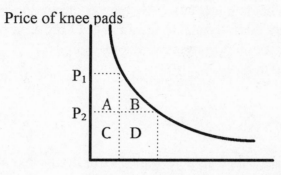

10.   Refers to Spike's compensated demand curve for knee pads as shown above. Area A + B measures:
      A.   the increase in Spike's consumer surplus when the price of knee pads decreases from P_1 to P_2 .
      B.   the decrease in Spike's consumer surplus when the price of knee pads increases from P_2 to P_1 .
      C.   the decrease in Spike's consumer surplus when the price of knee pads decreases from P_1 to P_2 .
      D.   Both A and B are correct.

11.   The substitution effect of a price change on the quantity demanded is also known as the:
      A.   uncompensated response.
      B.   compensated response.
      C.   Slutsky response.
      D.   Giffen response.

12. According to the Slutsky equation, the smaller is the initial amount of a good being consumed, then:
     A.   the larger is the income effect of a price change.
     B.   the larger is the difference between the compensated and observed responses to a price change.
     C.   the more likely is the good to be a Giffen good.
     D.   the less likely is the income effect of an inferior good to dominate the substitution effect.

13. If the federal government imposes a new tax on soft drinks and gives each consumer a cash rebate exactly equal to the amount of tax each pays, the opportunity cost of soft drinks in terms of all other goods:
     A.   remains unchanged.
     B.   increases.
     C.   decreases.
     D.   becomes negative.

14. If the federal government imposes a new tax on soft drinks and gives each consumer a cash rebate exactly equal to the amount of tax each pays, each consumer's:
     A.   real income falls, but money income remains unchanged.
     B.   money income falls, but real income remains unchanged.
     C.   real and money incomes remain unchanged.
     D.   real income rises, but money income remains unchanged.

15. A compensated demand curve eliminates the _____ of price changes embodied in the ordinary demand curve.
     A.   income effects
     B.   substitution effects
     C.   income and substitution effects
     D.   deadweight loss

Refer to the change in Lucas' consumption of blank videotapes and all other goods in response to a change in the price of blank videotapes as depicted below to answer questions 16-18.

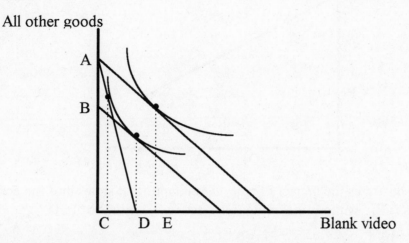

16.   The compensated response in Lucas' consumption of blank videotapes after the fall in their price is measured by:
    A.   distance AB.
    B.   distance CD.
    C.   distance DE.
    D.   distance CE.

17.   The income effect on Lucas' consumption of blank videotapes after a fall in their price is measured by:
    A.   distance AB.
    B.   distance CD.
    C.   distance DE.
    D.   distance CE.

18.   The distance AB measures:
    A.   an equivalent variation.
    B.   a compensated response.
    C.   a compensating variation.
    D.   an uncompensated response.

Questions 19-20 refer to the following:

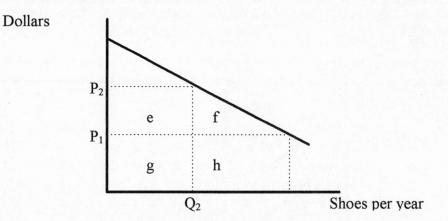

The figure above illustrates the impact of a quota on imports of shoes into the country. The price of shoes is P_1, without the quota, but rises to P_2 with the quota.

19.   The deadweight loss from the quota is equal to area:
    A.   e.
    B.   e + g.
    C.   f.
    D.   f + h.

20.   As a result of the quota, consumer surplus:
    A.   falls by area f + h.
    B.   rises by area e + f.
    C.   falls by area g + h.
    D.   falls by area e + f.

Problems

1. A father who was worried about the number of comic books his son bought each week proposed adding a "tax" of 25 cents on each comic. Every time the son's allowance was raised he bought more comic books. Currently the son buys 4 comics per week. The son claims it would be easier, and just as effective, to lower his allowance by $1 per week. Who is right? Explain using the Slutsky equation.

2. Which plan would cause greater welfare loss for the son? Explain.

3. After a few weeks, the son complained that this tax scheme wasn't fair -- that he deserved the full value of his allowance. After much discussion his father agreed to rebate the tax paid at the end of each week. Will this make the son as well off as before?

4. The adjacent states of Washington and Idaho treat food differently when applying sales taxes. Washington has a larger tax (7.5%) but excludes food, while Idaho has a lower tax rate (5%) but taxes food. Which tax scheme is more efficient in the sense that, for

a given amount of taxes collected from an individual, the welfare loss to the person is minimized?

5. The substitution effect for housing is fairly small, while the income effect is quite large. That being the case, would the change in the Marshallian consumer surplus be a good approximation of the gain consumer's enjoy from a housing subsidy? Use the Slutsky equation to explain why.

6. Suppose on average 5 percent of the people in Colfax, WA go annually to see the Spokane Indians baseball team but 15 percent of the people in Cheney, WA (which is much closer to Spokane) go to games because travel costs are $15 less. The price of a ticket is $10. Assuming Colfax and Cheney are of similar size, about 3000 people each, how can we get a measure of consumer surplus from this information?

7. Food coops usually offer price discounts of about 5 percent for members, who pay a nominal fee of $5 or $10 per year. Since the demand for food is inelastic, why would members choose to pay this fee?

CHAPTER 5. THE HOUSEHOLD AS SUPPLIER

Chapter Introduction

Most of us grow up in households where almost every weekday someone got up and went to work. To earn wages, mother, father or some other relative would sell what skills they had in the factor marketplace. If they were lucky, our household workers enjoyed their jobs. But the primary reason for such diligence was to provide an income to the household, so that we could play our role of consumers in the goods marketplace. And most of you either are already playing the same type role now, or expect to do so in the future. This may be the reason you are studying economics right now.

It may not seem that our decision to work is one over which we have much control. Most jobs demand a minimum commitment of hours, and, especially in times of high unemployment, our ability to find a job with characteristics we find desirable may seem well nigh impossible. But the reality is that our decisions play a large part in determining our incomes. We choose how much education to get, how many hours to work, and what profession to pursue. Our choice about these matters will depend quite a bit on the rewards that accrue to working and saving.

Increasingly, governments have recognized that policies that influence the rewards to working will alter work behavior. In the 1980s and 1990s the United States and many other countries cut income tax rates, thus increasing the percentage of disposable income people could spend as they wished. These policies attempted to stimulate the economy by increasing the reward from productive activities.

Chapters 2, 3 and 4 explained how households behave in the goods market. Those chapters assumed that people's income was fixed. In this chapter, the authors extend consumer choice theory to the household as a *supplier* of inputs - primarily of labor and capital. We see that households simply choose between work, which provides the means for consuming market goods, and nonmarket goods. Just like choice among different consumption goods, it turns out that we as suppliers of labor and capital choose from among many alternatives.

Chapter Outline

This chapter discusses how households use rational choice to make decisions as input suppliers. We use the same analytical techniques that were helped us to understand the household's role as a consumer in the goods market. It is important to realize that this chapter is an application of tools *already* developed - it simply uses the tools learned in chapters 2-4 to investigate something new.

Households get most of their income (about 89 percent) from the wages and salaries for supplying labor. Households have a **time endowment** that they can devote to **work** (or **labor**) or to **nonmarket activities**, usually lumped together into a generic good labeled **leisure**. Hours devoted to labor earn income that can be used to purchase **market**

goods, termed **consumption**. Households derive satisfaction (utility) by consuming market goods and leisure. Thus, work becomes the means to consume market goods by providing income. In this analytic framework, work itself provides no satisfaction.

Households are constrained by their time endowment. The number of hours worked, l, and the number of hours devoted to leisure, n, must sum to the time endowment, T. Thus, $T = l + n$. This situation sets up a typical consumer choice problem: choose the combination of work and leisure that maximizes utility subject to the constraint imposed by the time endowment. At the two extremes to a household's income, they can devote the entire time endowment, T, to work ($l = T$, $n = 0$), earning w per hour, thus giving an income of wT (and no leisure at all), or they can spend their entire endowment on nonmarket activities ($n = T$, $l = 0$), so they have no income. Alternatively, l_1 hours can be devoted to work, leaving $T - l_1 = n_1$ hours for leisure. Income in this case is wl_1. Algebraically, the amount, spent on market goods must equal the income, so

$$c = w \times (T - n)$$

where c is the amount of market consumption, with the price **normalized** to 1 (that is, set equal to 1 since only *relative* prices and incomes matter). This can be rearranged to

$$c + (w \times n) = w \times T$$

where the right hand side represents the **value of the time endowment** or the **full income**. The slope of the budget constraint is the negative wage rate. Leisure is not free: its price is the **opportunity cost** of the wage rate. When the wage rate increases both the value of the time endowment and the opportunity cost of leisure increase. The budget constraint gets steeper.

Households maximize utility by choosing among different combinations of work (consumption) and leisure that the time endowment and its value afford. A set of indifference curves indicate the household's preferences between consumption and leisure, and the budget constraint indicates the possible. The household maximizes its utility by finding the tangent between the budget constraint and the indifference curves, which determines how much time is spent in leisure, and how much at work.

Comparative statics techniques using the consumption-leisure model examines changes in the wage rate. Decreasing the wage makes leisure less expensive, since the wage is the opportunity cost of leisure. Thus, the substitution effect is *towards* leisure and away from work. This makes sense as consumption goods (bought using wages) now are relatively more expensive. At the same time, however, a lower wage decreases the potential income. Thus, if leisure is a normal good, the income effect of a wage decrease also decreases leisure consumption. Observed hours worked may increase or decrease depending on whether the substitution effect or income effect dominates. Rational reactions to a wage reduction run from working less because it is "no longer worth it" to working more to maintain a constant **standard of living**.

The **labor supply curve** shows the relationship between the quantity of labor supplied and the wage rate, *ceteris paribus*. It is derived simultaneously with the **leisure demand curve** by changing the wage rate and observing the utility maximizing amounts of labor and leisure. When the substitution effect dominates the income effect the labor supply curve slopes upward - increasing the wage increases the hours worked. It has a negative slope when the income effect dominates, and an increasing wage elicits fewer hours of work. One possibility that might apply to highly paid people like doctors and lawyers who work only four days a week is the **backward bending labor supply**. In this case, at first the substitution effect dominates, and the labor supply curve slopes upward, but as the wage rate gets extremely high, the income effect becomes dominant, and the curve "bends backward": the participants supply fewer hours of labor.

Income support programs affect work incentives by shifting the budget constraint. **Aid to Family with Dependent Children** (AFDC) was the most important **income maintenance program** in the US prior to 1997. Under this program, the government reduced the income subsidy one dollar for every dollar participants earned. This **implicit tax rate** of 100 percent made leisure very cheap (an opportunity cost of zero) causing a strong substitution effect towards leisure. Empirical evidence supports the conjecture that AFDC reduced the labor supply of recipients. In other words, people on welfare has absolutely no financial incentive to work.

Producer surplus is the amount of income a person receives for work above what would have been necessary to get them to supply that amount of labor. On a graph of the labor supply curve, it is the area above the labor supply curve and below the wage rate. In economic terms, when a person loses her job, her lost welfare is not the full amount of wages, but only the lost producer surplus. Thus, **unemployment insurance** may fully compensate a person for losing her job without fully replacing all lost income.

The **market supply curve of labor** shows the aggregate quantity of labor that all individuals in a market are willing to supply at each wage rate, *ceteris paribus*. It is **the horizontal sum** of individual labor supply curves. The market supply to particular occupations reflects **compensating differentials** for the desirable or undesirable characteristics of the job.

Households are also the source of **capital**. **Real capital** consists of machinery, buildings and other physical assets used in production. **Financial capital** is money that firms borrow to buy or rent real capital. Households supply capital through **savings**, by which they delay their consumption to the future. The **life-cycle model** says that consumption and savings decisions in any given year take into account expected lifetime economic conditions.

The **intertemporal budget constraint** shows the lifetime consumption possibilities that an individual (or household) can achieve by **lending** and **borrowing** at different stages of life. Feasible lifetime consumption is determined by the **endowment** point (which shows the income expected each time period) and the **interest rate**. The slope of the intertemporal budget constraint equals $-(1+i)$ where i is the interest rate. **Future consumption** can be increased above future income by saving some of current income, thus reducing **current consumption**. Alternatively, present consumption can be increased above current income by borrowing now to be paid back with future income, thus reducing future consumption. The **present value of the endowment** is the maximum amount of present consumption that could be obtained by borrowing against all future income.

The slope of the **intertemporal indifference curve** is the **marginal rate of time preference** between periods. Those with high levels of preference for present consumption will save little, while those with preference for future consumption will save more. We achieve equilibrium in the life-cycle model when the marginal rate of time preference between present and future consumption just equals the (1+i), the negative of the slope of the intertemporal budget constraint.

Comparative statics analysis of the life-cycle model examines changes in the interest rate. A decrease in the interest rate makes future consumption more expensive because savings earns less of a return and borrowing costs less. Thus, the substitution effect is *towards* current consumption, reducing savings. For someone who is initially a saver, decreasing the interest rate also lowers their income (they earn less interest). Current consumption is a normal good, so lower income means lower current consumption, thus higher saving. So the income and substitution effect on savers work opposite each other, and the net effect of a decrease in interest is uncertain. For the initial borrower, a decrease in the interest rate also causes a substitution effect towards current consumption. But since borrowers are paying interest, a decrease in the interest rate increases their income. Thus, the income effect also increases current consumption, and savings decreases.

Individual savings supply is determined by the equilibrium amount of savings in the life-cycle model at each interest level. If we add up the supply of savings for all individuals at each interest rate, we have the **market supply curve of savings**.

Present value (PV) is the maximum amount of money you would be willing to pay today for the right to receive a given amount of money at some specific time in the future. The **discount rate** is the interest used to compute present value in the formula

$$PV = M_0 + M_1/(1+i) + M_2/(1+i)^2 + \ldots + M_T/(1+i)^T$$

where M_k is the monetary payment in time k and T is the last period a payment is received. If the payment is a **perpetuity** with a constant payment M the present value follows the formula

$$PV = M/i.$$

PV allows us to compare different payments at different times on a common measure.

A third type of capital is **human capital**, which is the investment individuals make in skills and health that raise their productivity. Estimates suggest that human capital investment in the US is twice that invested in physical capital. Human capital investment requires taking less current consumption in exchange for higher earnings in the future. **The human capital production function** shows how an individual can transform current investment in human capital into future gains in income. The optimal amount of human capital investment, which maximizes the value of the endowment, is when the slope of the human capital production function equals the market rate of interest that is used for borrowing for physical capital. Borrowing allows people to keep their consumption up even as they invest in training, thus there is a **separation** of human capital production decision and consumption decision.

An Application of the Household as a Supplier

Taxes in the United States, especially the income tax system, have been a contentious political issue since Ronald Reagan was President. Even after taxes were simplified during the Reagan administration, many politicians, especially Republicans like Jack Kemp and Malcolm Forbes, have criticized the income tax system for its complexity, claiming a simpler system and lower taxes in general would stimulate economic growth and ensure a stable economy for years to come.

Question 1: The current tax system has lots of itemized and standard deductions and four marginal tax rates above the standard deduction, starting at 15%, then increasing to 23%, 28% and 33%. Tax credits and deductions exempt most people's first $10,000 of income. Ignoring the itemized deductions, draw the labor-leisure budget constraint that comes from this tax system.

Question 2: One issue of concern for the current tax system is its impact on work incentive. Contrast how this differs for a low wage individual and a high wage individual.

Forbes and others have championed the idea of a flat tax at a rate of about 20 percent of income. Forbes also advocates removing almost all itemized deductions and instead exempting the first $15,000 or so of income.

Question 3: Suppose a flat tax plan with a 20 percent rate replaced our current system. How would this change work incentive effects? Contrast how the work incentive effect might differ for low wage and high wage workers.

Proponents claim that this simplified system will reduce the excess burden inherent in the tax system, as well saving hundreds of millions of dollars in compliance and enforcement costs. Undoubtedly, simplifying the tax system will save on compliance costs. However, even the flat tax will have an excess burden.

Question 4: Using the tools developed in the previous chapter, show that even a flat rate income tax has an excess burden by finding the *equivalent variation*. Explain why it has the *excess burden*.

Another issue confronting policy makers is the disincentive that the tax system has on savings. One suggestion is to remove taxes on interest income, by making things like IRAs tax exempt, and exempting capital gains from taxes.

Question 5: Using the life-cycle model, show how these policies might stimulate savings. Will they necessarily work? Why or why not?

One aspect of these policies would to change from the current asymmetry in the way interest is treated. Currently, interest paid is not tax deductible, but interest earned is taxed. Proponents claim treating all interest the same (deducting that paid, taxes that earned) would improve savings. But with most people heavily in debt, it would require a radical change in people's behavior.

Multiple Choice Questions

1. Congratulations! You have just won a lottery in which the prize is a perpetuity that pays you $50,000 per year forever. The interest rate is 5%. The present value of your winnings is:
    A. $2,500.
    B. $50,000
    C. $1,000,000.
    D. infinite.

2. An investment involves a certain outlay in the present and a stream of returns in the future. If the market interest rate increases, *ceteris paribus*, the present value of an investment:
    A. increases.
    B. decreases.
    C. stays the same.
    D. Any of the above is possible.

3. Jan's intertemporal budget constraint has a constant slope if:
    A. she can only borrow money at a higher interest rate than she can lend money.
    B. she can actually lend money at a higher interest rate than she can borrow money.
    C. she can borrow and lend money at the same interest rate.
    D. her interest receipts are taxable but her interest payments are not tax deductible.

4. In the consumption-leisure model, the substitution and income effects of a wage change work in opposite directions:
    A. if leisure is a normal good.
    B. if leisure is an inferior good.
    C. regardless of whether leisure is normal or inferior.
    D. only for a wage decrease.

5. Tess works 40 hours a week when her wage is $25 per hour. If Tess becomes unemployed, her producer surplus:
    A. falls by $1,000 per week.
    B. falls by less than $1,000 per week.
    C. falls by more than $1,000 per week.
    D. remains unchanged as her increased leisure compensates for her lost earnings.

6.	Suppose that investment banking and teaching economics require exactly the same skills, but college teaching has more desirable characteristics, including shorter working hours. The salary of an investment banker is $100,000 while that of an economics professor is $55,000. The wage premium for an investment banker is known as:
	A.	a compensating differential.
	B.	compensated producer surplus.
	C.	the marginal rate of time preference.
	D.	the intertemporal budget constraint.

7.	Ms. Smith is initially a borrower. After a fall in the interest rate, Ms. Smith
	A.	borrows less.
	B.	borrows more.
	C.	borrows the same amount.
	D.	Any of the above are likely.

8. Assume a graph where future income is on the vertical axis and present income on the horizontal axis. If interest income is taxed but interest payments are not tax deductible, then the intertemporal budget constraint is:
   A. flatter above the endowment point than below it.
   B. a straight line with no kink.
   C. steeper above the endowment point than below it.
   D. kinked at the equilibrium point.

9. The amount of money an individual would have if she worked every available hour is known as:
   A. the value of the time endowment.
   B. full income.
   C. the time endowment.
   D. Both A and B are correct.

10. A wage increase:
    A. always increases the opportunity cost of an hour of leisure.
    B. increases the opportunity cost of an hour of leisure only if leisure is a normal good.
    C. increases the opportunity cost of an hour of leisure only if leisure is an inferior good.
    D. always reduces the opportunity cost of an hour of leisure.

This graph is for question 11.

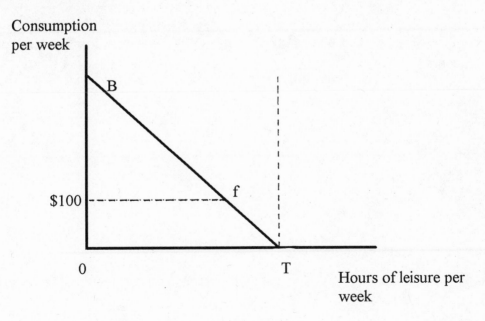

11. Suppose that line B in the figure above represents Daniel's consumption-leisure budget constraint in the absence of any government grants. Now Daniel becomes eligible for a monthly grant of $100 from the AFDC program, but the grant is reduced by $1 for each $1 that Daniel earns. Then Daniel's consumption-leisure budget constraint:
    A. becomes vertical above point f.
    B. becomes horizontal to the right of point f.
    C. becomes horizontal to the left of point f.
    D. remains unchanged.

This graph is for question 12

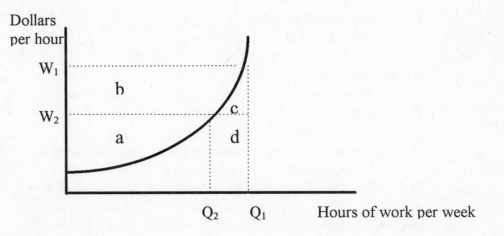

12. Suppose that Kathy's labor supply curve is represented in the figure above. A decrease in Kathy's wage rate from w_1 to w_2 results in a loss in producer surplus equal to:
    A. area b + c.
    B. area a + b.
    C. area b.
    D. area c + d.

13. Physical aids to production, such as tools and factories, are known as:
    A. real capital.
    B. financial capital.
    C. human capital.
    D. endowment capital.

14. According to the life-cycle model, peoples' consumption and saving decisions in a given year take into account:
    A. their economic circumstances in that year only.
    B. their economic circumstance over their lifetime.
    C. only their past economic circumstances.
    D. only their expected future economic circumstances.

15. If an intertemporal budget constraint is graphed with current consumption on the horizontal axis and future consumption on the vertical axis, the individual is a:
    A. borrower at points on the constraint below the endowment point.
    B. borrower at points on the constraint above the endowment point.
    C. saver at points on the constraint below the endowment point.
    D. saver at all points on the constraint.

16. At equilibrium in the life-cycle model where an individual can save and borrow at interest rate i, the marginal rate of time preference equals:
    A. 1 - i.
    B. 1 + i.
    C. 1/i.
    D. 1 x i.

17. Teri's weekly consumption is denoted by (c) and Teri's weekly leisure hours are denoted by (n). Suppose that Teri's total time endowment per week is 112 hours, and her hourly salary is $8. Teri's budget constraint is described by this equation:
    A. c = 8n - 896.
    B. 8c = 112 - n.
    C. c = 896 - 8n.
    D. c + n = 896.

Question 18 uses the following graph

Future consumption

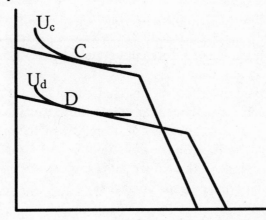

Present consumption

18. U_c and U_d represent Rodney's indifference curves. Suppose Rodney's optimal consumption choice if he takes the first job is represented by the point C, while his optimal consumption choice if he takes the second job is represented by the point D. If he takes either job, he is:

A.   a borrower.
B.   a saver.
C.   neither of the above.
D.   There is insufficient data to answer this question.

Questions 19-20 refer to the following graph

Consumption per
week

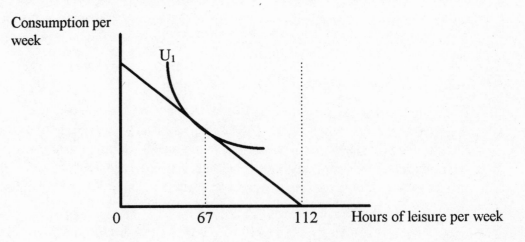

Hours of leisure per week

19. The figure above illustrates Molly's budget constraint and indifference curve between leisure and consumption.   If Molly can work as many hours as she wants at a wage rate of $9.
    A.   The budget constraint has a slope equal to -1/9.
    B.   The value of Molly's time endowment is $603 per week.
    C.   In equilibrium, Molly earns $405 per week.
    D.   All of the above are correct.

20. If Molly's wage rate falls,
    A.   she will work fewer hours.
    B.   she will work more hours.
    C.   she will work the same amount of hours.
    D.   she might work fewer, more, or the same amount of hours.

Problems

1. Current law requires that hourly wage earners get overtime pay (at least time and one-half) when they work more than 40 hours per week. Show graphically how this effects work incentive.

2. Many jobs require exactly 40 hours per week. Can this prevent an individual from maximizing her utility? Explain.

3. Discuss how borrowers and savers will react to an increase in the interest rate. Can we say for certain for both whether or not savings will increase or decrease? Explain.

4. Unlike the AFDC program which had a 100% tax on earnings, Social Security allows beneficiaries to keep all of their earnings up to about $9000 without any reduction in benefits, and above that only reduces benefits by 33 cents for every dollar earned. Show how the Social Security program affects an individuals budget constraint.

5. Describe a tax that does not have an excess burden. Use the context of a labor-leisure model and what you leaned in the application.

6. Until the Reagan tax reform of 1987 interest earned and interest paid were treated symmetrically by income taxes. Interest earned was subject to income taxes, and income paid was deductible from taxable income. The tax reform law of 1987 changed that. Interest consumers paid was no longer deductible. Interest earned, however, was still taxed. Explain how this change in the tax laws might affect savings incentives.

7. Find the PV of a 4 year annuity of $100 per year if the interest rate is 5% and if the interest rate is 10%.

8. Student loan programs have greatly increased how much individuals invest in education as human capital. Explain how individuals must have reacted to this new financial market.

9. Use the graph below to draw Sam's labor supply curve.

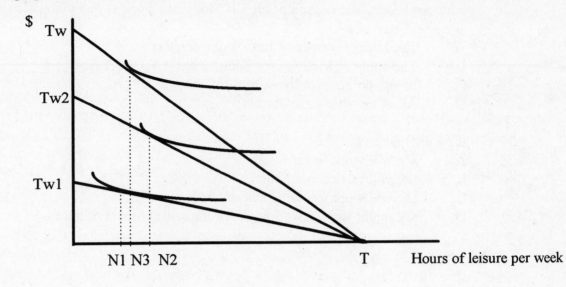

CHAPTER 6. CHOICE UNDER UNCERTAINTY

Chapter Introduction

Insurance is a strange commodity for it has its greatest value when something bad happens to us. Although most of us buy many different types of insurance, the basic premise is the same for all types - we protect our financial health against the costs we incur if something bad happens to us. With health insurance, we can't ensure that our health will be maintained (or even restored). The best we can do is guarantee the financial means to pay for our medical costs. Similarly, automobile insurance protects our financial health from the consequences of mistakes we might make when driving. It doesn't prevent us from having accidents.

Of course, we can't insure against everything. We buy things that turn out to be lemons, and have no recourse. After deciding to major in astrophysics, we graduate just in time to find the budget for space exploration has been cut. And sometimes we get the benefit of some change. You buy a house in an inexpensive neighborhood just before Intel announces it is building a new plant near it, bringing thousands or workers looking for housing to the area. Or you buy a lottery ticket, and it wins!

The world is filled with uncertainty, and usually consumer choices are made without full knowledge of the outcome. Chapters 2-5 developed consumer choice under conditions of *certainty*. Consumers knew the price of the good, what its exact characteristics were, and how they felt about it. In this chapter we relax these assumptions, but still apply the basic rules of consumer choice. We modify the familiar tools - budget constraints and indifference curves - and thus we can apply them to decisions made in the presence of uncertainty.

Chapter Outline

To incorporate **uncertainty** into choice theory requires one fundamental modification. We must allow for more than one possible **state of the world**. People do not know what the state of the world will be before making a decision. Thus, in the sense that the future is unknown, bringing uncertainty into the model makes it much more realistic. Uncertainty comes in because each person's consumption depends on the state of the world. No one knows before hand exactly what his or her consumption will be. Goods of this sort, whose level depends on which state of the world occurs, are called **contingent commodities**.

Gambling provides a simple illustration of contingent commodities. When you buy a lottery ticket there are two possible outcomes (really more, but let's ignore intermediate prizes). You will (most likely) have $1 less to spend on all goods other than the gamble, or you will have $1 million more to spend on other goods. If we think of all other goods as a composite commodity, it also becomes a contingent commodity if you take the bet.

How much of these other goods we have to consume depends on whether we win the lottery (one state of world) or not (the other state of the world).

The **budget constraint for contingent commodities** depends on the **endowment point** and the tradeoffs between states of the world. In this sense, the budget constraint for contingent commodities is similar to the ones we found in the previous chapter for consumption over time. People can make tradeoffs between states of the world by making **gambles** or **bets**, or they can consume their endowment points. The budget constraint always goes through the endowment point, and extends towards that payoff that the person taking the bet will have if he wins. Thus, if a bet pays 50 cents for every dollar bet, the slope equals -½. If only one side of a bet (the gambler can only bet that one state of the world will occur) the budget constraint moves from the endowment point in only one direction. But if both sides of the bet can be made, so the gambler can choose which state of the world she wants to bet will occur, the budget constraint moves from axis to axis.

An **actuarially fair gamble** is one for which the expected outcome is the endowment point. That means that the expected monetary gain is zero. The expected monetary gain is given by the formula

$$(1-\rho) \times W - \rho \times L$$

where $1-\rho$ is the **probability** that one state of the world will occur, the W represents the amount that is won if that state of the world occurs (termed the **payoff**), ρ is the probability that the other state of the world occurs, and L is the loss if that state happens. When a gamble is actuarially fair, on average there is neither a gain nor loss in monetary terms. The **fair odds line** is the budget constraint from an actuarially fair gamble. If a bet is not actuarially fair, the budget constraint differs from the fair odds line. **Odds** is simple the ratio of the probabilities of two events, thus the odds equal $\rho/(1-\rho)$. For an actuarially fair gamble $(1-\rho) \times W - \rho \times L = 0$ thus $\rho/(1-\rho) = W/L$. The slope of the fair odds line $= -\rho/(1-\rho) = -W/L$. The **expected value of consumption** is equal at every bundle on the fair odds line. The **certainty line** connects all possible endowment points. It is the locus of all possible certain consumption levels.

Just as individuals have preferences between different goods, they have preferences between consumption in different states of the world, that is, different combinations of contingent commodities. The normal assumptions about preferences that were discussed in chapter 2 still apply, as well as one additional assumption that the marginal utility of consumption is independent of the state of the world. Preferences between contingent commodities reflect an individuals' **attitudes towards risk**. **Risk averse** people do not like risk. They always prefer a sure thing, and will not accept an actuarially fair gamble. When their indifference curves intersect the certainty line, its slope is minus the odds. **Risk lovers** prefer uncertainty so they prefer a gamble to a sure thing. Their indifference curves are bowed out from the origin. **Risk neutral** people are indifferent among all alternatives with the same expected value; thus, their indifference curves coincide with the fair odds line.

Equilibrium occurs where the highest indifference curve possible is reached on the budget constraint. Risk averse people will only gamble if the bet is actuarially unfair *to* *their advantage*. Risk lovers will accept actuarially unfair gambles. State lotteries, as well as gambling in Atlantic City and Las Vegas, suggest that many people are risk lovers for small bets. But thriving insurance sales provides evidence that people are risk averse for many important aspects of their lives.

Investment and tax evasion are two examples of contingent commodities. Additional evidence that people are risk averse comes from the fact that riskier investments usually pay higher returns than safe investments. The extra compensation for risk is called a **risk premium**. **Diversification** allows people to reduce risk by using several investments at the same time. **Tax evasion** allows more consumption if a person gets away with it, but consumption is cut if they are caught. High penalties and high audit rates discourage tax evasion. Higher tax rates encourage it.

Insurance is a way for risk averse people eliminate risks. When insurance is actuarially fair, the **premium** equals the expected payoff of the insurance provider. For an actuarially fair insurance policy, the premium for $1 worth of insurance equals the probability of the "bad" state of the world occurring. The budget constraint with actuarially fair insurance has a slope $-\rho/(1-\rho)$. A risk averse individual will purchase **full insurance** when it is offered at actuarially fair odds. When a person is fully insured, consumption is the same no matter what state of the world occurs. Insurance allows an individual to equalize consumption over different states of the world.

Insurance policies generally are unfair in the sense that premiums exceed the expected monetary payment so that companies can make a profit, and because rates imperfectly adjust to actual probabilities. When an insurance policy is unfair, even risk averse individuals purchase less than full insurance.

Decision trees represents the choice problem when many outcomes are possible. They show how the outcomes are related to current decisions. Nodes are places where decision trees branch. One branch appears for each possible path at a node. At **decision nodes** individuals must take an action. At **chance nodes**, a random process determines which branch will be followed. A point representing an ultimate outcome is a **terminal node**. If the relative importance an individual attaches to a given contingency is exactly proportional to the probability of that state occurring, then the utility function is a **von Neumann-Morgenstern utility function**. In this case, the utility associated with an uncertain event is the expected value of the utility of each possible outcome. In a two state world utility equals $\rho \times U(c1) + (1-\rho) \times U(c2)$ where ρ is the probability of state 1 occurring, $(1-\rho)$ is the probability of state 2, c1 and c2 are the consumption in states 1 and c2 respectively, and $U(\bullet)$ is the utility function. Thus, $\rho \times U(c1) + (1-\rho) \times U(c2)$ is the **expected utility**. When the choice must be made among many alternatives, rational individuals choose that path with the highest expected utility. This same process works for **sequential decisions** by using **backward induction**.

An Application of Choice Under Uncertainty

Sometimes people don't seem rational. For example, even risk loving people should want to set their gambles so that they get the highest return possible. But when we look at what people do, it doesn't always seem that way.

In Las Vegas and Atlantic City, slot machines are about the worst bet someone can make. Card games, and even the roulette wheel, provide better returns, though the odds still favor the house. Thus, we should never see somebody playing the slots.

Question 1: Suppose a player with $100 goes to a casino and plays a coin flipping game. If heads comes up he wins 25 cents. If tails comes up, he pays a dollar. Show why only a risk loving person would play this game. (Hint: Figure out the expected monetary gain, and determine if the odds are fair.)

Question 2: Now suppose the player starts a card game instead with an Ace and two jokers. If he draws an Ace the gambler gets 25 cents. If a joker is drawn, the player pays a dollar. Show why only a risk lover would gamble on this game also.

Notice that if a risk loving player chooses to gamble, the odds do not change how much the person risks. In theory it is an "all or nothing" deal. Risk lovers are interested in the pay out, not the odds. Now give the same player a choice: At one table, if an Ace is drawn the player gets 25 cents. At another, she would get 30 cents.

Question 3: By putting both games on the same graph, show why the rational risk loving gambler would choose the table with a higher pay off for an Ace.

Not all risk lovers will take all gambles. The graph to the right illustrates a risk lover who prefers not to gamble on a game that pays 25 cents for a win, but takes one dollar for a loss. Again, we don't need the fair odds line to make this judgment. Risk lovers choose to take or not take a bet based on the potential gain.

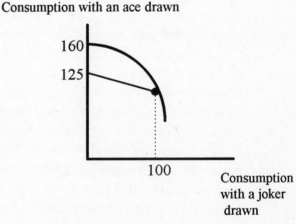

Consumption with an ace drawn

160

125

100

Consumption with a joker drawn

Question 4: For the person in the graph, how large would the payment for a win need to be for her to take the bet?

To address the original issue, why do some gamblers take the worse odds? It may be a budget limitation. The graph at the right shows two possible games. The first game pays 75 cents for every win against minus one dollar for every loss. It requires a minimum bet of $200. The second game pays 50 cents for a win against minus one dollar for every loss. It requires only a $100 minimum.

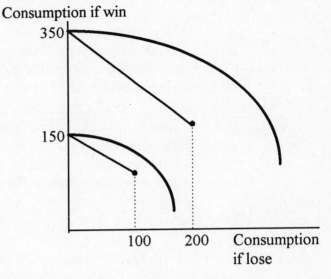

Question 5: Which game would a risk loving player choose if she could afford both?

Question 6: What might make a player choose to play the lower game, with odds of ½ instead of the game with odds of ¾?

Multiple Choice Questions

1. If Jennifer is risk averse, her indifference curves for contingent commodities:
    A. are convex to the origin.
    B. are bowed outward from the origin.
    C. are a set of parallel straight lines.
    D. have constant slopes equal to minus the odds.

2. Which of the following provides evidence that most people are risk adverse?
    A. The existence of risk premia.
    B. The popularity of mutual funds.
    C. The purchasing of insurance.
    D. All of the above.

3. The process of buying several investment assets in order to reduce risk is known as:
    A. diversification.
    B. actuarially fair insurance.
    C. sequential decisions.
    D. a decision tree.

4. A risk-averse person facing actuarially fair insurance will:
    A. buy full coverage.

C.   buy less than full coverage.
D.   Any of the above is possible.

5.   Alex's utility function satisfies the von Neumann-Morgenstern axioms. Thus he will:
A.   maximize his expected utility.
B.   maximize his expected income.
C.   maximize the utility of his expected income.
D.   minimize his expected loss.

6.   If Karen plays a game at a casino, and the casino on average makes money at that game, then the game has:
A.   a positive expected value for Karen.
B.   a zero expected value for Karen.
C.   a negative expected value for Karen.
D.   an expected value for Karen greater than 1.

7.   Steffi will win $100,000 in a tennis match with a probability 0.75 and receive a consolation prize amount of $50,000 if she loses. Steffi's expected winnings are:
A. $50,000.
B. $62,500.
C. $75,000.
D. $87,500.

8.   Jill and Kris are contestants on a game show. Each is faced with the choice of receiving $2,000 for sure or receiving $4,000 if a fair coin lands heads and nothing if the coin lands tails. If Jill is risk loving and Kris is risk averse:
A.   Jill would pick the $2,000 for sure.
B.   Jill would pick the fair coin gamble.
C.   Karen would pick the fair coin gamble.
D.   both women would be indifferent between the two options.

9.   Karen works as a waitress at Content Pebble in Malibu. One of her tables has a $200 check total. Karen believes that she will receive a tip of $10, $20, $30, or $40, with each of these amounts being equally likely. The expected value of Karen's tip from this table is:
A. $20.
B. $25.
C. $30.
D. $35.

10. Mav and Iceman are the only two pilots in contention for Top Gun honors. Suppose that the probability of Mav winning is 60%. Viper offers Mav this bet: for each dollar he bets, Mav wins $1 if he wins Top Gun honors, but loses $2 if he does not get Top Gun honors. If Mav initially has an income of $50, he will bet:
    A. $0.
    B. $25.
    C. $30.
    D. $50.

11. A commodity whose level depends on which state of the world occurs is known as a:
    A. contingent commodity.
    B. fair odds commodity.
    C. probable commodity.
    D. von Neumann-Morgenstern commodity.

12. An actuarially fair gamble is one for which the:
    A. actual monetary gain equals zero.
    B. maximum monetary gain equals zero.
    C. minimum monetary gain equals zero.
    D. expected monetary gain equals zero.

13. Along the fair odds line, the expected value of consumption:
    A. is higher for bundles to the left of the endowment point than for bundles to the right.
    B. is higher for bundles to the right of the endowment point than for bundles to the left.
    C. is equal at every bundle.
    D. equals zero since the expected monetary gain of the gamble equals zero.

14. Consider the indifference map for contingent commodities. For a risk-averse individual, the slope of each indifference curve _____ equals minus the odds in favor of the event on the horizontal axis.
    A. at every point on the curve
    B. to the right of the endowment point
    C. to the left of the endowment point
    D. at the curve's intersection with the certainty line

15. When confronted with an actuarially fair bet, a risk-averse individual maximizes utility by electing:
    A.   a bundle to the left of the endowment point.
    B.   a bundle to the right of the endowment point.
    C.   the endowment point.
    D.   a bundle anywhere along the fair odds line.

16. Suppose that taxpayers face an average income tax rate of 25 percent and that the odds of being audited are 20 percent. According to the tax-evasion model in the text, the government should establish a fine of _____ for each $1 of income not reported in order to eliminate evasion.
    A. $0.63
    B. $1.00
    C. $6.00
    D. $1.50

17. Actuarially fair insurance is a policy for which the premium for $1 worth of insurance equals:
    A.   1 - p, where p is the probability of occurrence of that state of the world for which the insurance coverage is purchased.
    B.   the expected pay-out by the insurance provider.
    C.   1/p, where p is the probability of occurrence of that state of the world for which the insurance coverage is purchased.
    D.   1 + p, where p is the probability of occurrence of that state of the world for which the insurance coverage is purchased.

Question 18 refers to the following graph.

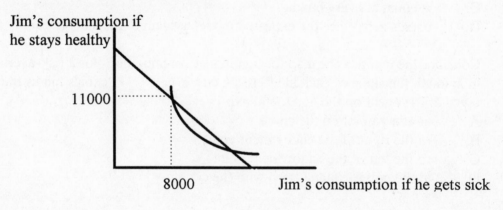

18. Jim earns $20,000 per year. If Jim gets sick he loses all income. He can buy an insurance policy that pays him $8,000 if he gets sick for $9,000 now. According to this graph, Jim will
   A. maximize his utility with the insurance policy
   B. would prefer a larger policy that pays at the same rate of $9 of premium for $8 of insurance.
   C. would prefer a smaller policy that pays at the same rate of $9 of premium for $8 of insurance.
   D. buy no insurance since his indifference curve indicates Jim is a risk lover.

19. For a risk averse individual who buys an actuarially fair insurance the MRS is
   A. equal to $\rho/(1-\rho)$.
   B. equal to $(1-\rho)/\rho$
   C. equal to $1/(1-\rho)$
   D. equal to $1/\rho$

20. Suppose that Marisa is faced with a choice between a certainty of receiving $10 and a gamble with a 40 percent chance of winning $100 and a 60 percent chance of losing $50. If Marisa prefers the gamble, she is:
   A. risk averse.
   B. risk loving.
   C. risk neutral.
   D. either B or C.

Problems

1. Most insurance policies have deductibles, meaning that the party buying the insurance is responsible for part of the cost if a "bad" outcome occurs. For example, in a car accident, you might have to pay the first $500 of costs. Are you fully insured? Does this mean you are not risk averse? Is it unfair insurance?

2. One conclusion in the textbook is that people with a greater risk of accident purchase more insurance, *ceteris paribus*. Yet young males, the most likely group to have a car accident, are the least likely to buy it when not required, and most likely to buy minimum amounts when it is required. How do these two facts reconcile?

3. In equilibrium, a risk averse individual buys insurance so that the MRS=p/1-p where p= the premium per $1 of coverage. Suppose the insurer mispecifies the risk, so p<ρ where ρ is the probability of the bad outcome. Show in this case the individual will buy more insurance and, in fact, her consumption will be higher under either outcome.

4. Jim is a risk averse individual who earns $30,000 per year. If he stays healthy he has no medical costs. If he gets sick, it will cost him $10,000 to restore his health. If the probability of getting sick is 1/10, how much insurance would Jim like to buy if premiums are fair?

5. Suppose you have the following game. You are given $500 to start. Three cards are laid face down on a table. One is the Ace of spades, the other two are jokers. If you choose the Ace you get $1 for every $1 you bet, plus you get back the amount you bet. Sketch your budget for this bet. If you are risk neutral, show graphically how much you would bet?

6. Now suppose the game is changed so you start with nothing, you get $1000 if you choose the Ace of spades, and get nothing otherwise. Since you can't lose, of course you take the game. After you make your choice, but before the card is revealed, one of the other cards, a joker, is revealed. You are now given the opportunity to switch to the other card you did not choose? Should you? Explain.

7. Suppose you are choosing between two investment strategies, a Treasury bill (T-bill) or stocks. The T-bill definitely pays a return of $500 but stocks will either pay a return of $0 with 1/5 probability, $400 with 1/5 probability or, $1500 with 1/5 probability. Alternatively, for $100 you can buy some investment advice, which changes the probability of the return to stocks to 1/4 that your return is 0 gain and 3/4 that your gain is $1200. If your utility function is to maximize your return, should you buy the investment advice?

CHAPTER 7. THE FIRM AND ITS GOALS

Chapter Introduction

So far, we've focused on the role households play in markets. Even in centrally planned economies, consumers usually face choices. Facing a set of prices, households make decisions that they hope will give them the highest possible level of utility. Thus, they are demanders in the goods market and suppliers in factor markets. But to fully understand market economies, we need to look at the other principal player in the marketplace for, as we saw in Chapter 1, it is the interaction of the demand *and* supply sides of marketplaces that determines the prices charged and quantities produced, and ultimately the level of activity and distribution within the economy. Firms fulfill these roles. They are suppliers in product markets and demanders in factor markets.

Our concept of a firm is often colored by popular media notions of "big business." Recent reports of layoffs, wage and benefit cuts, and reorganizations have given an impression that firms are large, anonymous entities led by greedy CEOs who make millions of dollars a year at the expense of exploited workers towards whom the firm has no loyalty. But firms cannot be defined so simply. Nor are they inherently evil. Firms range in size from General Electric and Microsoft to the independent pizza parlor and the small general store in rural Idaho and Vermont. What they *do* have in common is a set of principles and goals that define a theory of the firm. Just as the theory of consumption gave us a set of rules for household behavior, the theory of the firm lays out a set of rules that are valid for any firm that meets its assumptions.

This is the first of three chapters that examine what firms do and how they make decisions. Our basic assumption is that firms seek to maximize profit. The first task is to fully understand what economists mean by profit and how their definition differs from what you might normally think of profit. You'll find that some earlier concepts, especially opportunity cost, are important to this understanding. We then move on to see why profit maximization is a reasonable assumption to describe the way firms behave, and then derive basic rules of behavior that apply to any firm meeting a rather loose set of assumptions.

Chapter Outline

This chapter presents a general framework, called the **theory of the firm**, for how **firms** make decisions about **prices** and **output**. Firm decision making is grounded in the idea that firms **maximize profit**. They apply to any firm regardless of other characteristics of the market in which it operates.

Firms must address four basic issues to maximize profit:

- What goods should the firm produce?

- How should the product be produced?

- How much should be produced, and at what price sold?

- How should the product be promoted?

Firms exist to answer these questions in the most effective manner possible. A firm is any organization that buys and sells goods and services. Three types of individuals make up firms: **workers**, who are paid fixed wages and told what to do; **managers**, who are responsible for making decisions and monitoring the workers, and **owners**, who fund the **investment** and bear the **financial risk** associated with the firm. A single person can play more than one role. In a small stationary store, for example, the owner may also manage the shop and work the counter 5 hours a day. Or, in large corporations, the owners (stockholders) are separate from the managers who usually own only a very small share of the stock, and manage the production employees. Firms like United Airlines have a mix: owned primarily by the pilots, many United employees are owners and managers, but some are not.

Firms exist to minimize **transactions costs** by clarifying the relationships between workers, managers, and owners. The organization of the firm sets specific contractual relationships between the parties that minimizes exchange costs. Although contracts between separate entities can (and often are) used to produce goods, within a firm hierarchical relationships and responsibilities are already spelled out, so that the costs of contingencies are minimized. For example, if a worker fails to perform his work, the managers of the firm has clear rights about firing the worker.

The foundation of the theory of the firm is the assumption that the firm's goal is to maximize **economic profit**. Economic profit is the difference between **total revenue** and **total economic cost**. It is what is left over for the owners of the firm after paying for all the factors of production - labor, management skill, and capital. Economic profit differs from the normal interpretation of profit, say one given by an accountant, in the way total cost is calculated. **Economic cost** includes the **opportunity cost** of capital and labor that the owners contribute to the production process. Thus, while we might normally view the profit to a small stationary store just the total return the owner takes out of the store, economists would count as a cost the wages the owner could make elsewhere for the five hours a week she spends serving customers. Once we realize that the wages paid to workers and the interest paid on capital are also their opportunity costs, it becomes clear that total economic cost is the sum of the opportunity cost of all **inputs** to production.

Sunk expenditures (sunk costs) are those which, once made, cannot be recovered. Firms must pay sunk costs no matter what they produce. Sunk expenditures are not an economic cost. When firms invest in capital to be used for production those costs are not sunk unless the capital is unrecoverable and nontransferable. If the capital can be sold, the difference between the purchase price and the resale price is called **depreciation**. For example, used computers are cheaper than new computers, but can be used by lots of businesses. Depreciation indicates the fall in the value of an asset over time. The **user cost of capital**, the opportunity cost of owning and using an asset, consists of depreciation plus the interest forgone by buying the asset.

Firms maximize profit by output, input and promotion levels, often simultaneously. We simplify the analysis by looking at them separately. Profit depends on revenue and costs at each output level. **Total revenue** is the number of units sold times the price of each unit. The **firm-specific demand curve** shows the quantity demanded of a specific firm's output at a particular price charge by that firm. We use the firm specific demand curve to derive the **total revenue curve**, which relates total revenue to output, for the firm. The **total economic cost curve** shows the relationship between a firm's output and the level of total economic cost. It depends on **factor prices**, **technology** and **product characteristics**. The **maximum profit** a firm can make comes at the output where the total revenue curve is the greatest distance above the total economic cost curve.

The **change in profit** is equal to the **change in total revenue** minus the **change in total cost**. The change in total revenue that occurs when one more unit of output is sold is called **marginal revenue**. **Marginal cost** is the change in total cost when one more unit of output is produced. The **marginal output rule** says as long as the firm does not shut down profit is maximized at the output where marginal revenue equals marginal cost. This rule is valid for any profit maximizing firm.

A firm **shuts down** when the profit from not producing exceeds the highest possible profit when it does produce. When a firm shuts down, it has no output and thus no revenue. Since all inputs will be put to their best alternative use when a firm shuts down the opportunity cost, and thus the economic cost, also equals zero. Thus, if it shuts down, a firm has an economic profit of zero. Shutting down is better than staying in business if staying in business results in **economic losses**. The **shut-down rule** says a firm should shut down if the firm's average revenue is less than its average cost for all possible choices of output level. Since economic profit is always less than or equal to accounting profit, a firm may find it best to shut down even if accounting profit is positive. A simple application of the shut down rule is if economic profit is negative when marginal revenue equals marginal cost, the firm should shut down, since at its best output, average revenue is less than average cost.

The profit maximizing assumption has been criticized for several reasons:

- units of output are unclear,
- firms use **markup rules** instead of marginal revenue and marginal cost in deciding price,
- firms can't be perfect when applying profit maximizing rules, and, most importantly,
- since owners and managers are often separate, there is no incentive for managers to maximize profit.

But many characteristics of markup rules show them to be consistent with profit maximization. And the models give consistent ideas of general behavior even if they are not perfectly applicable. Although it is clear that owners want the firm to maximize profit, the goals of the managers must be addressed.

Managers incentives may differ from profit maximization for several reasons. Managers' **consumption of leisure** may conflict with the work necessary to maximize profit. Alternatively, managers may wish to **maximize the amenities** they consume from managing the firm. A third alternative, since prestige often comes to managers of large firms, is **sales revenue maximization**. When managers' goals differ from owners' goals, we have what is termed a **principal-agent relationship**, where the **principals** (the owners) have hired the **agent** (the managers) to perform a task, running the firm, on their behalf. Owners set up **internal control mechanisms** and **external control mechanisms** to try to ensure that the managers do in fact maximize profit. Internal control mechanisms include **corporate governance schemes** (including the responsibilities of managers and the **board of directors**), **proxy fights** and **performance-based compensation**. **Free-riding** on the part of most stockholders limits the effectiveness of many internal control tools. External control mechanisms include **corporate raiding** in the **market for corporate control** and **product market competition**. Lenders and other suppliers of capital may also refuse to supply capital to firms that are not maximizing profit. This is called **discipline from capital suppliers**.

Firms must make decisions over time under uncertainty. Often the costs of hiring and investment decisions and production come before sales and revenues. As a result, firms must analyze profit over time instead of period to period. Similarly, it may not know the revenues that it will have when production decisions must take place.

When costs and revenues come at different times, firms make investment decisions to maximize the **present value** of its profit. The distribution of a firm's profit that are paid to stockholders is called the **dividend payment**. Because stockholders care about **capital gains** in the price of the stock, even short term stockholders want the firm to maximize the present value of the entire future dividend stream, which is the present value of all future profits.

Because returns to investment are uncertain, managers must balance **risk** and **expected return**. Stockholders can reduce risk by diversifying their holdings. Thus, stockholders may wish firms to maximize **expected returns**. Managers cannot diversify away the risk associated with different investments. Thus, from an owner's point of view, a risk averse manager may be biased against risky (but potentially well paying) projects. External control mechanisms mitigate against this happening.

An Application of the Firm and Its Goals

In a much ballyhooed (and much hooted) move, in February 1997 McDonald's Corporation convinced its franchisees to adopt a new marketing strategy that called for 55 cents prices on breakfast and lunch sandwiches when a customer also buys a drink and fries. Although franchisees have long resisted discounting, they went along with it as McDonald's struggled to maintain growth in its business. In 1996, McDonald's US sales 3.3% while its arch rival, Burger King, saw an increase of 2.6% that year (*The Wall Street Journal*, February 27, 1997, page B1).

Question 1: McDonald's tied the low price to the purchase of a drink and fries. As a customer, how would you define the good being offered?

Owners of McDonaldÕs franchises make their money on the sales of goods to customers. McDonaldÕs Corporation makes most of its money by making sales to franchises. The franchise owners dislike price discounts because it cuts into their profits. But McDonald's expects that the pricing strategy could add $50,000 to average store sales within 18 months because of increased sales of fries and soft-drinks.

Question 2: What did McDonald's executives expect to happen to the quantity sold if the price of sandwiches were lowered? What does that say about the slope of the firm-specific demand curve?

Question 3: How are the roles of McDonald's Corporation management and that of the owner of a franchise different?

Question 4: Why would McDonald's Corporation propose a pricing scheme that hurts the profits franchise owners make?

Question 5: Just because sales go up $50,000 at a typical McDonald's restaurant, does that mean profit will go up as well? If profit goes down, what does that mean about marginal revenue and marginal cost? Why might we expect that profit would go down?

Burger King went through four CEOs while finding a strategy to threaten McDonald's dominance of the fast food industry. It was widely believed that the 55 cents pricing strategy was a very risky one for McDonald's to pursue. Some analysts suggest a more conventional advertising strategy, such as a tie-in with a new movie, would be safer.

Question 6: Is McDonald's choice of the risky strategy consistent with the profit maximizing assumption?

The day *The Wall Street Journal* disclosed the price cutting strategy, the stock prices of McDonald's, Burger King and Wendy's all fell.

Question 7: What would cause the stock price of all three companies to fall?

Multiple Choice Questions

1.   Which of the following is an example of an internal control mechanism?

A. Discipline from capital suppliers.
B. Proxy fights.
C. The market for corporate control.
D. Product market competition.

2. Which of the following is an example of an external control mechanism?
A. Performance-based compensation schemes.
B. Corporate governance schemes.
C. Discipline from capital suppliers.
D. All of the above.

3. Stockholders want a firm to maximize:
A. the present value of all future profits.
B. current dividends.
C. total revenue.
D. the present value of profits earned only while the stockholder holds shares in the firm.

4. The marginal output rule states that if a firm does not shut down, then it should produce output at a level where:
A. average revenue equals average cost.
B. marginal revenue equals marginal cost.
C. marginal revenue equals average cost.
D. marginal cost equals average revenue.

5. A firm should shut down if every possible output level results in:
A. average cost less than marginal revenue.
B. marginal revenue less than average cost.
C. average revenue less than average cost.
D. average cost less than average revenue.

6. The economic theory of the firm is based on the assumption that the firm's goal is to maximize:
A. economic profits.
B. accounting profits.
C. market share.
D. revenues.

7.   Accounting profit _____ economic profit.
      A.   can be greater than
      B.   can be less than
      C.   always equals
      D.   can be greater or less than

8.   The goal of the economic theory of the firm is to predict how the firm answers the question of:
      A.   what price to charge.
      B.   what combination of inputs to use in making its product.
      C.   how to promote its product.
      D.   All of the above are correct.

9.   Total economic cost must be calculated as the:
      A.   sum of the accounting cost of all of the inputs.
      B.   difference between the accounting and imputed costs of all of the inputs.
      C.   sum of the opportunity cost of all of the inputs.
      D.   difference between the opportunity and imputed costs of all of the inputs.

10.   Suppose that Firm A has eight years remaining on a ten-year lease for a machine. Annual lease payments are $2,000. The firm can use the machine itself or sublease it for $500 per year.
      A.   The annual economic cost of the machine is $2,000.
      B.   The firm has a sunk expenditure of $1,500.
      C.   The firm has a sunk expenditure of $2,000.
      D.   The annual economic cost of the machine is $1,500.

11.   The opportunity cost that an owner incurs as a consequence of owning and using an asset is known as:
      A.   a sunk expenditure.
      B.   depreciation
      C.   capital loss.
      D.   the user cost of capital.

12.   Marginal revenue is defined as:
      A.   the change in total revenue due to the sale of one more unit of output.
      B.   the change in total revenue divided by quantity of output.
      C.   total revenue divided by quantity of output.
      D.   the change in total revenue divided by the change in total cost.

13. The change in economic profit when the firm produces one more unit of output equals:
    A. total revenue minus total cost.
    B. marginal revenue minus marginal cost.
    C. average revenue minus average cost.
    D. average revenue minus marginal cost.

14. The firm's total cost divided by the number of units produced is the:
    A. marginal cost.
    B. average cost.
    C. imputed cost.
    D. user cost.

15. When costs and revenues occur at different dates, the firm should make its investment decisions to:
    A. maximize the present value of its profit.
    B. maximize the future value of its profit.
    C. minimize the present value of its costs.
    D. minimize the future value of its costs.

Questions 16-17 refer to the following:

The demand curve and total costs for Alice's Boutique are given below:

Total Output	Price	Total Cost
0	$70	$7
1	$66	$8
2	$62	$11
3	$58	$16
4	$54	$23
5	$50	$32
6	$46	$43
7	$42	$56
8	$38	$71

16. Alice's Boutique should produce a total output equal to:
    A. 0 units.
    B. 3 units.
    C. 7 units.
    D. 8 units.

17.   Alice's Boutique's maximum profit is:
       A.   -$7.
       B. $158.
       C. $233.
       D. $238.

Questions 18-19 refer to the following graph:

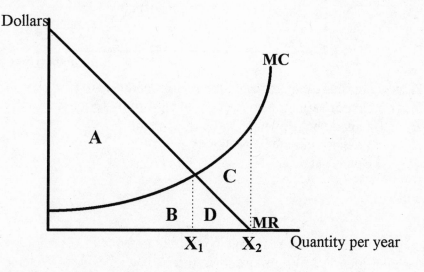

18.   At output level x_2, total revenue equals _____, total cost equals _____, and economic profit equals _____ for this firm.
       A.   areas A + B + D; areas B + C + D; area A - area C
       B.   areas A + B + D; areas B + C + D; areas A + C
       C.   areas A + C; areas B + D; area D - area C
       D.   areas A + C; areas B + D; - area C

19.   A manager desiring to maximize economic profit chooses:
       A.   output level x_1.
       B.   output level x_2.
       C.   an output level between x_1 and x_2.
       D.   an output level less than x_1.

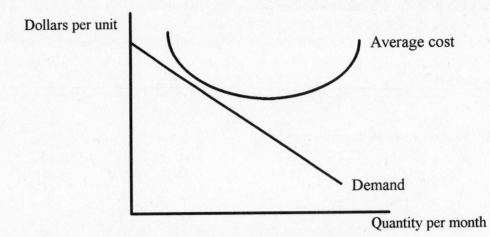

Dollars per unit

Average cost

Demand

Quantity per month

20.   According to the curves drawn in the figure, this firm
    A.   cannot earn a positive economic profit by producing output.
    B.   should shut down.
    C.   should continue to produce.
    D.   Both A and B.

Problems

1. Helen opens up her own economic consulting practice in her home. The fee that she charges per hour is $100. In order to start her own business, Helen quit a job which was paying $50,000 per year and cashed in a $10,000 certificate of deposit that was yielding 5 percent
    interest. During the first year, expenses for items such as paper and utilities totaled $5,000. Find Helen's imputed cost for her own labor. Then find her economic costs for the first year.

2. Suppose Helen provides 1000 hours of consulting services in her first year. Find her economic profit and her accounting profit.

3. Suppose you are in charge of production for a company that uses labor in its production process. After a labor strike and negotiation, wages will increase 10 percent. You must make a recommendation to the board about output. Discuss how your recommendation might differ if a) the firm is profit maximizing, and b) the firm is a nonprofit firm which sets economic profit to zero.

4. In 1991 *The Wall Street Journal* reported that Bear Sterns and Company estimated that for the second quarter American Airlines would earn only about 60 cents per share, compared to $1.30 the previous year. At that time, stock for American Airlines was selling for $60 per share. At the same time the rate of return on a 90 day government bond was 7 percent. Calculate American Airlines the economic profits or losses per share.

5. The early 1990s was a period of bank closings that was unprecedented since the Depression. Many of the troubled banks replaced the managers that had got them in trouble, and were being operated in a manner which covered only economic costs but not sunk costs. Nevertheless, the Federal Deposit Insurance Corporation closed many of these banks. Was the FDIC move in the best interest of taxpayers, who had to cover the costs of closing the banks?

6. The banks that got into trouble did so because of taking risky investments in real estate markets, particularly in major southern cities. Discuss whether this was reasonable behavior on the parts of the banks, or whether it betrayed the faith of the stockholders.

7. In 1991 two entrepreneurs in Chicago, Mark Weinberg and Mark Finch, started the *Blue Line*, an unofficial alternative to the program published by the Chicago Blackhawks. Weinberg and Finch collected about $2,280 revenue per week from the publication. The cost of printing, graphics, distribution. And other items came to about $1200 per week. Their initial investment was $12,000 for advertising, permits and other such nonrecoverable items. Assuming both partners (at least one was a lawyer) left jobs paying $50,000 per year, find their accounting and economic profit or loss.

8. Republican policy makers often claim that lowering the rate of tax on the profits business firms make will stimulate the economy. Daniel Moynihan, a Democratic Senator from New York suggests that as an alternative, the Social Security payroll tax should be lowered. He claims lowering profit taxes will do nothing to stimulate the output of existing firms, while lowering payroll taxes will. Assuming firms are profit maximizers, and the profits tax is on economic profits, who is correct?

CHAPTER 8. TECHNOLOGY AND PRODUCTION

Chapter Introduction

Consumption goods that households buy in product markets come from firms that combine raw materials and talent to produce finished goods. Usually we think of production as a process that involves physical inputs and physical outputs. Mills combine heat, iron ore and tin with labor to give us steel. Water, seeds, equipment and labor produce agricultural crops. In the service sector, much, if not most, inputs involve the effort of labor. Other inputs play a secondary role. And the output itself often lacks any physical presence. Legal assistance is more important for increasing the security of our lives than it is for producing contracts, *per se*. In this chapter we learn how technology constrains the production decisions that all firms must make.

A problem common to all production -- whether it involves a physical output like a car or a service output like cleaning -- is how to best combine different inputs to get the desired output. As Professors Katz and Rosen point out, a car can be built by hand, by using robots in an automated process, or by some combination. Similarly, paraprofessionals can replace some time a lawyer might spend on a contract without adversely affecting the product. No matter what the product, firms must decide what combination of inputs to use to produce its output.

We don't answer the question about *which* input combination to use in this chapter: that is left for chapter 9. Instead, our focus here is on the physical relationship that transforms inputs to output. Thus, we won't talk about dollars or costs. At the same time, keep in mind that what we do here is the prelude to understanding costs of production. And we know you are not engineers -- neither are we. So the production relationships are by necessity vague. We'll develop an understanding of production, not its engineering.

Before moving on, you might be interested about the "production" of economics. Economists use mathematical tools. Efficiency dictates that we find the least cost method of understanding new areas. Such is the case with technology and production. You will find, with minor modification, that the theory of production is similar to the theory of consumer choice. A lot of what you see in this chapter is old tools with new labels. Use this fact -- it makes lots of the stuff in this chapter easier.

Chapter Outline

Technology is the firm's options for combining inputs to produce some specific output. The **production function** shows the highest level of output, called the **total product**, that the firm can produce from a given level of inputs. Algebraically the production function can be represented $F(L, K)$ where L is the level of labor used, K is the level of capital used, and the function $F(\bullet, \bullet)$ represents technology. $F(L, K)$ denotes the level of total product that firms obtain when they put specific values for L and K into the function. It is similar to the utility function used in chapter 2, with the important distinction that production is **cardinal** while utility was **ordinal**. Thus, while we were unable to compare specific levels of utility, especially between individuals, the cardinal characteristic of production allows us to make comparisons about the *level* of production within a firm and between firms.

An **isoquant** is a graphical representation of the production function, showing different combinations of L and K which give the *same* level of output. (You can think of it as the production equivalent of a consumer's indifference curve.) When all the isoquants corresponding to a given production function but showing different levels of output are put on the same graph we have an **isoquant map**.

Although isoquants show different possibilities a firm can use to produce a specific level of output, all of those possibilities may not be available all the time. The **decision-making horizon** can limit which combinations a firm can use. In the **short run,** only one input (usually labor) is a **variable factor** while all other inputs are **fixed factors**. In the **long run** all inputs are variable. Thus, isoquants describe the choices for production in the long run.

Marginal physical product (MPP) is the additional output that is produced when a firm uses one more unit of an input, holding all the other inputs at their previous levels. Algebraically,

$$MPP_L = \Delta X/\Delta L$$

where MPP_L is the marginal physical product of labor, ΔX is the units of additional output we get, and ΔL is the units of additional labor used. When the technology shows **increasing marginal physical product** of an input, it is said to exhibit **increasing marginal returns**. Graphically, the MPP curve has a positive slope, and the slope of the total product curve, which equals the MPP is increasing. With **constant marginal returns**, the MPP is unchanged as the amount of the input used increases. The MPP curve is flat and the total product curve has a constant slope. If the MPP of an input falls as the amount of the input used goes up, the technology exhibits **diminishing marginal returns**. The MPP slopes downward, and the total product curve has a diminishing slope. Thus, while total product may still increase, it does so at a slower rate.

The marginal returns in a single production function may change as the level of input used changes. We commonly expect increasing marginal returns at first, followed by a period of constant marginal returns, and finally as the amount of the input used gets large, diminishing marginal returns set in. Because this pattern is true for so many production activities, economists often refer to the **law of diminishing marginal returns**.

In the long run, firms can choose to employ different levels of all inputs simultaneously. **Factor substitution** is the firms' ability to choose its **long run input mix**. Isoquants graphically show how factors can be substituted. The negative of the slope of the isoquant, called the **marginal rate of technical substitution (MRTS)**, shows the rate at which available technology allows the substitution of one factor for another. Along an isoquant, the change in output is zero, thus

$$MPP_L \times \Delta L + MPP_K \times \Delta K = 0$$

which, by rearranging, gives

$$-\Delta K/\Delta L = MPP_L/ MPP_K.$$

The left hand side of this equation is the negative of the slope of the isoquant so we have that

$$MRTS = MPP_L/ MPP_K.$$

Thus the marginal rate of technical substitution between two inputs equals the ratio of the marginal physical products of the inputs. When the MRTS of one factor for another falls as the amount of the first factor goes up, the technology exhibits **diminishing marginal rate of technical substitution**. Most technologies exhibit diminishing marginal rate of technical substitution, which derives from diminishing marginal physical products.

When factors are **perfect substitutes**, they exhibit a constant marginal rate of technical substitution. In this case isoquants are linear. If factors cannot substitute for one another at all,, isoquants are right angles with the angles all on a ray from the origin. This is called a **fixed proportion production function** and is the production equivalent to the indifference choice between **perfect complements** that we saw in the theory of consumer choice.

The **degree of returns to scale** shows the rate at which the amount of output increases as all inputs are changed **proportionately**. Depending on the technology, firms can experience increasing, constant or decreasing returns to scale. With **increasing returns to scale**, output changes **more than proportionately** to the **proportionate change** in inputs. **Constant returns to scale** show proportionate changes in output, while **decreasing returns to scale** show less than proportionate changes in output. Returns to scale are largely independent of the marginal physical product curves.

An Application of Technology and Production

Agricultural biotechnology is finally proving itself. In 1996, according to a report in *The Wall Street Journal* ("Huge Biotech Harvest is a Boon for Farmers - And for Monsanto," October 24, 1996, page A1), farmers planted millions of commercial acres of genetically altered crops for the first time in 1996. And it paid off. Farmer Dennis Greiner reported that an acre planted with genetically engineered soybean seeds yielded 7 more bushels of soybeans than the 45 that were harvested from a nearby field planted with conventional seed.

Question 1: Think of a production process that uses seed and other inputs. Graphically show how agricultural biotechnology has shifted the isoquants.

One of the big changes from using genetically altered seed is that the plants that come from the altered seeds are rendered *immune* to the herbicide Roundup. Thus, the entire field can be sprayed, killing off the weeds that normally compete with the soybeans for sun and nutrients. Farmers can get the same number of bushels from less land by using more herbicide.

Question 2: Graphically show how the altered seeds changes the production choice farmers make between land and Roundup.

Question 3: What has happened to the MPP_{land} and the $MPP_{Roundup}$? What about the MRTS between land and Roundup?

Question 4: Alternatively, if we include biotechnology in "other inputs" we can build a production function between land and other inputs. For a given output, show how biotechnology has changed the point on an isoquant farmers might choose.

When a farmer can full spray a field with Roundup, rather than needing to spot spray the weeds, he saves both his labor time and wear and tear on farm equipment.

Question 5: What will happen to the total product of the farmer's labor time and of the farm equipment? Draw the total product curve for labor before and after genetically altered seed became available.

Question 6: Does the change in the marginal physical products and the MRTS change the returns to scale? Explain your answer.

Mr. Greiner, the farmer mentioned above, planted only 65 acres of 200 in genetically altered seeds last year. Suppose he wants to keep his output the same next year.

Question 7: Is it a short run or long run decision if he decides to plant more acres in genetically altered seed next year? Is Mr. Greiner substituting one input for another? If so, which inputs are being increased, and which decreased? Explain your answer.

Multiple Choice Questions

1. A production function with diminishing marginal returns can exhibit:
   A. increasing returns to scale.
   B. constant returns to scale.
   C. decreasing returns to scale.
   D. all of the above.

2. In the short run, _____ variable, while in the long run, _____ variable.
   A. no factors are / all factors are
   B. all factors are / only one factor is
   C. only one factor is / all factors are
   D. all factors are / no factors are

3. If a production function exhibits a diminishing marginal rate of technical substitution, then the corresponding isoquants are:
   A. bowed toward the origin.
   B. bowed away from the origin.
   C. straight lines.
   D. vertical lines.

4. Let MPP_L represent the marginal physical productivity of labor and MPP_K the marginal physical product of capital. The marginal rate of technical substitution between capital and labor is equal to:
   A. $MPP_L \times MPP_K$.
   B. MPP_L/MPP_K.
   C. $MPP_L - MPP_K$.
   D. $MPP_L + MPP_K$

5. The production function $Q = F(K, L) = K^2L^2$ exhibits:
   A. decreasing returns to scale.
   B. constant returns to scale.
   C. increasing returns to scale.
   D. no effect of scale.

6. Suppose that ice cream and milk must be used in a fixed proportion to make ice cream shakes. This means that, on a graph with ice cream on one axis and milk on the other, the isoquants for ice cream shakes:
   A. have a constant downward slope.
   B. are right angles.
   C. are horizontal lines.
   D. are vertical lines.

Question 7 refers to the following graph:

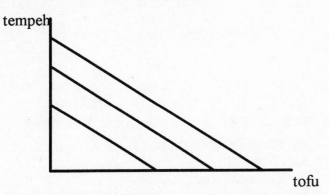

7. According to the isoquant map for the production of soy burger patties:
   A. tofu and tempeh are perfect substitutes.
   B. the marginal rate of technical substitution between tofu and tempeh must equal one.
   C. the marginal rate of technical substitution between tofu and tempeh equals zero.
   D. Both A and B are correct.

Question 8 refers to the following graph:

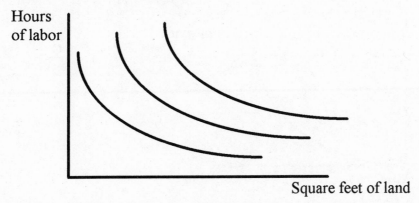

8. Moving downward along a given isoquant for the production of bonsai trees:
   A. labor and land are perfect substitutes.
   B. the marginal rate of technical substitution between labor and land is diminishing.
   C. the marginal rate of technical substitution between labor and land is increasing.
   D. there is no factor substitution between labor and land.

9.   A curve that shows all of the input combinations that yield the same amount of output is known as:
    A.   an isocost line.
    B.   an indifference curve.
    C.   a total product curve.
    D.   an isoquant curve.

10.   For a given output level, the firm's feasible input combinations are indicated by:
    A.   a single point on an isoquant in the long run.
    B.   the entire isoquant in the short run.
    C.   a single point on an isoquant in the short run.
    D.   Both A and B are correct.

11.   Diminishing marginal returns refers to a decrease in:
    A.   total output when the amount of one input increases, ceteris paribus.
    B.   the rise in total output when the amount of one input increases, ceteris paribus.
    C.   total output when the amount of all inputs increases.
    D.   the rise in total output when the amount of all inputs increases.

Question 12 refers to the following graph:

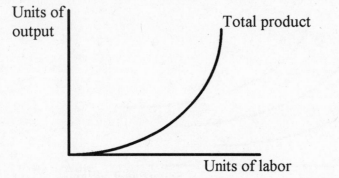

12.   The total product curve exhibits:
    A.   increasing marginal returns to labor.
    B.   decreasing marginal returns to labor.
    C.   an increasing marginal rate of technical substitution.
    D.   a diminishing marginal rate of technical substitution.

13. The rate at which the firm can substitute one factor for another while still producing the same level of output is known as the:
    A. degree of returns to scale.
    B. rate of substitution.
    C. rate of marginal returns.
    D. rate of technical substitution.

14. Consider an isoquant curve that is graphed with units of labor on the horizontal axis and units of capital on the vertical axis. Suppose that, at a given point on the isoquant, the marginal physical product of labor is 10 and the marginal physical product of capital is 20. At that point:
    A. the marginal rate of technical substitution equals 2.
    B. the slope of the isoquant is -2.
    C. the marginal rate of technical substitution is 0.5.
    D. Both A and B are correct.

15. If a firm increases the amounts of all of its inputs by 10 percent and its output therefore increases by 20 percent, the firm's production function exhibits:
    A. increasing returns to scale.
    B. decreasing returns to scale.
    C. increasing marginal returns.
    D. decreasing marginal returns.

16. The highest total amount of output that a firm can produce given the amount of its inputs is known as the:
    A. marginal physical product.
    B. degree of returns to scale.
    C. marginal rate of technical substitution.
    D. total product of L and K.

17. The slope of the total product curve as the firm changes the amount of labor while holding the amount of capital fixed is equal to the:
    A. marginal rate of technical substitution.
    B. marginal physical product of labor.
    C. marginal physical product of capital.
    D. degree of returns to scale.

Use the following table for questions 18-19

Total Number of Capital	Total Amount of Laborers	Output
100	0	0
100	1	5
100	2	12
100	3	21
100	4	30
100	5	37
100	6	42

18. According to the input and output data in the table, the marginal physical product of labor between the second and third units of labor equals:
    A.   21 bicycles.
    B.   9 bicycles.
    C.   33 bicycles.
    D.   12 bicycles.

19. According to the input and output data in the table, the production of bicycles exhibits:
    A.   increasing marginal returns to labor for all output levels shown.
    B.   decreasing marginal returns to labor for all output levels shown.
    C.   constant marginal returns to labor for all output levels shown.
    D.   first increasing, then constant, and finally decreasing marginal returns to labor.

Question 20 refers to the following graph:

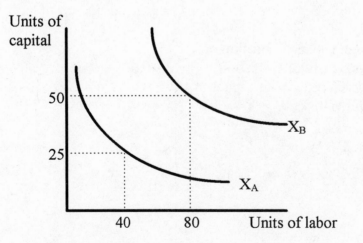

20. Suppose X_A represents the isoquant for 100 units of output and X_B represents the isoquant for 150 units of output in the figure. The production function for this firm exhibits:
    A. increasing returns to scale.
    B. decreasing returns to scale.
    C. constant returns to scale.
    D. increasing marginal returns.

Problems

1. Workers in a factory work 8 hour shifts. The machinery used in production needs oil and gasoline each day. It can hold enough gasoline to operate 8 hours without a refill. Once a day oil must be added. Refilling with gasoline, which is done automatically without labor when the machine needs it, takes 1 hour. Adding the oil takes 1/2 hour and cannot be done when gasoline is being refilled. As long as it is added once a day, the oil can be scheduled for any time. The machine must be shut off when it is refilled with either gasoline or oil. When it is operating, it produces 10 units of output per hour. Find the total product and marginal physical product curves for workers using this machine. Assume the union contract sets the shifts from 8 AM to 4 PM, 4 PM to Midnight, and Midnight to 8AM, and no deviation from this schedule is permitted.

2. What type of returns to scale exist for the factory in question 1? Now suppose the refilling must be done manually, and machine operators don't have the skills necessary to refill the machines. The factory must hire a worker specifically refill the machines with gas and oil. Does that change your answer? Explain why or why not.

3. Finally, suppose the machines cannot work without an operator. Draw the isoquant map for machines and workers.

4. A major hospital in Washington state reported that a certain procedure requires 3 nursing hours to perform. A nursing hour is defined as 1 nurse working 1 hour. One unit of the procedure can be accomplished by 1 nurse working 3 hours, 2 nurses working together for 1.5 hours each, and so forth (so for $Q = 1$, $N \times H = 3$). Describe the production function and the returns to scale for this procedure.

5. New rules require that nurses doing the procedure discussed in question 4 have special on-sight training that takes four months. Describe the short run and long run, and discuss ways the hospital can increase the number of procedures it can perform in the long run and short run.

6. A production function is such that the $MPP_K = 1/K$ and the $MPP_L = 2/L$. Does this production function show diminishing MPP of labor and capital? What is the MRTS if $K = 10$ and $L = 30$? What if $K = 40$ and $L = 60$? Is there diminishing MRTS?

7. Show that if a firm has the production function $Q = aK + bL$ where a and b are constants that it has constant returns to scale. Now suppose the production function is $Q = K^a L^b$. Show that if $a + b = 1$, there are constant returns to scale, if $a + b < 1$ there are decreasing returns to scale, and if $a + b > 1$, there are increasing returns to scale.

8. Feedlots buy young cattle and raise them to market weight. A feedlot's output is pounds of cattle. Traditionally feedlots buy year-old cattle that weigh about 700 pounds, feed them for 90 days, and sell them when they reach about 1050 pounds. It takes about 2450 pounds of grain to get the 700 pound feeder calf to market weight, at which point it is called a steer. Feedlots can also buy younger cattle that weigh about 550 pounds, feed them 3250 pounds of grain, and have a 1050 pound steer to sell. Find the MRTS between young cattle weight and grain if the output is 1 market weight steer.

CHAPTER 9. COST

Chapter Introduction

We saw in the last chapter that various technologies provide firms many options about how to produce goods. With many choices available, a firm must somehow decide which combination of inputs it will use within available technological limits. Depending on the production function, it may be very easy to substitute one input for another, or almost impossible. Usually, as we see in the textbook's example of Toyota and Nissan, substitution is possible, but not perfect. So a firm's manager must decide what inputs to use and how to combine them. In this chapter we see *how* firms make those decisions. Technology defines the options. Now we see why firms will choose one particular option.

Firms care about input combinations because of their profit maximization goals. Some input combinations are cheaper than others. More profits can be made, given *any* level of output, by minimizing the cost of producing that output. By knowing how inputs combine physically and incorporating input costs, firms can calculate marginal and average cost curves. As we saw in chapter 7, firms need to consider their economic costs if they are to find the profit maximizing level of output. Although they probably don't consciously plot their cost curves, by trial and error firms reveal what their costs look like, and take them into account when deciding how much to produce.

Chapter Outline

Firms make production decisions over two time horizons, the **short run** and the **long run**. Consequently, the analysis of costs of production must be made over similar decision horizons.

Firms choose among different combinations of inputs that give the same output based on the **economic costs** of production. Firms must somehow measure the **opportunity cost** of production inputs if they are to make logically sound decisions. **Short run opportunity cost** excludes expenditures on **fixed factors**, like capital, since by definition there is no alternative use for a fixed factor in the short run. In the short run, expenditures on capital and other fixed factors are considered **sunk expenditures** – this assumes that firms cannot retool machinery or other fixed assets to produce other goods in the short run. Costs that represent the short run opportunity cost of producing a given output is called the **short run economic cost** of producing that output. In the short run, only variable factors have opportunity costs, so another name for the short run economic cost is **short run variable cost (VC_{SR})**.

We use the isoquant to find the short run variable cost of any particular output with the following procedure:
- Using the isoquant or production function, find the level of capital that is fixed in the short run.
- Find the level of labor needed given that capital to produce the desired output.

- Multiply the quantity of labor found by the wage rate. This is short run variable cost.

To find the entire short run variable cost schedule, repeat these steps at each output level.

Short run variable cost does not capture all the expenditures that firms must make in the short run. Although not relevant for decision making, payments for fixed factors, called **short run fixed costs**, can provide useful information to the firm, first for planning future production and second for evaluating past decisions. The sum of short run variable cost and short run fixed cost is know as **short run total cost**.

Firms must hire more variable inputs to increase output in the short run. Since they have to spend more to get more output, the short run variable cost curve slopes upward. Capital contributes to the productivity of variable inputs – for example, a tractor makes a farmer more productive than a horse does -- so the position of the short run variable cost curve depends on the amount of fixed inputs. Usually an increase in capital lowers short run variable cost. **Short run marginal cost (MC_{SR})** is the change in short run variable cost that comes from increasing output by one unit. In the short run, marginal cost is the amount of variable input needed to increase output by one unit times the cost of the additional variable input.

The cost of one additional unit of the variable input is called **the marginal factor cost (MFC)**. To find MC_{SR} we first note that MPP_L is the additional output from one more unit of labor. Thus, 1 more unit of output requires $1/MPP_L$ units of labor. Then the additional cost of one more unit of output, MC_{SR} equals $1/MPP_L \times MFC$ so $MC_{SR}=MFC/MPP_L$.

When a firm is a **price taker**, the marginal factor cost is equal to the price of the factor, including wages, benefits and other costs associated with labor, denoted by w. Thus for the price taking firm, $MC_{SR}=w/MPP_L$. The lower the marginal physical product of labor, or the higher the wage rate, the higher the marginal cost of output. Thus, when the production function exhibits the usual diminishing marginal product of labor, the short run marginal cost curve slopes upward.

Short run average variable cost (AVC_{SR}) is variable cost divided by the number of units being produced, so $AVC_{SR}= VC_{SR}/x$ where x is the number of units produced. It equals the average amount of labor used per unit of output times the wage rate. When production is characterized by increasing marginal product labor short run average cost is diminishing as output goes up, simple because the average amount of labor per unit of output is decreasing. When there are diminishing marginal products of labor, short run average cost is increasing.

Short run average total cost (ATC_{SR}) is short run total cost divided by output, and **short run average fixed cost (AFC_{SR})** is short run fixed costs divided by output. Since fixed costs don't change as output goes up, AFC_{SR} always decreases as output increases. Since $TC_{SR}=VC_{SR}+FC_{SR}$, dividing both sides by output gives the relationship $ATC_{SR}=AVC_{SR}+AFC_{SR}$. Because AFC_{SR} is always decreasing, at large outputs, $AVC_{SR}+AFC_{SR}$ come close together. Also, whenever marginal cost is below average variable cost, average variable cost falls, and whenever marginal cost is above average variable cost, average variable cost goes up. Using these two facts, we know that the short run marginal cost curve will always cross the short run average variable cost curve at the point where average variable cost is at its minimum.

In the long run all inputs may be varied, so expenditures on all factors are economic costs and firms can substitute one factor for another. The **economically efficient** input combination to produce a specific level of output is the one that has the lowest opportunity cost. We measure the cost of different combinations of inputs with **isocost curves**, which show the different input combinations that cost the same amount. In absolute value, the slope of the isocost curve is equal to the ratio of the input prices. The **isocost map** is the collection of isocost lines that exist given a set of factor prices.

The economically efficient input combination for producing a specific level of output is at that point where the isoquant for that output is tangent to an isocost line. That isocost line determines the economically efficient cost, and the level of inputs at the **tangent point** is the economically efficient combination. Since slopes are equal at tangents, the MRTS = w/r where r is the user cost of capital and w is the price per unit of labor. Thus, we find that $MPP_L/MPP_K = w/r$ or $MPP_L/w = MPP_K/r$. A firm that takes factor prices as given should operate at a point where, *at the margin*, the inputs' marginal physical products are proportional to their prices. We can use this fact to understand how firms respond to changes in factor prices, technology or output amount or characteristics.

Since in absolute value the slope of the isocost line is equal to the ratio of the input prices, a change in the price of labor (w) pivots the line. If w increases, the line pivots inward, and if w decreases, the line pivots outward. The pivot point is the intercept on the capital axis since the price per unit of capital has not changed.

Suppose the price per unit of labor goes up. If labor lies on the horizontal axis, the isocost curve gets steeper. Thus, to find a tangent to a given isoquant, we need to find a point on the isoquant with a steeper slope. We'll find it further up on the isoquant, where more capital and less labor is used. When the price of an input goes up, the firm substitutes away from the factor whose price has risen, and towards the factor whose price is unchanged. Even with this substitution, however, total cost must always increase when the price of one of the factors used in production rises.

Technological improvements allow firms to produce the same amount of output with fewer inputs. This will not effect factor prices, so the isocost map is unchanged. However, isoquants will shift inward. Technological improvements lower firms' total costs, and fuel **economic growth**.

The nature and the amount of output also affect isoquants but not isocosts for the price taking firm. If the quality of the products improves, firms must usually add more inputs to produce the same output: Thus, isoquants move outward. Since input prices have not changed, the isocost lines all have the same slope as before. But since more inputs are needed, total cost is higher. In the same way increasing the output quantity requires moving to an isoquant that is further from the origin. More inputs are used, and thus the tangent indicating the optimal input combination lies on a higher isocost line. Total cost goes up. If we find the set of tangents between isoquants and isocosts at various levels of output, we show the **expansion path** for the firm's production. This path shows the different input combinations that should be used for the least cost production of all output levels, holding technology, input prices and product characteristics constant (e.g., *ceteris paribus*).

We can use the expansion path to find the **long run total cost (C_{LR}) curve**. **Long run total cost** is the minimum total opportunity cost needed to produce a given amount of output in the long run. We find long run total cost by finding the tangency between the isoquant and isocost line and computing the cost of the input combination at that point. If we do this for all output levels, we have the long run total cost curve.

Long run marginal cost of output is the change in long run total cost to produce one more unit of output. Long run marginal cost is simply the difference between the tangent isocost lines if output is expanded by one unit. **Long run average cost (AC_{LR})** is long run total cost divided by the number of units being produced. Since all costs are economic costs in the long run, AC_{LR} can be used to determine a firm's shut down rule. That is, a firm should shut down if, in the long run, it cannot cover all of its long run average cost at any output level.

Long run average cost may increase or decrease as output goes up. If AC_{LR} decreases as output increases, there are **economies of scale**. Alternatively, if AC_{LR} increases as output goes up, there are **diseconomies of scale**. Economies of scale can come from many sources. One of the more common sources is derived from the **technological returns to scale** that we studied in the last chapter. When there are constant returns to scale, doubling the amount of input gives the double the amount of output. But doubling inputs will also double costs. By definition $AC_{LR} = C_{LR}/Q$. If we double both C_{LR} and Q, the ratio remains unchanged, and so AC_{LR} is the same. Thus, with constant returns to scale in production comes constant long run average cost.

Further analysis shows us that increasing returns to scale in production creates a long run average total cost curve that exhibits economies of scale. Looking again at the relationship between doubling inputs and output, increasing returns to scale implies that output *more than doubles* as we double input quantities Since total cost has just doubled, by the formula $AC_{LR} = C_{LR}/Q$ long run average cost must decline. Similarly, with decreasing returns to scale in production the long run average total cost curve will show diseconomies of scale. It is very important for you to realize these are different, though related, concepts. Returns to scale is an aspect of the physical production of a good. Economies of scale refers to an economic analysis of the costs of producing a good.

Economies of scope is a related concept to economies of scale. "Economies of scope" means a firm can produce two products together more cheaply than it would cost if two separate firms produced the two products independently. Economies of scope come from the ability of the production processes to share some skills or facility, or if the byproduct of one production process can be used as an input for producing the other good, like a cereal factory also producing high fructose corn syrup as it mills the grain for its cereal.

Two key differences exist between long run and short run costs. In the short run sunk inputs do not impose economic (opportunity) costs. But in the long run, all costs are economic costs since all inputs are variable. This tends to raise long run economic costs relative to short run economic costs. But since all factors can be varied in the long run but not the short run, the ability to substitute one input for another may help the firm to lower average cost. In terms of *economic costs*, substitutability of inputs and opportunity cost of all inputs have opposite effects - so it is possible that the short run variable cost exceeds the long run total cost. For total expenditures on inputs, only the second difference matters, so short run total cost is always at least as large as long run total cost.

The appendix to chapter 9 uses calculus to analyze production functions **and cost minimization**. It uses a **Cobb-Douglas production function** to illustrate how we can express the properties of production functions using calculus. The marginal physical product of a factor is the **partial derivative** of the production function with respect to that factor (i.e., $MPP_L = \partial F/\partial L$ where F represents the production function and L represents the factor, in this case labor). Diminishing marginal returns to labor holds if $\partial MPP_L/\partial L < 0$. Since the $MRTS = MPP_L/MPP_K$ we find that the $MRTS = [\partial F/\partial L]/[\partial F/\partial K]$. Returns to scale are found by comparing $F(\beta L, \beta K)$ to $\beta F(K, L)$.

By using the rule that for cost minimization the $MRTS = w/r$ along with the production function we can find that the derivative of the cost function with respect to a factor price is the cost minimizing quantity of that factor. The Lagrangean method is used to find the cost minimizing method of production with more than two inputs. To do so, form the Lagrangean problem

$$L = wL + rK + tE + \mu[x - F(L,K,E)]$$

where the three inputs are L, K, and E with respective per unit prices of w, r, and t, x is the specific amount of output, $F(\bullet,\bullet,\bullet)$ is the production function, and μ is the Lagrangean multiplier. **Differentiate** the Lagrangean with respect to L, K, E and μ, and solve the resulting first order necessary conditions for specific values of L, K, E and μ.

Economists often try to **estimate** production functions using **time-series, cross-sectional or panel data studies**. An alternative approach is to use **engineering data**. One serious problem that economists face when estimating production functions is **aggregation**: how can we lump many types of workers together into measures of labor and many types of machines and physical inputs into measures of capital? Additionally, production functions require that firms be operating **efficiently**, but firms often make errors or face constraints that prevent them from using optimal input combinations.

An Application of Cost

In the last chapter we applied the analysis of technology and production to agricultural biotechnology. As you should recall, Monsanto Corporation had genetically altered soybean seeds to make them immune to the herbicide Roundup. When farmers used the new seeds they could spray the entire field, killing more weeds than spot spraying could. If the intensive spraying was used, yield per acre increased from 45 bushels to 52 bushels.

Question 1: Once a field is already planted in the new seeds, what is the variable input? If a farmer has no other use of his time, is there an economic cost to using it as labor on the farm? Explain.

Suppose regular spraying of a field takes 3 gallons of Roundup, while the more intensive spraying that can only be done on fields with genetically altered seeds takes 5 gallons of Roundup. Both types of spraying take about the same amount of time and equipment. After a field has been planted with the genetically altered seed, either method of spraying can be used. (Ignore the option of not spraying at all.) If farmers use the old, less intensive method, their yields are about the same as if regular seed had been planted.

Question 2: At that point, what is the variable input? Should a farmer make decisions based on the fact that the more expensive genetically altered seed was planted? What type of cost do we call that?

Question 3: If a gallon of Roundup costs $5, what is the approximate short run marginal cost of 1 more bushel of soybeans?

Dennis Greiner, a farmer showcased in the story, farms 200 acres of land. Suppose he had planted all 200 acres with the genetically altered seed. For each acre, he now must choose between the spraying methods. Suppose, in 20 acre increments, he can choose either method. Assume there are no costs but the cost of the Roundup.

Question 4: Construct short run variable cost and marginal cost curves for using the intensive spray. What shape does the short run average variable cost curve have? Why?

The technology yields a relatively straightforward production function for soybeans. For each acre planted, the farmer can get 52 bushels if he uses genetically altered seed and 5 gallons of Roundup, or 45 acres with regular seed and 3 gallons of Roundup. Seeding an acre of land with the genetically altered seed costs $15. Planting an acre with regular seed costs $5 per acre. Before he plants, Mr. Greneir will decide which method of planting to use for each 20 acre parcel.

Question 5: Using this information, construct short run variable cost and marginal cost curves for Mr. Grenier at the time of *planting*. Assume the amount of land he has is fixed and can't be used for any other crop.

We don't know the rental rate of land that Mr. Grenier faces, but suppose it is $100 per acre. Now allow for the idea that the land has other uses (that is why there is a rental rate for it).

Question 6: Think of using the genetically altered seed and the extra Roundup as 1 unit of "innovative technology." Construct an isoquant between land and innovative technology if output is to be 2,000 bushels of soybeans. Do the same for 5,000 bushels and 9,000 bushels. What is the MRTS?

Question 7: Innovative technology costs $25 per unit based on the extra cost of seed and the extra Roundup used. Find the optimal combination of land and innovative technology for each level of output. Label the expansion path.

Monsanto originally planned to sell the genetically altered seed for the same price as regular seed, thinking it would make higher profit by selling more Roundup, as well as selling more seed than its competitors. Instead, Monsanto has decided to put its efforts towards producing many types of genetically altered seeds. The same scientists can work on many different crops at the same time, and the same plant can be used to produce different types of seeds.

Question 8: What economic phenomenon from this chapter does this decision illustrate?

Multiple Choice Questions

1. The short-run total cost curve:
    A. slopes upward as output rises.
    B. slopes downward as output rises.
    C. is horizontal as output rises.
    D. initially slopes downward, then upward, as output rises.

2. The short-run marginal cost curve intersects the short-run average cost curve at the:
    A. minimum point of the marginal cost curve.
    B. maximum point of the marginal cost curve.
    C. maximum point of the average cost curve.
    D. minimum point of the average cost curve.

3. You are considering producing lecture notes for this course. Your one-time cost of hiring a note-taker is $420. Once you have the notes, it costs $2.00 per copy of notes produced. Your long-run average cost function for output is given by:
    A. $420 + $2x.
    B. $420/x + $2.
    C. $420/x + $2x.
    D. $422x.

4. Suppose that the production of bonsai trees requires only two inputs, land and labor. The isoquants for the trees are convex to the origin. If the price of land increases, ceteris paribus, then there will be:
    A. factor substitution away from land to labor.
    B. factor substitution away from labor to land.
    C. an outward shift of the firm's isocost line along the axis measuring units of land.
    D. a parallel inward shift of the firm's isocost lines.

5. Suppose that the firm's amount of capital is perfectly fixed in the short-run. The firm has 100 machines with a daily user cost of $50 per day. The total short-run opportunity cost of the machines is equal to:
    A. $0 per day.
    B. $50 per day.
    C. $500 per day.
    D. $5,000 per day.

6. Because alternative uses of inputs typically are _____ limited in the short run than in the long run, the opportunity costs of the inputs are lower in the _____.
    A. less / short run
    B. more / short run
    C. less / long run
    D. more / long run

7. Assume that the firm uses only two inputs: labor and capital. The amount of capital is fixed in the short run; the amount of labor is variable. The firm's short-run total cost curve:
    A. is independent of the level of capital.
    B. shifts upward with a higher capital stock.
    C. becomes steeper with a higher capital stock.
    D. shifts downward with a higher capital stock.

8.   The additional amount that the firm has to pay when it adds one additional unit of
       its variable input is known as the:
       A.   marginal factor cost.
       B.   short-run marginal cost.
       C.   long-run marginal cost.
       D.   short-run average cost.

9.   Suppose that the firm is a price taker in the market for labor, its only variable
       input. The wage rate is $50 per day, and the firm is producing at an output level
       where the marginal physical product of labor per day is 0.2. The daily user cost of
       capital is $200 per unit. At that output level, the short-run marginal cost equals:
       A. $10 per day.
       B. $450 per day.
       C. $1,000 per day.
       D. $250 per day.

10.   Technology that involves high set-up costs that must be incurred once no matter
       how much output is produced tends to exhibit:
       A.   economies of scale.
       B.   diseconomies of scale.
       C.   no effect of scale.
       D.   rapidly rising average costs with rising output.

Questions 11-12 refer to the following:

Metropolis, Inc. faces a wage rate of $80 per day and a daily user cost of $120 per
machine. The firm is a price taker in both factor markets. Imagine a graph with the
number of workers on the horizontal axis and machines on the vertical axis.

11.   An isocost line for Metropolis, Inc. has a slope of:
       A.   -4/3.
       B.   -3/4.
       C.   -2/3.
       D.   -3/2.

12.   If Metropolis is producing 600 units of output using an input combination
       involving a MPP for labor of 4 and MPP for robots of 3, then Metropolis, Inc. is:
       A.   using an economically efficient input combination.
       B.   using too many machines and not enough labor.
       C.   using too much labor and not enough machines.
       D.   minimizing the total input cost of producing 600 units.

Question 13 refers to the graph below

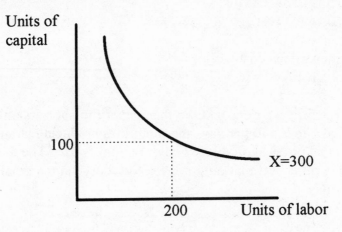

13. Consider the isoquant in the figure for an output level of 300 units. The firm's amount of capital is fixed at 100 units in the short run. The user cost of capital is $200 per day, and the wage rate is $80 per day per worker. The short-run total cost of producing 300 units is equal to:
   A. $20,000 per day.
   B. $36,000 per day.
   C. $16,000 per day.
   D. $24,000 per day.

Question 14 refers to the graph below:

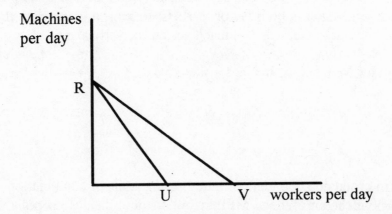

14. Suppose that the firm's initial isocost line is shown by line RU. Which of the following could explain a shift in the isocost line to line RV?
   A. An increase in the daily user rate of capital, ceteris paribus.
   B. A decrease in the daily user rate of capital, ceteris paribus.
   C. A decrease in the wage rate, ceteris paribus.
   D. An increase in the wage rate, ceteris paribus.

Questions 15-18 refer to the graph below:

Machines per day

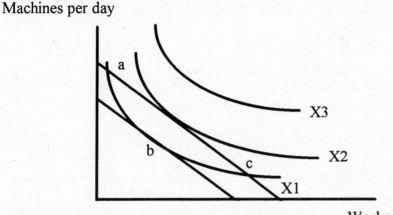

Workers per day

15. Consider the isocost lines and isoquants in the figure. Suppose that the wage rate is $100 per worker per day and the daily user cost of capital is $250 per day. At point b, the marginal rate of technical substitution equals:
 A. 0.4.
 B. 2.5.
 C. 150.
 D. 350.

16. Consider the isocost lines and isoquants.
 A. Points a, b, and c all represent the same level of factor expenditures by the firm.
 B. Point a represents the same level of output as points b and c but at a lower cost.
 C. Point b represents the same level of output as point d but at a higher cost.
 D. Points a, d, and c all represent the same level of output by the firm.

17. Suppose that the firm represented in the figure initially is operating at point b. Then the wage rate rises, ceteris paribus. If the firm continues to produce the same output level in the long run with the economically efficient combination of inputs:
 A. the firm's total cost will rise.
 B. the firm will be on a steeper isocost line.
 C. the firm will substitute capital for labor.
 D. All of the above are correct.

18. Suppose that isoquant X2 in the figure represents just one more unit of output than isoquant X1. Further suppose that total factor expenditure equals $125,000 along isocost line IC and $127,000 along isocost line IC. Between points b and d, the firms:
    A. short-run marginal cost equals $2,000.
    B. long-run marginal cost equals $2,000.
    C. short-run average cost is $126,000.
    D. long-run average cost is $126,000.

19. Suppose a firm has the production function $F(L,K)=2L^3K^2$. Then the firm exhibits
   _____
    A. diseconomies of scale
    B. economies of scale.
    C. constant average cost.
    D. constant marginal cost

20. Suppose a firm has the production function $F(L,K)=2L^3K^2$. Then the firms marginal rate of technical substitution equals:
    A. 2K/3L
    B. K/L
    C. 3K/2L
    D. 4K/6L

Problems

1. In problem 1 of the previous chapter, we found the following table of marginal physical product for labor when one machine was used.:

Worker	TP	MPP
1	80	80
2	150	70
3	215	65

   If workers earn $10 per hour, find the short run total cost, average (variable) cost and marginal cost curves.

2. Problem 2 of chapter 8 asked whether the production process showed increasing, constant or decreasing returns to scale. Assume a special worker is needed to refill the gasoline and oil in that problem. Assume also, the scheduling of workers can be flexible so one refiller can take care of more than one machine. Would there be economies of scale? Explain.

3. In the 1980s the State of Washington implemented a "comparable worth" plan for state employees that raised the wages paid to workers in jobs that were identified as traditionally dominated by female workers, like secretaries. On average, the wages state employees earned went up. What should happen to the mix of jobs the state has? What should happen to the mix of labor and capital the state uses to produce government? Explain.

4. Using an isoquant map, show the expansion path for Washington state government before and after comparable worth was implemented. What happened to the short run and long run average cost curves for government after the plan was implemented?

5. Draw an isoquant for a good that is produced using capital and labor. Label the isoquant through the point that represents 1 unit of capital and 1 unit of labor as Q1, and the isoquant that goes through the point that represents 2 units of capital and 2 units of labor as Q2. Suppose the isocost line C1 is tangent to the first isoquant and the isocost line C2 is tangent to the second isoquant. If there is increasing returns to scale, what is the relationship between C1 and C2? Explain. How does your answer change if there is decreasing returns to scale?

6. Suppose a company has the production function $Q=5L^{3/4}K^{1/4}$ where Q is the output, L is labor hours used and K is units of capital used. The price of labor is $15 per hour and the price of capital is $5 per unit. Find the cost minimizing input combination for 100 units of output. Find the approximate short run and long run marginal cost if suddenly 200 more units of output were needed.

7. Suppose a production function requires that capital and labor be combined in a fixed proportion of 2 units of labor for every unit of capital. Draw the long run expansion path, and the short run expansion path if K=100. Why don't you need to know input prices? If the price of capital is $2 per unit and the price of labor is $1 per unit, find the short run and long run average and marginal cost curves.

CHAPTER 10. THE PRICE-TAKING FIRM

Chapter Introduction

Some firms cannot influence the price they are able to charge to consumers. Wheat farmers are a classic example. They can sell all the grain they wish to the local grain elevator operator at the going rate. If they wish to sell at a higher price, they must wait in hope that the price will rise over and above the costs they incur to store their crops.

Agriculture provides many such examples of price-taking behavior because there are so many close substitutes for one farmer's crop, namely, the crops of all other farmers. If one farmer attempts to charge a higher price, consumers always can find more of nearly the same crop from another farmer.

This chapter details the output decisions by such price-taking firms. While no industry is really perfectly competitive, the pure competition model can generate important insights into how firms operating in a reasonably competitive environment behave.

Chapter Outline

A **price-taking firm** chooses its actions under the belief that it cannot effect the price it charges by changing its level of output or its use of inputs. We study such firms because many real-life firms are much more like price-takers than they are like other firms you will study later in this book. Another reason to study price-taking firms is that their choices are easy to analyze. They make a good "beginners" study of the theory of the firm.

Remember the **two rules for profit maximization**. The **Marginal Output Rule** says: If the firm does not shut down, then it should produce where marginal revenue equals marginal cost. The **Shut-Down Rule** says: If the firm can find no output level where marginal revenue exceeds average economic cost, then it should shut down. Matters are especially easy for the price-taking firm. Its demand function is **perfectly elastic**: demand is horizontal and equal to the price dictated by the market. Thus, average and marginal revenue are each equal to the market-given price!

The two rules for profit maximization are pretty easy for this type of firm. The **Marginal Output Rule for a Price-Taker**: If the firm does not shut down, then it chooses output so that price equals marginal costs. The **Shut-Down Rule for a Price-Taker**: If price is less than average economic cost for all levels of output, then the firm should shut down.

Now, each of these rules must hold in either the **short-run** (when some inputs are fixed for the firm) or the **long-run** (when the firm makes decisions as if all inputs are variable). Look first at the short-run. Suppose the firm has chosen its scale of operation and written contracts that generate overhead payments that it must pay even if it produces nothing. Under the shut-down rule, output will be zero if price is less than average variable cost.

But if price is above average variable cost, then output is determined by setting the market-given price equal to marginal cost. The **short-run supply curve** for a price-taking firm, then, is zero up to the minimum of the average economic cost curve, and then follows the marginal cost curve above that. The **long-run supply curve** is zero for prices below long-run average cost (remember, there are no fixed costs in the long run!) and output is determined by setting the market-given price equal to long-run marginal cost for prices above the minimum of long-run average cost.

If you compare short-run and long-run supply curves, you will find that their relationship makes good economic sense. In the long-run, firms have more time to substitute between inputs. In the short-run, firms are pretty much stuck if there is much of a change in the input prices. Thus, long-run supply is much more elastic than short-run supply.

What about the price-taking firm's input choices? In the short-run, the firm has few choices to make (since some inputs are fixed). The profit-maximizing, price-taking firm should continue to hire an input up to the point where its price is equal to its **marginal revenue product** (that is, marginal physical product multiplied by the price of output). In the short-run, if an input price rises, so do the firm's marginal costs and it cuts back on the use of the input. This **output effect** causes short-run input demand to slope downward. In the long-run, all inputs are variable so that the firm has more choices to make. But the profit-maximizing choice remains; hire all inputs until the input's price is equal to its marginal revenue product. Long-run input demand also slopes down, for two reasons. First, since the firm can also change its use of all other inputs in the long-run, the **factor substitution effect** leads the firm to move away from expensive inputs. Second is an output effect: as input prices rise, the firm reduces its output. Both factors lead the long-run input demand function to slope downward.

A Price-Taking Application

Professional athletes were not always paid such astronomical salaries. Prior to 1975, major league baseball players were bound to their team by contract. They could not sell their services on the open market and had only two options: play for the team owner that held their contract, at the agreed upon salary, or not play at all. As you can imagine, this contractual restriction greatly depressed salaries. "Free agency" changed all of that in 1976. Some of the first crop of free agent players saw their salaries rise nearly ten-fold!

Question 1: Even though firms are willing to pay up to the player's marginal revenue product, wouldn't they like to pay them less? Prior to free agency, how did owners set players' salaries? (Hint: Think about the opportunity costs of players.)

Question 2: Free agency essentially created a perfectly competitive market for players. Using a graph of the supply and demand for sports labor, show how free agency increased salaries.

Question 3: What single factor determines the salary paid to any player under free agency?

According to the theory in this chapter, team owners as price-takers in the short-run should have adjusted their output level downward. But the number of teams increased and the number of games per season did not decrease.

Question 4: Explain this apparent contradiction to the theory of pure competition. (Hint: It might help to think about what happened to the profits of team owners.)

In the long-run, both factor substitution (move away from higher priced player inputs) and output effects (reducing output) should take occurred. But, again, there was no reduction in the number of games and the number of teams actually has increased over time!

Question 5: Again, explain this apparent contradiction to the theory. Now, think in terms of what would have happened if fan interest and other factors had remained constant.

Question 6: Using a graph of the baseball player labor market, discuss who was better off after free agency, players or owners.

The astronomical rise in salaries also happens to coincide with huge increases in viewership and interest in sports memorabilia collectibles.

Question 7: Show how rising player salaries is consistent with the idea that firms pay up to and including the marginal revenue product of an input. Do ticket prices rise because players get paid more, or vice versa?

Multiple Choice Questions

1. For a price-taking firm, marginal revenue is everywhere:
   A. less than the price taken as given by the firm.
   B. greater than the price taken as given by the firm.
   C. equal to the price taken as given by the firm.
   D. independent of the price taken as given by the firm.

2.   If a firm is a price taker in its output market, its firm-specific demand curve is:
     A.   perfectly elastic.
     B.   a horizontal line at the market price.
     C.   equal to its average revenue curve.
     D.   All of the above are correct.

3.   The marginal output rule for a price-taking firm is, unless it shuts down, produce the output level where:
     A.   marginal revenue equals marginal cost.
     B.   price equals marginal cost.
     C.   price equals average cost.
     D.   Both A and B are correct.

4.   The shut-down rule for a price-taking firm says:
     A.   shut down if average variable cost is less than average revenue for all output levels.
     B.   shut down if price is less than average variable cost for all output levels.
     C.   shut down if price is less than average total factor expenditures for all output levels.
     D.   Both B and C are correct.

5.   The short-run supply curve of a price-taking firm:
     A.   is the marginal cost curve above the average variable cost curve.
     B.   is the average variable cost curve above the marginal cost curve.
     C.   is zero for price below average variable cost.
     D.   Both A and C are correct.

Question 6 and 7 refer to the following:

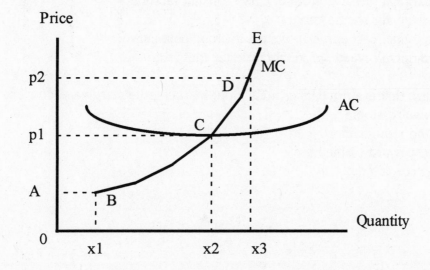

Refer to the marginal cost and average cost curves for output in the figure, above.

6. In the figure, MC and AC are short-run cost curves. Which of the following line segments form part of the firm's short-run supply curve?
   A. Segment OA.
   B. Segment BC.
   C. Segment CDE.
   D. Both A and C are correct.

7. In the figure, if the firm's output price is $p1, how much should this firm supply?
   A. Zero.
   B. Output level x2.
   C. An output level between zero and x2, such as x1.
   D. The firm is indifferent between the output levels of zero and x2.

8. For a firm that is a price taker in its output market, the marginal revenue product of a factor is found by multiplying the:
   A. marginal physical product of that factor and marginal revenue.
   B. marginal physical product of that factor and the price of the output.
   C. marginal factor cost and marginal revenue.
   D. Both A and B are correct.

9. The firm's marginal revenue product is the change in:
   A. total revenue that results from selling one more unit of output.
   B. total revenue that results from hiring one more unit of an input.
   C. total output that results from hiring one more unit of an input.
   D. marginal revenue that results from hiring one more unit of an input.

10. The short-run derived demand curve for a firm that is a price taker in the market for the variable input coincides with the firm's:
    A. marginal physical product curve for that factor.
    B. marginal revenue curve.
    C. marginal cost curve above the average cost curve.
    D. marginal revenue product curve for that factor.

11. For a firm that is a price taker in its input markets, the marginal factor cost is:
    A. upward-sloping.
    B. a horizontal line.
    C. downward-sloping.
    D. a vertical line.

12. The factor hiring rule states that a profit-maximizing firm should hire a factor up to the point at which its:
    A. marginal revenue product equals its marginal factor cost.
    B. marginal revenue product equals marginal revenue.
    C. marginal revenue equals its marginal factor cost.
    D. marginal physical product equals its marginal revenue product.

Question 13 refers to the following:

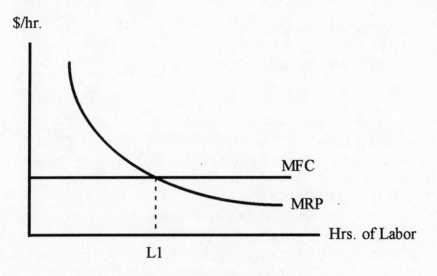

13. What is the equilibrium number of hours of labor for this firm?
    A. L1, where the MFC intersects the MRP.
    B. Since MFC is constant, it is always better to hire more hours of labor, but exactly how much more cannot be determined based on this graph.
    C. Since MRP is decreasing and MFC is constant, it is always beneficial to hire more hours of labor; so, an infinite amount of labor should be purchased.
    D. None of the above is correct.

14. In the short run, the sign of the output effect of a change in an input price:
    A. is always negative.
    B. is always positive.
    C. is always zero.
    D. may be negative or positive.

15. In the long run, the output effect of a change in an input price:
    A. is always positive.
    B. is always negative.
    C. is always zero.
    D. may be negative or positive.

16. In the long run, the sign of the sum of the factor substitution and output effects of a change in an input price:
    A. is always positive.
    B. is always negative.
    C. is always zero.
    D. may be negative or positive.

17. The output effect of a change in factor prices causes the firm's derived demand for the factor to:
    A. slope downward throughout its range.
    B. slope upward throughout its range.
    C. initially slope downward, then upward.
    D. initially slope upward, then downward.

18. Which is larger, the responsiveness to output price changes of the firm's long-run supply or the responsiveness of its short-run supply?
    A. Long-run supply is more responsive.
    B. Short-run supply is more responsive.
    C. They respond equally to such a change.
    D. Cannot be determined from the given information.

19. When the amount of a firm's fixed factor is at its long-run equilibrium:
    A. short-run average cost is less than long-run average cost.
    B. short-run average cost is greater than long-run average cost.
    C. short-run average cost equals long-run average cost.
    D. short-run average cost can be less than, equal to, or greater than long-run average cost.

20. When the amount of a firm's fixed factor is at its long-run equilibrium:
    A. short-run marginal cost is less than long-run marginal cost.
    B. short-run marginal cost is greater than long-run marginal cost.
    C. short-run marginal cost equals long-run marginal cost.
    D. short-run marginal cost can be less than, equal to, or greater than long-run marginal cost.

Problems

1. Sometimes, we observe the prices of a particular item rising almost simultaneously at all outlets. One example is gasoline. Prices at all stations appear to rise at the same time even if none of the usual reasons holds (for example, summer seasonality or world-wide political turmoil). Typically, consumers cry foul and, occasionally, there are investigations by agencies responsible for fair pricing. But is this collusion? Given the theory in this chapter provide an explanation based on perfect competition.

2. A price that is low enough to cause a price-taking firm to shut-down in the long-run may not be low enough to make it shut-down in the short-run. Explain this possibility using a graph of long-run and short-run supply.

3. Short-run and long-run supply functions intersect at a particular point. Explain how a short-run result is also a long-run result.

4. Using the theory of competitive input hiring, explain how it is that entertainers and top-level corporate executives make so much money. Be sure to explain how you would find their marginal revenue product. Also, using the same theory, explain how you would determine whether or not such extremely expensive labor inputs are over-paid.

5. Suppose the price of labor rises. Describe how the firm will respond in the short-run. What is different about how the firm will respond in the long-run? Demonstrate these responses with a graph of each situation.

6. In the short-run, only the output effect dictates supply. In the long-run, there are both factor substitution and output effects. Does this mean that the firm will supply more in the long-run than in the short-run? Why or why not? Use a graph to demonstrate your answer.

CHAPTER 11. EQUILIBRIUM IN COMPETITIVE MARKETS

Chapter Introduction

To understand how prices and quantities are determined, we bring the supply and demand sides of the market together. Since we did this already in earlier chapters, you might well wonder what else there is to know from this exercise.

The answer lies in the details. You now have a much deeper understanding than you had in Chapter 1. Demand is driven by many underlying factors which are now familiar to you. The same goes for the supply side. Your understanding of how preferences, budgets, technologies, and input prices impact supply and demand will lead to a deeper understanding of market outcomes.

The point is to find the market price. Once you have it, your detailed approach to changes in supply and demand will allow you to understand two key points about equilibrium. The first is the impact on individuals and individual firms, rather than just upon market aggregates. The second is the impact among individuals and individual firms in terms of welfare. This section builds on the last one; the equilibrium you will study assumes perfect competition. In later chapters, other types of market structure will determine equilibrium.

Chapter Outline

Many important markets come closer to meeting the competitive ideal than they do to some other market structure. This means that a competitive market model can provide insights into real-world economic outcomes.

Perfect competition relies on four basic characteristics. **Sellers are price-takers**: they cannot effect the price of output by their output choices. **Sellers do not behave strategically**: they need not take actions of others into account when they decide their output levels. **Entry and exit** are not hindered in any way: if one firm decides it would be better off producing another economic output, it simply doe so cost free. **Buyers are price-takers**: the only way that buyers can tell firms apart is by the prices these firms charge.

Most of these assumptions seem pretty heroic, but they may hold in some situations. The assumptions are more likely to hold if there are many buyers and sellers, outputs of different firms are very close substitutes, information flows freely, and new firms wishing to enter a given industry encounter no barriers of any kind.

Once again, the distinction between the short-run and the long-run comes into play. In **the short-run**, the number of firms is fixed. To get market supply, just determine how much output all firms will provide over the range of possible prices. This is **the horizontal sum** of individual firm supply functions. Similarly, market demand is just the horizontal sum of individual demand functions. **Equilibrium** occurs at the intersection of supply and demand. If the price is above equilibrium, sellers compete with sellers by dropping the price. If the price is below equilibrium, buyers compete with buyers to obtain output by bidding up the price. At the intersection of supply and demand, neither buyers nor sellers have any incentive to attempt to alter the price of output.

In **the long-run**, of course, the number of firms is variable. In response to price changes, firms enter (if there are profits) and exit (if there are losses). Three possible outcomes arise in response to, say, an increase in output price. If input prices are unaltered even if individual firm choose to expand and/or additional firms choose to enter the industry, this is a **constant cost industry** and the long-run supply function is horizontal. If input prices rise as individual firms choose to expand, or as other firms enter, this is an **increasing cost industry** and the long-run supply function slopes upward. Finally, and least likely, if input prices fall with increased output and entry, this is a **decreasing cost industry** and the long-run supply function would slope downward.

Economic rent is an important concept. The basic idea is as follows. Suppose a farmer can grow wheat on a piece of land and that piece of land would be brought into production at a price of $4.00 per bushel. If the price of wheat rises to $5.00 per bushel, the land remains in production and earns more than is required to keep it in wheat production. This return over and above what it takes to keep the land in production is called economic rent. Economic rent determines the uses to which resources will be put, since resources will be used where they generate the highest economic rent.

All of these results help you to gain insight into individual and individual firm choices when output prices change. But the perfectly competitive equilibrium provides more insights than these. For example, **total surplus** (the sum of consumers' and producers' surpluses) is maximized at the intersection of supply and demand. This is a desirable characteristic since no gains from trade go uncollected. In addition, the competitive model helps you understand just why it is that the **statutory incidence** of public policies, that is, the intended or expected impact on buyers and sellers, may not be what policy makers expect or intend! For example, **tax incidence**, or who pays the tax, may not take place as intended. Indeed, the more elastic demand is relative to supply, the higher the **tax burden** on suppliers. As another example, **price ceilings** and **price floors** need not make the intended beneficiaries any better off and may actually make them worse off.

A Competitive Equilibrium Application

The current "market" situation for human organs for transplant and research purposes can be characterized as a market shortage. Typically, it is illegal to offer to sell human organs for money. This usually is due to some moral repugnance: the human body is not an old junker car to be "parted out." Thus, the "supply" side consists of charity at a price equal to zero. Organ donor driver's licenses and living wills are the only sources of such organs.

But it is instructive to wonder just what would happen if trade in organs were allowed and functioned in a perfectly competitive market. The place to start is a characterization of the "market" as it currently exists. Let's examine kidney donation. It seems more likely that people would consider a market for donations of kidneys, since a person can function with only one, as opposed to other organs like hearts.

Question 1: In general terms (unless you wish to research the levels of current organ shortages), graph the current demand and supply situation for human kidneys.

Question 2: Identify the level of the shortage at price equals zero. Are there any consumers' surpluses? Identify them in your graph. Do the same for producers' surpluses (if you can).

Now, it would be reasonable to expect two things if a market is allowed. First, some reduction in charitable donation of kidneys would be expected; why give it away if you can earn a return? Second, individuals who would not give their kidney away at a zero price may now consider such donations.

Question 3: Is there any reason to think that the demand for kidneys may change if a competitive market is instituted? If so, what are they?

Question 4: Graph the new supply for human kidneys. Identify the perfectly competitive equilibrium. Is the shortage eliminated? Ask around among your friends and classmates and see if you can get any idea about what the equilibrium price might be.

Proponents of such a market approach argue that the shortage of kidneys would be eliminated. Implicit in their argument is that more kidneys will be made available, relative to the current situation where kidney sales are illegal. Do you think this is true?

Question 5: Show the conditions under which *fewer* kidneys would be available. What reaction on the part of kidney suppliers would cause this to happen?

It also is reasonable to assume that those who now enter on the supply side will be those with the lowest opportunity costs. The "fairness" of such a market may ultimately be called into question.

Question 6: Identify consumers' and producers' surpluses in the competitive market situation. Who earns the most producer's surplus? (Hint: Is it sellers with high or low opportunity costs?) Think about a general profile of this type of supplier.

Question 7: Would you support the institution of such a market? Why or why not?

Multiple Choice Questions

1. The perfectly competitive model assumes that:
    A. buyers and sellers are price-takers.
    B. there is free entry into the market.
    C. sellers do not behave strategically.
    D. All of the above are correct.

2. The perfectly competitive model is most likely to apply when:
    A. there are many sellers in the industry, producing homogeneous goods.
    B. there are few buyers, who are ill-informed about the available alternatives.
    C. there are many barriers to entry.
    D. All of the above are correct.

3. Which of the following occurs when a competitive market is in equilibrium?
    A. Buyers are choosing their optimal purchase levels, given the prevailing market price.
    B. sellers are choosing their optimal output levels, given the prevailing market price.
    C. suppliers are willing to produce as much as buyers wish to purchase at the prevailing market price.
    D. All of the above are correct.

4. In a competitive industry, a short-run equilibrium cannot persist in the long run if:
    A. the firms are earning positive economic profits.
    B. the firms are suffering economic losses.
    C. the firms are earning zero economic profits.
    D. Both A and B are correct.

5. The number of firms in a competitive industry:
    A. can vary in both the short run and the long run.
    B. is fixed in the long run.
    C. is fixed in the short run.
    D. if fixed in both the short run and the long run.

6. Consider a competitive industry which is initially in long-run equilibrium. After the long-run adjustment to an increase in market demand, the new equilibrium price will be:
    A. lower for a decreasing-cost industry.
    B. higher for a decreasing-cost industry.
    C. higher for a constant-cost industry.
    D. lower for an increasing-cost industry.

7. In a competitive industry with heterogeneous suppliers, new firms will continue to enter the market until:
    A. every firm just earns zero economic profit at the prevailing price.
    B. the firm with the highest cost of those in the market just earns zero economic profit at the prevailing price.
    C. the firm with the lowest cost of those in the market just earns zero economic profit at the prevailing price.
    D. the firm with the average cost of those in the market just earns zero economic profit at the prevailing price.

8. Suppose that all the firms in a competitive industry have access to the same technology and that input prices are not affected by the size of the industry. If the minimum value of the long-run average cost curve is $5, then entry of new firms will occur until the market price:
    A. equals $6.
    B. equals $7.
    C. equals $5 or less.
    D. exceeds $5.

9. Consider a competitive constant-cost industry. The long-run supply curve would be:
    A. upward sloping.
    B. downward sloping.
    C. horizontal.
    D. none of the above.

10. Consider a competitive increasing-cost industry. The long-run market supply curve would be:
    A. upward sloping.
    B. downward sloping.
    C. horizontal.
    D. none of the above.

11. Consider a competitive decreasing-cost industry. The long-run market supply curve would be:
    A. upward sloping.
    B. downward sloping.
    C. horizontal.
    D. none of the above.

12. In a competitive market:
    A. total surplus is maximized at the equilibrium output level.
    B. consumer surplus is maximized at the equilibrium output level.
    C. producer surplus is maximized at the equilibrium output level.
    D. All of the above are correct.

13. Suppose the market elasticity of demand for nectarines is 1, while the market elasticity of supply is 3. A $1-per-unit tax on nectarines causes the net price received by nectarine sellers to:
    A. fall by less than $1.00.
    B. fall by more than $1.00.
    C. rise by less than $1.00.
    D. rise by more than $1.00.

14. Suppose the market elasticity of demand for nectarines is 1, while the market elasticity of supply is 3. A $1-per-unit tax on nectarines causes the price paid by the consumers of nectarines to:
    A. fall by less than $1.00.
    B. fall by more than $1.00.
    C. rise by less than $1.00.
    D. rise by more than $1.00.

15. If the market for consumer retail credit is competitive, then a law imposing a maximum interest rate below the equilibrium annual interest rate results in a:
    A. loss of consumer surplus for all consumers.
    B. loss of producer surplus.
    C. gain of consumer surplus for all consumers.
    D. gain of producer surplus.

16. If the market for consumer retail credit is competitive, then a law imposing a maximum interest rate below the equilibrium annual interest rate:
    A. increases total surplus.
    B. has no effect on total surplus.
    C. reduces total surplus.
    D. may increase or decrease total surplus.

Questions 17-18 refer to the following:

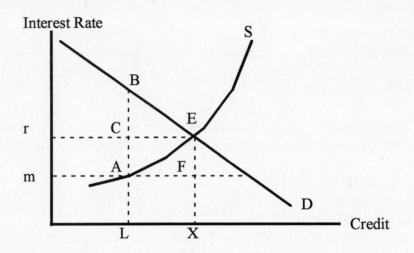

Refer to the graph above of the California retail credit market for which the government has imposed a maximum interest rate of m.

In the graph, compare the competitive equilibrium of r to the maximum allowable interest rate of m.

17. The loss in consumer surplus from the interest rate ceiling for households who would have borrowed at r but do not borrow at m is represented by the area of:
    A. region ABE.
    B. region BCE.
    C. region CAE.
    D. region ABEF.

18. The loss in producer surplus from the interest rate ceiling is represented by the area of:
    A. region rCAm.
    B. region rEAm.
    C. region CAE.
    D. region CEXL.

Questions 19-20 refer to the following:

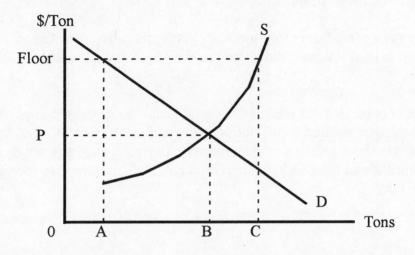

Refer to the figure above, which illustrates the market for almonds. Suppose the government imposes a minimum price on almonds.

19.   At the price floor shown, the actual quantity of almonds bought and sold is:
    A.   amount A.
    B.   amount B.
    C.   amount C.
    D.   zero almonds.

20.   At the price floor shown, there will be a _____ of _____.
    A.   shortage / amount AC.
    B.   shortage / amount BC.
    C.   surplus / amount AC.
    D.   surplus / amount AB.

Problems

1.   Explain how a short-run supply curve can be upward sloping but a long-run supply curve can be downward sloping. Doesn't this mean that opportunity costs are falling in long-run?

2.   Using the concept of economic rent, explain why rent control on apartments in big cities results in the demolition of some apartment units.

3.   It is common during natural catastrophe for the price of necessities such as food and water to rise dramatically for a short time. It is just as common for government to step in and prosecute price gougers. Discuss the impacts of this government action on the amount of basic necessities that will be forthcoming in times of tragedy. Do you think the government should step in and prosecute price gougers in this way?

4.   In emerging economies, private property is being reinvented. Discuss the impacts of instituting a competitive market in residential land and housing. In particular, what will

happen to the quantity and price of housing? In terms of consumers' and producers' surpluses, will such markets be efficient? Will they be fair?

5.   Entry barriers can come from many sources. Many states have enacted ceilings on liability payments due in legal actions. Show that this will drive down the price of legal services in divorce cases.

6.   A windfall profits tax extracts returns to good fortune. For example, suppose the price of oil rises due to some political supply interruption such as the Gulf War. A windfall tax would simply tax these gains away. Demonstrate that such a tax will not change anything about the allocation of resources to oil production. Do you think that such a tax is fair? Why or why not?

CHAPTER 12. GENERAL EQUILIBRIUM AND WELFARE ECONOMICS

Chapter Introduction

Thus far, we have looked at closely related markets such as consumption substitutes and close substitute inputs. But almost all markets are interrelated in some way. Broadening your scope of analysis can yield insights into how changes in one market generate ripples felt throughout all related markets.

For example, the federal government is rethinking pollution control policy. Opponents cite far-reaching implications that may stunt the growth of the entire economy. Clearly, politicians understand how one piece of the "puzzle of the economy" will fit into all of the other pieces! If you want to make sense of such policy questions, broaden your scope of analysis to include as many impacts as possible.

The rest of this chapter covers the limited way that economics can define "good" results. The branch of economics concerned with the societal desirability of alternative economic results is called welfare economics. Under very precise, and therefore limited, definitions, welfare economics can help identify socially beneficial and socially detrimental economic outcomes.

Chapter Outline

All of the seemingly widespread sectors of the economy are linked together. A focus on closely related sectors is called **partial equilibrium analysis**. Broadening the scope of analysis to include the simultaneous determination of all related market outcomes is called **general equilibrium analysis**.

Like partial equilibrium analysis, general equilibrium analysis traces changes in supply and demand. Markets for commodities are linked if one commodity is an input for the production of another, or if they are substitutes or complements in production or consumption. For all of the relationships to be covered, prices must satisfy the following **conditions for general equilibrium**: Every firm maximizes profits, every consumer maximizes utility, and supply and demand are in equilibrium in all markets.

The simplest general equilibrium analysis uses the **pure exchange model**, sometimes referred to as the "Robinson Crusoe" economy, since nobody produces anything and the only way that welfare is enhanced is through exchange of a given total amount of commodities. Given two individuals' indifference curves, a given amount of each commodity, and price ratios that represent the marginal rate of substitution, comparisons of voluntary trade inside an **Edgeworth box** can show the **efficient allocations** between the two individuals. These allocations represent the simplest sort of general equilibrium.

While general equilibrium provides an understanding of how all sectors of an economy react to one another, **welfare economics** precisely specifies desirable economic outcomes. The criteria for a change that enhances welfare are summarized by the idea of Pareto efficiency: an economic outcome is **Pareto efficient** if no other rearrangement of goods can make one person better off without hurting another person. For an economic result to be Pareto efficient, it must be **consumption efficient** (all consumers have equal marginal rates of substitution between any pair of goods which means they are on the **contract curve**), **production efficient** (all producers have equal marginal rates of technical substitution between any pair of inputs which means that output occurs along the **production possibilities curve**), and **allocation efficient** (the marginal rate of substitution equals the marginal rate of transformation).

Pareto efficiency helps us determine how market structures measure up. As long as markets exist for all commodities, the **First Fundamental Theorem of Welfare Economics** states that perfect competition is Pareto efficient. The **Second Fundamental Theorem of Welfare Economics** is a bit more involved. As long as indifference curves all are convex, this theorem states that any Pareto efficient result came from some general competitive equilibrium. Of course, there can be many such equilibria.

The power of these two fundamental theorems appears when we consider how other types of market structure fail to measure up. Two market situations that clearly do not measure up are market power situations where price exceeds marginal cost and markets that fail to exist (which can lead to externalities or asymmetric information). Both of these violate one of the theorems, that is, they violate the criteria for Pareto efficiency.

The fundamental theorems, based on the Pareto criteria, only concern efficiency. But what about fairness? One possible Pareto efficient outcome is that one person has nearly all of the goods and another has nearly none. This demonstrates that "welfare economics" only describes welfare within its carefully set criteria. A given society need not find a Pareto efficient outcome to be meet its **equity criteria**, or sense of fairness. One last area of welfare analysis tries to portray the ethical considerations of a society by developing a **social welfare function**. Such a function shows how a given society is willing to trade-off between the levels of happiness enjoyed by members of that society. But this is a dicey issue. Economists have no more standing than any other members of society in determining whether such an analysis is either valid or useful.

A General Equilibrium Application

CAFE (Corporate Average Fuel Economy) standards require that car manufacturers attain a certain fuel efficiency (miles per gallon) across their whole fleet. While making cars more fuel efficient may be a laudable goal, what are the efficiency impacts of the particular way that government chose to do it? Some have argued that this approach is just like asking for nails by weight in the former Soviet Union where factories could satisfy production requirements by producing one huge nail. While this meets the requirements, it surely violates Pareto efficiency since the incentives get misdirected.

Question 1: What do you think was the impact of CAFE on the mix of small and large cars? Thinking about a starting place where price equals marginal cost, what can you say about the quantity of small and large cars supplied?

Question 2:   Can this satisfy consumption efficiency? Production efficiency?

Hopefully, you noticed that firm responses to CAFE only can produce a dis-equilibrium result. But producers and consumers must surely respond in the long-run.

Question 3:   Given your answers, above, how can firms bring supply and demand back together again?

Question 4:   Now what happens to consumption efficiency? Production efficiency?

Question 5:   Can allocation efficiency be satisfied? (Hint: Think about whether or not MRS can be equal to MRT, given that MRT is just the ratio of marginal costs of large and small cars.)

Your analysis should lead you to the conclusion that society could attain a higher place on its production possibilities curve (more large, fewer small) without CAFE. This would be a Pareto-improvement!

Question 6:   Why would government lawmakers choose CAFE in the first place? Can you think of another way to raise fuel efficiency without violating Pareto efficiency?

Multiple Choice Questions

1.   Suppose the government imposes a new sales tax on vanilla ice cream. General equilibrium analysis would indicate the impact of the tax on the market for:
   A.   vanilla ice cream.
   B.   chocolate ice cream.
   C.   hot fudge sauce.
   D.   all of the above.

2.   At the general equilibrium set of prices for an economy:
   A.   consumers are maximizing their utility subject to their budget constraints.
   B.   producers are maximizing profits.
   C.   the quantity supplied equals the quantity demanded in all markets.
   D.   All of the above are correct.

3. In the Edgeworth box, the contract curve is the locus of:
   A. production-efficient points.
   B. mutual tangencies of the consumers' indifference curves.
   C. allocation-efficient points.
   D. All of the above are correct.

4. Along the contract curve in an Edgeworth box:
   A. nobody can be made better off without harming someone else.
   B. the marginal rates of substitution are equal for all consumers.
   C. all allocations of commodities are consumption efficient.
   D. All of the above are correct.

5. Along the production possibilities curve:
   A. it is possible to increase the output of one commodity without changing the output of the other commodity.
   B. the marginal rates of technical substitution are equal for all commodities.
   C. the allocations of inputs are consumption efficient and production efficient.
   D. All of the above are correct.

6. The rate at which the economy can substitute one output for another by shifting its resources between the outputs is known as the marginal rate of:
   A. substitution.
   B. transformation.
   C. technical substitution.
   D. reallocation.

7. Consider an economy that produces only two goods: coffee and doughnuts. At current production levels of the two goods, the marginal cost of coffee is $0.05 and the marginal cost of doughnuts is $0.20. If the production possibilities curve is drawn with coffee on the vertical axis and doughnuts on the horizontal axis, the slope of the curve equals:
   A   -10.
   B.   -1/10.
   C.   -4.
   D.   -1/4.

8. In order for the allocations of commodities and inputs in an economy to be Pareto efficient:
   A. the total quantities consumed must be on the production possibilities curve.
   B. the allocation of the commodities must be on the contract curve.
   C. the marginal rate of substitution for all consumers must equal the marginal rate of transformation.
   D. All of the above are correct.

9.   To have a Pareto-efficient allocation of resources, the ratio of output prices:
   A.   must exceed the ratio of marginal costs.
   B.   must be less than the ratio of marginal costs.
   C.   must equal the ratio of marginal costs.
   D.   can be greater than or less than the ratio of marginal costs.

Questions 10-12 refer to the following:

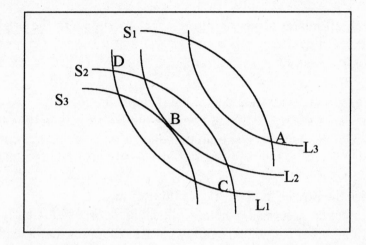

Refer to the Edgeworth box in the figure above. L_1, L_2, and L_3 are Laverne's indifference curves. S_1, S_2, and S_3 are Shirley's indifference curves. Points A through D represent alternative allocations of milk and Pepsi.

10.   Which of the allocations labeled in the figure is consumption efficient?
   A.   Allocation A.
   B.   Allocation B.
   C.   Allocation C.
   D.   Allocation D.

11.   According to the figure, which of the following reallocations would be a Pareto improvement?
   A.   From allocation A to allocation B.
   B.   From allocation B to allocation A.
   C.   From allocation C to allocation B.
   D.   From allocation D to allocation C.

12.   Which of the following reallocations would improve the welfare of both Laverne and Shirley?
   A.   From allocation A to allocation D.
   B.   From allocation B to allocation C.
   C.   From allocation C to allocation D.
   D.   From allocation D to allocation B.

13. "As long as producers and consumers act as price takers and there is a market for every commodity, the equilibrium allocation of resources is Pareto efficient." This is the definition of the:
    A. First Fundamental Theorem of Welfare Economics
    B. Second Fundamental Theorem of Welfare Economics
    C. Theory of the Second Best
    D. Theory of General Equilibrium

14. Provided that all indifference curves and isoquants are convex to the origin, for each Pareto-efficient allocation of resources:
    A. government intervention is required to generate a set of prices that can attain that allocation.
    B. commodities are fairly distributed among the consumers in the economy.
    C. commodities are unfairly distributed among the consumers in the economy.
    D. there is a set of prices that can attain that allocation as a general competitive equilibrium.

15. If some firms have the power to affect their output prices:
    A. freely operating markets will generally allocate resources efficiently.
    B. freely operating markets will generally allocate resources inefficiently.
    C. the firms may be able to raise price above marginal cost by supplying more output than would occur in competitive equilibrium.
    D. the firms may be able to raise price above marginal cost by allocating an inefficiently large quantity of resources to their output.

16. If production or consumption of a commodity generates a negative externality, a freely operating market generates:
    A. an inefficiently small amount of the commodity.
    B. an inefficiently large amount of the commodity.
    C. the efficient amount of the commodity.
    D. Cannot be determined by the given information.

17. A function that shows how the well-being of society depends upon the utilities of its members is known as the:
    A. contract curve.
    B. social welfare function.
    C. utilities possibilities function.
    D. production possibilities curve.

Questions 18-20 refer to the following:

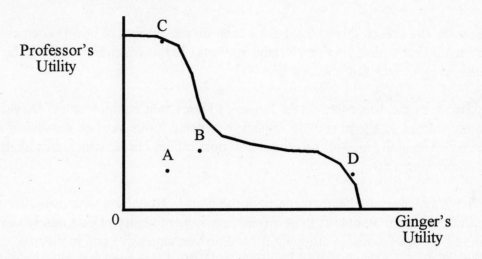

Refer to the utility possibilities frontier of Professor and Ginger (on Gilligan's Island) in the figure above. Points A through D represent alternative utility allocations.

18. Which utility allocations in the figure are Pareto efficient?
    A. Allocations A and B.
    B. Allocations B and C.
    C. Allocations C and D.
    D. Allocations D and A.

19. Which utility allocations in the figure are Pareto inefficient?
    A. Allocations A and B.
    B. Allocations B and C.
    C. Allocations C and D.
    D. Allocations D and A.

20. According to the figure, which of the following reallocations would involve a Pareto improvement?
    A. Allocation A to allocation B.
    B. Allocation B to allocation C.
    C. Allocation C to allocation D.
    D. Allocation D to allocation C.

Problems

1. Just recently, the French government put a limit on the amount of non-French music programming that is aired by French radio stations. Is this restriction likely to be Pareto efficient? Why or why not?

2. During harvest time, it is common for farmers to pool their equipment and harvest everybody's crops as a joint activity, especially when it looks like bad weather may hamper the harvest. Using the idea of the production possibilities curve, why is this likely to be a Pareto-improving act.

3. Firewood is a primary fuel in many parts of the world. But along with using firewood comes deforestation. People strip new (and immature) forestry efforts nearly as fast as they are planted. Policies aimed at stopping it have proven expensive and ineffective. What is the relevance of the First Fundamental Theorem of Welfare Economics to this situation?

4. Identify whether or not each of the following are Pareto improvements. If so why and if not, why not?
   a. Federal crop insurance.
   b. First-home buyers' subsidies.
   c. Environmental restrictions.

5. Using the criteria for Pareto efficiency, discuss the efficiency aspects of legalizing currently illegal drugs. If you find that legalization would enhance efficiency, would it be fair?

6. "Social welfare theory is crazy; it is impossible to trade-off one person's happiness for another person's happiness." Comment in light of the social welfare theory in this chapter.

CHAPTER 13. MONOPOLY

Chapter Introduction

As we saw in the last chapters, perfect competition requires many close substitutes for any given producer's output. A firm that faces no other firms producing the same output is called a monopolist. Since no other firms serve the market, the monopolist faces the market demand function by itself. The monopolist is thus a price-maker; the price it can charge depends upon how many units it chooses to produce.

Both positive and normative consequences arise from monopoly. Positive, as we use it, answers "what if" questions about a particular economic situation. Judgments of "should we" questions are the domain of normative analysis. The positive consequences concern the level of output, the price, innovation, and any inefficiency that results from these choices by the monopoly firm. Put another way, the positive analysis would examine how monopoly shapes up relative to the First Fundamental Theorem of Welfare Economics. The answer is that markets with price-makers may not satisfy Pareto efficiency criteria. Other positive questions concern what happens if monopolists are taxed. Or, whether any means can push monopolists toward a more efficient outcome and what the consequences are of doing so.

Some monopolists cannot tell which of their customers are willing to pay more than other customers. They must charge all customers the same price. But monopolists who can tell buyers apart based on their willingness to pay may be able to practice price discrimination. Price discriminating monopolists either charge different prices to different consumers or charge different prices for subsequent units sold to the same consumer. Output choices are different for price discriminating monopolists than output choices for single-price monopolists. As a result, the analysis of positive and normative consequences differs for price discriminators.

The normative consequences, as with all normative problems, concern "should we" questions, primarily how "should we" regulate monopoly. All normative considerations are driven by equity, or fairness, considerations.

Chapter Outline

Monopoly indicates only a single supplier in the market. Since monopolists will earn positive economic they must somehow block entry by other firms if they are to maintain their market power.

Unlike price-taking firms, monopolists know that they are **price-makers**; the price that they can charge will be determined by how many units of output they choose to produce. This happens because monopolists face the entire market demand function, which slopes downward. If they want to sell more, they must lower the price in order to sell more units. The **fundamental assumptions about a monopolists** are: they are price-makers, they exhibit no strategic behavior, entry is blocked, and buyers are price-takers. Blocked entry is essential to being a monopolist.

Factors that block entry include lack of access by other firms to key inputs, declining costs throughout the relevant range of production, and government actions such as licensing and franchising. The most likely setting for monopoly would have plenty of buyers, one seller, a low degree of substitutability among outputs, perfect information about the monopolist's price and output, and limited entry.

If the monopolist cannot tell which consumers are willing to pay how much, it must charge the same price for all units of output. Since demand slopes downward, it knows that some consumers are willing to pay more than the existing price. But not knowing which consumers will pay more, if it really wants to sell that level of output, then it must charge the same price to all. The **single-price monopolist** follows both the Marginal Output Rule (if it produces, it sets marginal revenue equal to marginal cost) and the Shut-Down Rule (shut-down if price is below average cost at all output levels).

For this single-price monopolist, marginal revenue lies below the demand function. This happens because the single-price monopolist must lower its price on all units, not just the marginal units, in order to increase output. It is relatively easy to show **MR=P[1-1/ε]**; we know that marginal revenue, price, and elasticity are all related. Further, the smaller the elasticity of demand, the lower marginal revenue will be. Marginal revenue is greater than zero, equal to zero, and less than zero as demand is elastic, unitary elastic, and inelastic, respectively.

Obvious consequences arise out of having marginal revenue below the demand curve. When the single-price monopolist follows the Marginal Output Rule and sets marginal revenue equal to marginal cost, price is greater than marginal cost. Further, output is lower than would occur at the intersection of marginal cost and demand. This means that there will be units valued by society at more than their marginal costs of production, but the monopolist will not produce them. This lost value is called the **deadweight loss of monopoly** to society. One final observation about the monopolist's profit maximizing output level is that it cannot occur in the inelastic portion of the demand function; if marginal costs are positive, marginal revenue be greater than zero.

The monopolist clearly violates Pareto efficiency criteria. While it satisfies production and consumption efficiency, it violates allocation efficiency. Since price exceeds marginal cost, no binding tie equates the marginal rate of substitution and the marginal rate of transformation. This would be remedied if the monopolist increased output; total surplus would rise if output were increased. Many regulatory approaches aim to curb the monopolist's tendency to reduce output and raise price, including **antitrust** and **public utility** approaches.

But some monopolists can separate consumers into groups willing to pay different amounts for the same output, or can tell how much more people are willing to pay for subsequent units of consumption. If this type of monopolist can identify consumers with different willingness to pay and prevent any sort of arbitrage between those willing to pay less and those willing to pay more, then it can practice **price discrimination** and raise its profits. **First-degree price discrimination** involves charging all demanders a different price for the same type of good. **Second-degree price discrimination** occurs when the same set of prices for different levels of consumption is only separate its customers into groups and offers each group a different price for the same type of output. Price discrimination still violates allocation efficiency since price is equal to marginal cost only on the last unit of output sold and price exceeds marginal cost on all previous units.

A Monopoly Application

Airlines often are offered as one of the best examples of an industry where a few firms are price-makers.

Question 1: Describe how the setting of the airline industry is or is not consistent with the requirements for price-making. In particular, which factors block the entry of potential competitors?

Question 2: Even though they are price-makers, occasionally an airline cancels a flight or discontinues particular routes. Why do you think this happens?

Airlines definitely do charge different people different prices to fly.

Question 3: Which type of price discrimination do airlines practice? First-degree? Second-degree? Third-degree? Justify your choice.

Question 4: Using the idea that $MR=P[1-1/\varepsilon]$, show just why it is that business travelers pay more than week-end fliers to the same destination.

A particularly interesting practice is holding some seats open for immediate (nearly same-day) purchase. The price of such tickets, even thought the flight goes to the same place at exactly the same time, is much higher than advance tickets.

Question 5: Give a cost-difference justification for the price difference between "same-day" tickets and advance tickets.

Question 6: Give a price discrimination justification for the difference between these two types of tickets.

Question 7: Why are there so many restrictions on the redemption of frequent-flier miles? (Hint: Think about the requirements for successful price discrimination.)

Multiple Choice Questions

1. The monopoly market model assumes that:
    A. buyers are price makers.
    B. there is free entry into the market.
    C. sellers do not behave strategically.
    D. sellers are price takers.

2. A non-discriminating monopolist facing the same demand and cost environment as a perfectly competitive industry:
    A. produces more output.
    B. charges a lower price.
    C. creates a deadweight loss.
    D. creates more total surplus.

3. At a monopolist's equilibrium output and price levels, market demand:
    A. must be inelastic.
    B. must be unitary elastic.
    C. must be elastic.
    D. may be inelastic or elastic.

4. Assume that no firms in the economy engage in price discrimination. A profit-maximizing monopolist who is a price taker in its input markets chooses an output level that is:
    A. production efficient.
    B. consumption inefficient.
    C. allocation efficient.
    D. All of the above are correct.

5. Which of the following would be inconsistent with an assumption of free entry of new firms into an industry?
    A. Patents held by existing firms.
    B. The lack of new suppliers who know how to produce the product.
    C. The lack of access to needed inputs.
    D. All of the above are correct.

6. Suppose a non-discriminating monopolist decides to sell one more unit of its output. At the new output level, the monopolist receives:
    A. higher revenue from the infra-marginal units than at the old output level.
    B. lower revenue from the marginal unit which sells for a lower price than at the old output level.
    C. lower revenue from the infra-marginal units which now sell for a lower price than at the old output level.
    D. Both A and B are correct.

Questions 7-11 refer to the following:

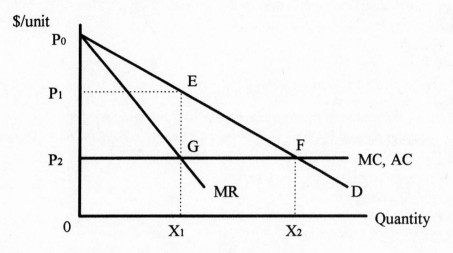

Refer to the figure above, where line D is the market demand curve.

7. If the industry illustrated in the figure is perfectly competitive, the equilibrium industry output level is _____ and the equilibrium price level is _____.
   A. X_2 / P_2.
   B. X_1 / P_2.
   C. X_2 / P_1.
   D. X_1 / P_1.

8. If the industry illustrated in the figure is a non-discriminating monopoly, the equilibrium industry output level is _____ and the equilibrium price level is _____.
   A. X_2 / P_2.
   B. X_1 / P_2.
   C. X_2 / P_1.
   D. X_1 / P_1.

9. If the industry illustrated in the figure is a non-discriminating monopoly, the monopolist's profit at equilibrium is measured by the area of the region:
   A. $P_0 P_1 E$.
   B. $P_1 E G P_2$.
   C. $O P_1 E X_1$.
   D. $O P_1 E F X_1$.

10. If the industry illustrated in the figure is a non-discriminating monopoly, the deadweight loss caused by this industry being monopolized is measured by the area of the region: .
    A.   G E F.
    B. P_1 E G P_2.
    C. P_0 F P_2.
    D. P_0 P_1 E.

11. If the industry illustrated in the figure is a non-discriminating monopoly, the loss in consumer surplus caused by this industry being monopolized is measured by the area of the region:
    A.   G E F.
    B. P_1 E G P_2.
    C. P_1 E F P_2.
    D. P_0 E P_1.

Questions 12-13 refer to the following:

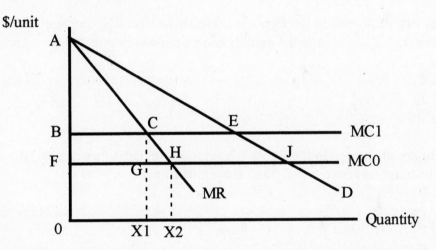

Refer to the figure above, which illustrates the impact of a unit tax on the output of a non-discriminating monopolist. MC0 is the firm's marginal cost curve before the tax; MC1 is the marginal cost with the tax.

12. As a result of the unit tax on the output of the non-discriminating monopolist in the figure, the firm's equilibrium profit falls by the sum of:
    A.   areas ABC, BCGF, and CGH.
    B.   areas ACE and CEJH.
    C.   areas ABC and ACE.
    D.   areas BCGF and CGH.

132

13. As a result of the unit tax on the output of the non-discrimination monopolist in the figure, the total tax payment by the firm to the government equals:
    A. the sum of areas BCGF, CGH, and CEJH.
    B. area CGH.
    C. area BCGF.
    D. the sum of areas ABC, BCGF and CGH.

14. Suppose a natural monopoly producing an output level of 500 is broken up into 10 firms, each producing an output level of 50. The average cost for each of the 10 firms:
    A. exceeds the average cost of the monopolist.
    B. is equal to the average cost of the monopolist.
    C. is less than the average cost of the monopolist.
    D. may exceed or be less than the average cost of the monopolist.

15. Under third-degree price discrimination, a monopolist:
    A. produces less than the output level that maximizes total surplus.
    B. produces exactly the output level that maximizes total surplus.
    C. produces more than the output level that maximizes total surplus.
    D. may produce more or less than the output level that maximizes total surplus.

16. Which of the following conditions must exist in order for price discrimination to be profitable for a producer?
    A. Buyers must be able to perform arbitrage.
    B. That producer must be a price taker.
    C. That producer must be able to identify a customer's willingness to pay.
    D. All of the above are correct.

17. The marginal revenue curve of a monopolist engaged in perfect price discrimination:
    A. lies everywhere below the market demand curve.
    B. lies everywhere above the market demand curve.
    C coincides everywhere with the market demand curve.
    D. intersects the market demand curve at its midpoint.

18. Burns, Inc. practices third-degree price discrimination by charging different prices to residential versus business customers. Burns, Inc. should determine its total output level by equating combined marginal cost with:
    A. the horizontal sum of the residential and business demand curves.
    B. the horizontal sum of the residential and business marginal revenue curves.
    C. the vertical sum of the residential and business marginal revenue curves.
    D. the vertical sum of the residential and business demand curves.

Questions 19-20 refer to the following:

R. J.'s is a well-known restaurant in Beverly Hills that serves a unique chili made with secret herbs and spices. R. J.'s has a daily seating capacity of 100 patrons. Half of the people that walk into R. J.'s are willing to pay up to $7 for a bowl of chili, while the other half are only willing to pay up to $3. The marginal cost of making a bowl of chili is constant at $1.

19. If R. J.'s charges everybody $3, its daily profits are:
    A. $600.
    B. $300.
    C. $200.
    D. $100.

20. If R. J.'s could somehow perfectly price discriminate, then its daily profits would be:
    A. $600.
    B. $400.
    C. $300.
    D. $200.

Problems

1. How much would you pay for a monopoly? How much would you sell it for, once you owned it? Are there any true monopoly profits earned after the monopoly changes hands? Why or why not?

2. Your university probably contracts some campus services, for example, supplying pop machines and pop campus-wide. The winner of the contract then becomes a monopoly seller. What happens to the price of soda pop, relative to a competitive situation? What about the variety of different brands of pop? Do you think that the university should just identify vending areas and let competition determine who installs machines? Think carefully about the rent that is charged under the current practice and how that influences your costs.

3. Pro sports teams have a monopoly in their cities. Think about what would happen if they were forced to compete. Would cities be as likely to build stadiums and arenas for teams? What would happen to the price of attendance? What would happen to the number of games? What would happen to the quality of games? Do you think it would be desirable to force competition onto the world of professional sports? Why or why not?

4. What determines the number of taverns in a given town or city? What is the impact on price and output? What would happen if anybody who wanted to simply could open a bar?

5. Wal-Mart should have failed. The popular wisdom at the time was that a department store required a threshold level of sales volume in order to succeed. Such volume, according to the popular wisdom of the time, could not be had in lower population areas. But Wal-Mart, in 20 years, has grown to over 2,000 stores in precisely those areas where they were predicted to fail. How did they do it?

6. Businesses in the student union building have a monopoly position. Why do they care if a small competitor shows up and pushes price down a little since it can only cost a little positive profit. (Hint: Think about how the rent is determined.)

CHAPTER 14. MORE ON PRICE-MAKING FIRMS

Chapter Introduction

This chapter extends the theory of price-making to situations that will enhance your understanding of the world around you. Technically, "monopoly" refers to a situation of a sole seller, and none of the situations in this chapter satisfy this definition. But the predictions of price-making theory under monopoly provide insights over a fairly broad range of topics.

A cartel is a group of firms acting together to create monopoly power over output decisions. Successful collusion of this nature that the cartel as a whole be able to organize production and price, deal with potential competition, distribute monopoly profits to all its members, and overcome the incentives to cheat on the cartel's provision of a monopoly price (above marginal cost).

Monopolistic competition occurs when a number of firms each exercise price-making power in the same market. Each firm must differentiate its output from the other firms. But this tends to raise their costs until there are zero economic profits in the long-run.

Monopsony could just as easily be called monopoly over inputs. If one firm faces the entire industry supply function for an input, it has a special problem whenever it wishes to increase its use of that input. Whenever the firm hires more of the input, it must pay all units, not just the additional ones, a higher price. This problem will make the firm's extra costs of hiring curve lie above the input supply function.

Throughout this chapter, the efficiency and equity implications of these price-making situations are examined in the short-run and in the long-run.

Chapter Outline

This chapter examines market structures with price-making sellers and price-making input buyers. As always, the objects of analysis are price and output results, the distribution of surplus between buyers and sellers, and the efficiency and equity implications that follow from the distribution of surpluses.

If price-making suppliers can coordinate their production decisions they can increase their profits relative to those they can achieve acting independently. A **cartel** is an organization of price-making firms aiming to monopolize the supply of some good. The goal of the cartel is to **restrict output**, raise **price above marginal cost**, and **earn positive economic profits** in the long-run.

A cartel must **organize production and price** at monopoly levels, **exclude entry** by other firms outside the cartel (entry would dissipate the positive economic profits the cartel organized to capture in the first place), and **distribute the monopoly profits** to all its members in such a way that each member is happy to remain with the cartel, rather than going out on their own. But that's not the end of the cartel management problem. Once member shares of production are set, incentives to cheat on the cartel's provision of a monopoly price (above marginal cost) arise and members are tempted to sell more units than would maximize cartel profits. As a result of this **incentive to cheat**, the cartel confronts **monitoring and enforcement problems**.

Interestingly, government action often creates and/or reinforces cartel behavior. In such situations, where governments grant price-making power, **rent-seeking theory** predicts that social losses due to monopoly will be even larger than the deadweight loss that occurs under the usual monopoly model. Resources spent competing over such preferred market positions are wasted and each firm competing for the rents is willing to expend the expected level of monopoly profit to be gained! The problem can be even worse if substantial uncertainty exists over who will win in the competition for these rents.

Monopolistic competition occurs when a number of price-makers compete in the same market. Even though there may be many firms, and reasonably free entry and exit, price-making power may be maintained if each firm practices **product differentiation**. Part of their costs go to convincing consumers that their output is different from the other firms' products, for example, through advertising product features. The analysis of monopolistic competition assumes that **sellers are price makers**, **sellers do not behave strategically**, **free entry** into the market, and **price-taking buyers**. These assumptions are most likely met under a market structure with many buyers, many suppliers, **heterogeneous output** (as opposed to **homogeneous output**) by different producers, buyers may be either well-informed or poorly-informed, and entry must not be restricted.

Advertising, brand names, or introduction of new brands of the same product may accomplish this differentiation in the eyes of consumers. Short-run equilibrium is similar to the monopoly result; each firm in the industry prices above marginal cost and earns positive economic profit. But "keeping up with the Joneses" through continued expenditure on product differentiation raises costs until, despite the fact that each firm faces a downward sloping firm demand curve, each firm earns zero economic profits in long-run equilibrium.

An interesting question is whether monopolistic competition produces the **socially efficient level of variety** for consumers. This is the same thing as asking whether the number of firms is efficient, since the model specifies one brand for each firm. Many find the "**excess-capacity theorem**" appealing; decreasing the number of brands would lower average cost. While this is true, it misses the point that variety is valuable. The theory, which includes both the costs and benefits of variety, shows that whether or not monopolistic competition gives the efficient number of firms depends on cost and demand conditions. The theory is indeterminate on this question overall and we must examine each product market as a separate case.

A **monopsony** is a market with a single buyer. While it's possible for a consumer to be the sole buyer of a particular output, the most prevalent examples of monopsony concern a single buyer of an input. For example, one firm might purchase all of a particular type of labor. The assumptions under the monopsony model are **price-taking sellers**, **sellers do not behave strategically**, widely **variable entry conditions**, and **buyers are price-makers**.

If one buyer faces the entire industry supply function, it has a special problem whenever it wishes to increase its purchases. As it purchases more, it must not only pay a higher price for the marginal units, but it must raise the price to all units purchased. This problem will make the firm's **marginal factor cost greater than the price** of each unit of input given by the supply curve. Since the price is determined by input demand, the upshot of monopsony is that the price of the input is less than its marginal revenue product.

The partial equilibrium result is that less of the input is hired under monopsony than would be the case competitively and **the input is paid less than its marginal revenue product**. Since some units of the input carry higher marginal revenue product than marginal cost, a deadweight loss to monopsony arises when these units of input are not hired. If the monopsonist hired more of the input, total surpluses would rise. General equilibrium analysis reveals that the monopsonist chooses a socially inefficient means of production because society's perception of the extra benefits and extra costs of the input are not equal.

A Price-Making Application

Recently, quite a debate over the impact of the minimum wage has emerged. Newspapers such as the Wall Street Journal have had a field day with what appears to be a refutation of fundamental economic theory. According to "classical theory," increasing the minimum wage results in dis-employment and employers trying to slough non-wage costs of employment off on employees. But some recent empirical work based on data from Pennsylvania fast-service firms shows no impact on hiring when the minimum wage is increased. The question may simply be one of theoretical misapplication, since the debate assumes that these minimum wage markets are competitive.

Question 1: Why might minimum wage labor markets not be very competitive? Draw a graph that shows a monopsonized minimum wage labor market just before the minimum wage is imposed.

Question 2: Now, on the same graph, show what happens to employment and the wage if a minimum wage is imposed that is less than the wage that equates supply and demand. Does this level of minimum wage help explain the seeming rejection of the "classical theory?"

While this much of an analysis of monopsonized minimum wage markets helps sort out some policy disagreement, more insight is available.

Question 3: On the same graph (if it's too cluttered, you may want to start over with your graph of the market before any minimum wage is imposed), show the impacts on employment and the wage of imposing a minimum wage that is less than the wage that equates demand and marginal factor cost.

Question 4: Is there any unemployment in this case? Would an examination of whether or not the level of employment changed at the firms reveal this type of unemployment?

Finally, maybe the reason that a look at employment at particular firms with monopsony price-making power reveals no change in employment when the minimum wage is imposed just depends on how high the minimum wage is set.

Question 5:   (By now, you'll probably need a "clean" initial starting graph.) Show the impacts on employment and the wage of imposing a minimum wage that is greater than the wage that equates demand and marginal factor cost. Is there any dis-employment? Any other unemployment?

Question 6:   Given your answer in Question 5, what sort of policy advice would you give to the President concerning setting the minimum wage in monopsony labor markets?

Multiple Choice Questions

1.   When suppliers jointly act like a monopolist by restricting output and raising price, they are said to form:
    A.   monopolistic competition.
    B.   a monopsony.
    C.   a natural monopoly.
    D.   a cartel.

2.   The full cartel outcome requires that:
    A.   the price and joint quantity produced be at the levels that maximize joint profit.
    B.   the firms collectively produce the amount of output for which industry marginal revenue equals industry marginal cost.
    C.   there be no cheating on the cartel agreement by individual firms.
    D.   All of the above are correct.

3.   A successful cartel must be able to:
    A.   prevent its members from cheating on the agreement.
    B.   limit entry by new suppliers.
    C.   collectively produce where the industry marginal revenue equals the vertical summation of the firm-specific marginal cost curves.
    D.   Both A and B are correct.

4.   If a cartel currently produces an output level at which industry marginal cost equals industry marginal revenue, and the cartel price exceeds marginal cost, then:
    A.   industry profit would rise if all members increased output.
    B.   it is in each cartel member's self-interest to cheat by reducing output.
    C.   it is in each cartel member's self-interest to cheat by expanding output.
    D.   industry profit would rise if all members reduced output.

5.   If a cartel succeeds in maintaining the cartel price but cannot prevent the entry of new firms into the industry:

A. the industry's total output level will rise.
B. entry continues until the equilibrium average cost equals the fixed price.
C. entry continues until the equilibrium marginal cost equals the fixed price.
D. All of the above are correct.

6. The government is more likely to rely on structural remedies rather than conduct remedies in its antitrust policy, ceteris paribus, for an industry:
A. with significant economies of scale.
B. with significant technological barriers to entry.
C. with significant product differentiation.
D. without significant economies of scale.

7. The monopolistic competitive model assumes that:
A. sellers do not behave strategically.
B. buyers are price makers.
C. there are barriers to entry.
D. sellers are price takers.

8. In the short run, equilibrium for monopolistic competitive firms resembles equilibrium for a monopolist in that:
A. marginal cost exceeds price.
B. price exceeds marginal cost.
C. price equals marginal cost.
D. marginal revenue exceeds marginal cost.

9. In long-run equilibrium, monopolistic competitive firms:
A. must earn positive economic profit.
B. must earn zero economic profit.
C can earn negative economic profit.
D can earn positive economic profit.

10. As the number of firms in a monopolistic competitive industry increases, ceteris paribus, the aggregate consumer surplus:
    A   should decrease.
    B.   should increase.
    C.   should stay the same.
    D.   may decrease or increase.

11. The private incentive for a new firm to enter a monopolistic competitive industry differs from the social incentive by the:
    A.   increase in consumer surplus.
    B.   decrease in profit-per-firm for already existing firms.
    C.   increase in the new firm's profit.
    D.   changes in both consumer surplus and the profit-per-firm for existing firms.

Questions 12-13 refer to the following:

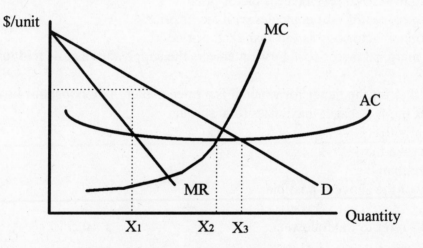

Refer to the figure above, which illustrates the demand and long-run cost conditions for a representative firm in monopolistic competition.

12. In long-run equilibrium, the representative firm in the figure will produce _____ units of output.
    A. X_1.
    B. X_2.
    C X_3.
    D.   less than X_1.

13. The figure illustrates the current situation for the representative firm. In the long run, firms will _____ the market, and the representative firm's demand curve will _____.
    A.   enter / shift outward
    B.   enter / shift inward
    C.   exit / shift outward
    D.   exit / shift inward

14. The monopsony model assumes that:
    A.   sellers behave strategically.
    B.   buyers are price makers.
    C.   sellers are price makers.
    D.   entry of new suppliers must be free.

15. Consider a monopsonist facing a supply curve for its input that is upward sloping. In equilibrium in the factor market:
    A.   marginal factor cost exceeds factor price.
    B.   marginal factor cost coincides with factor price.
    C.   marginal factor cost is less than factor price.
    D.   the marginal factor cost curve intersects the supply curve at its midpoint.

16. In the market for the factor for which it is a price maker, a monopsonist buys _____ amount of the factor that maximizes total surplus.
    A.   exactly the
    B.   less than the
    C.   more than the
    D.   Any of the above is possible.

Questions 17-19 refer to the following:

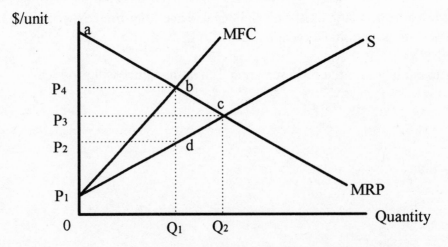

Refer to the figure above, which illustrates the marginal factor cost and marginal revenue product curves for a monopsonist in the factor market.

17. In equilibrium, the monopsonist in the figure will purchase _____ units of the factor.
    A. Q_1.
    B. Q_2.
    C. Q_2-Q_1.
    D. Q_1+Q_2.

18. In equilibrium, the monopsonist in the figure will pay a price of _____ for the factor.
    A. P_1.
    B. P_2.
    C. P_3.
    D. P_4.

19. If the monopsonist in the figure is a price-taking seller of output, the deadweight loss of the monopsony equals:
    A. region a b P_1.
    B. region a c P_1.
    C. region P_4 b d P_1.
    D. region b c d.

20. A profit-maximizing monopsonist produces its equilibrium output with:
    A. production efficiency, but not allocation efficiency.
    B. allocation efficiency, but not production efficiency.
    C. neither production nor allocation efficiency.
    D. both production and allocation efficiency.

Problems

1. Many instructors grade on a curve. They compare classmates to each other in setting grades. If students agreed to only answer the five questions on all quizzes, home works, and exams that they were sure they knew, then all students would be identical, leaving the instructor in a bind. Essentially, there would be no variation on which to base grades. Explain why instructors don't worry about this problem. Why would such a "curve cartel" be expected to break down?

2. Many colleges within a university are accredited by some outside agency. For example, many schools of business are accredited by the American Association of Collegiate Schools of Business. What impact should accreditation have on the value of member school degrees? Why? Why is it difficult to get accreditation? Once they are accredited, why does the accrediting agency review its members on a periodic basis?

3. Muster the best case you can for why the beer industry is monopolistic competitive.

4. Business people commonly state that product differentiation is essential to the long-run profitability of their firm. Evaluate this in light of the monopolistic competition theory of this chapter. What do you think these business people really are trying to say?

5.   Are there too many espresso stands where you live? What is the right number of espresso stands? Explain using the theory in this chapter.

6.   In almost all workplaces, the discussion of salaries among employees is forbidden. Why are there taboos on the discussion of salaries in the workplace? Whose interests do such a taboo serve? Why would it be in the best interest of all workers to know the salary of newly hired workers and to fully disclose their salary each time they got a raise?

CHAPTER 15. OLIGOPOLY AND STRATEGIC BEHAVIOR

Chapter Introduction

In all models developed thus far, we have explicitly assumed that firms exhibit no strategic behavior. In monopoly, with only one firm, there are no other firms to act against. In perfect competition, there is no because no firm has price-making power in the first place. In monopolistic competition, even though each firm has price-making power, they do not consider the impact of their choices on other firms, or the choices that other firms make on their own price and output.

But firms *do* account for each others' actions. A more precise, but also more complicated, model recognizes that firms take each other's actions into account when one firm's actions effect the demand curves faced by all members of the industry. The consequences are important. Each firm must observe or predict what other firms are going to do with their price and output. But each firm must also consider how the others will respond to its own price and output choice. All firms must choose their actions based on the actions and reactions of other firms in the industry. This is what is economists mean by strategic behavior.

This chapter aims to develop a model that includes the mutual interdependence of firms in an industry. The approach will be familiar: lay out the fundamental assumptions, identify the sort of structure where these assumptions are most likely to hold, and show the results on price, output, and the distribution of total surpluses. In this case, no single comprehensive model can capture or predict real behavior. Instead, we will develop a common underlying theme to a variety of strategic behavior models.

Chapter Outline

The focus of this chapter is on **strategic behavior** in oligopoly markets. **Oligopoly** is characterized by a few price-making firms that recognize the interdependence of their price and output choices. The assumptions underlying oligopoly analysis are that **sellers are price-makers**, **sellers behave strategically**, **conditions of entry vary** widely, and **buyers are price takers**. The type of market structure most likely to be characterized by oligopoly has the following characteristics: many buyers, relatively few firms, a wide range of output substitutability, either poorly-informed or well-informed buyers, and a wide range of entry situations.

Duopoly is the simplest of oligopoly models in which two firms compete, entry is blocked, output is homogeneous, and identical, and marginal costs remain identical and constant. Equilibrium must include the firms' strategic choices. This requires that **self-enforcing agreements** occur. It is in each firm's individual best interest to abide by an "agreement" given that other firms also abide by it. **Tacit agreements** are never discussed (since such discussions would usually be illegal); firms can come to a common understanding about price and output without actually discussing either one.

Firms make price and output choices based on the assumptions one firm makes about the behavior of the other firm. Once chosen, the firm then makes its choices taking the other firm's action as given. The result is the firm's best response, given its assumption about the behavior of the other firm. Equilibrium now can be defined as the situation in which all firms are exercising their best response relative to all other firms. This is a **Nash equilibrium**.

A Nash equilibrium where both duopolists choose their best *quantity* responses toward each other is called a **Nash-Cournot equilibrium**. Here's how to find such an equilibrium. Each firm takes the other firm's output and price choice as given; each thinks that it addresses the **residual demand** left-over after the other firm makes its profit maximizing choice. Each firm calculates its **best-response** to the other firm's profit maximizing choices, sequentially, until the residual demand is zero. The set of best-responses is called the firm's **reaction curve**. Since equilibrium requires each firm to be on their reaction curves, the intersection of the two reaction curves determines the Nash-Cournot result.

A number of interesting comparative static results arise in Nash-Cournot models. Starting from equilibrium, using reaction functions, **comparative statics** look at how each firm would adjust output and maintain the equilibrium. For example, a firm's profits falls when its own costs rise but rise when its rival's costs increase.

A Nash equilibrium where both duopolists choose their best *price* responses to each other is called a **Nash-Bertrand equilibrium**. Equilibrium is a bit more complicated to derive. One firm's best-response to the other's price choice now depends on the initial relationship (one firm's price is either greater than, equal to, or less than the other firm's price). Price comparisons result in an equilibrium where all firms charge price equal to marginal cost (under the assumption that marginal costs are constant and equal for both firms).

Now for the $64,000 question: Which model should we use to analyze strategic settings of oligopoly in the real world? The answer is indeterminate. Sometimes Cournot works best and sometimes Bertrand. The key question hinges on whether it takes firms longer to adjust their prices or their quantities. Cournot works best when it takes longer to adjust quantity, while Bertrand seems best when prices are "sticky."

Unlike Cournot and Bertrand models, **models of repeated interaction** allow firms to form beliefs about the actions of rivals and take them into account, simultaneously. For example, even though Nash-Cournot equilibria are self-enforcing agreements, each firm must consider the benefits and costs of "**cheating**" on these tacit agreements. The benefits are the value of increased sales. The costs come from the other firm forcing the cheater to live with lower profits over an extended time by setting price closer to marginal cost. These penalties must be **credible threats**: if the firm threatening a penalty would be harming itself by imposing the penalty, the potential cheater will not respond. The potential cheater then weighs the near-term benefits against the discounted present value of the far-off penalty.

We can make some general predictions when thinking about repeated interaction. The lower the costs of cheating, the more likely it will occur. The harsher the punishment, the less likely a firm will cheat. The simpler the agreement, the less likely cheating will take place. These general predictions, in turn, lead to some ideas about how elements of a market's structure will effect cheating. Cooperation is more likely when costs are similar, demand is constant over time, it is easy to monitor firm output, negotiations with all customers happen at the same time, individual orders are small relative to the market level of output, only a few firms participate. The impact of product differentiation on cooperation is ambiguous; substitution is less when price falls, but credible threats are less believable when your product is not substantially like your rival's.

An Oligopoly Application

Burger King has gained enough of the fast-service food market to finally emerge as a threat to McDonald's. Indeed, McDonald's has now adopted responses to Burger King's marketing strategies. At first, the two chains competed in terms of quality, for example, when McDonald's came out with its "adult" deluxe sandwiches. But now the strategy is in terms of price. McDonald's has embarked on the "throw-back" price strategy of 55¢ sandwiches, tied to the introduction of the franchise in 1955.

Question 1:   Following the market structure requirements in the chapter, make the case that Burger King and McDonald's are competing in a duopoly market.

Question 2:   Is the interdependence of these two firms best described by a Nash-Cournot setting or a Nash-Bertrand setting? Why?

One prediction of the duopoly model in the chapter is that equilibrium will be characterized by self-enforcing agreements, usually of the tacit variety. But this doesn't appear to be the case for Burger King and McDonald's, who appear to be on the verge of a price war.

Question 3:   Why aren't the two duopolists reaching a tacit agreement? Explain in terms of the factors that facilitate such agreements.

Question 4:   What would have to happen for the two firms to reach agreement, that is, for a strategic Nash equilibrium to occur?

Question 5:   McDonald's clearly is the duopolist pushing for price reductions. Why isn't Burger King trying to adopt some sort of punishment strategy, like forcing price toward marginal cost for a long period of time?

While the verdict is not in completely, reports are that McDonald's 55¢ strategy has failed.

Question 6:   Using the reaction function concepts in the chapter, how could you have predicted that this approach would fail? Do you expect Burger King to respond by lowering its price? Why or why not?

Multiple Choice Questions

1.   An oligopoly model assumes that:

    A.   sellers are price takers.
    B.   sellers do not recognize their mutual interdependence.
    C.   sellers behave strategically.
    D.   buyers are price makers.

2.   An oligopoly model is most likely to apply when:
    A.   there are few sellers in the industry.
    B.   there are many sellers in the industry.
    C.   there is just one seller in the industry.
    D.   there are few buyers in the industry.

3.   In order to be self-enforcing, a collusive agreement must satisfy:
    A.   the Nash condition only.
    B.   the credibility condition only.
    C.   both the Nash and the credibility conditions.
    D.   neither the Nash nor the credibility conditions.

4.   A collusive agreement in which each firm finds that abiding by the agreement is its profit-maximizing course of action, given that other firms are abiding by the agreement, is known as a:
    A.   tacit agreement.
    B.   best-response agreement.
    C.   credible agreement.
    D.   self-enforcing agreement.

5.   In a duopoly:
    A.   the price received by either firm depends only on its own output level.
    B.   the price received by either firm depends on the output levels of both firms.
    C.   each firm's profit depends only on its own output level.
    D.   each firm's residual demand curve equals one-half of the market demand curve.

6.   If one firm in a duopoly increases output by one unit, the marginal revenue to the industry
     _____ the marginal revenue to the firm that changes its output.
     A.   exceeds
     B.   is less than
     C.   equals
     D.   may exceed or fall below

7.   A market is in Nash equilibrium when each firm is choosing the strategy that:
     A.   gives the firm a long-run profit of zero.
     B.   gives the firm a positive long-run profit.
     C.   maximizes its profit, regardless of the strategies of the other firms in the market.
     D.   maximizes its profit, given the strategies of the other firms in the market.

8.   A Cournot equilibrium is a _____ equilibrium in a market in which each firm's strategy
     consists of its choice of _____ level.
     A.   Nash / price
     B.   Bertrand / price
     C.   Nash / output
     D.   Bertrand / output

9.   Under a Nash-Cournot equilibrium, the level of industry output is _____ than the joint-
     profit-maximizing level and _____ than the competitive level.
     A.   greater / greater
     B.   less / less
     C.   greater / less
     D   less / greater

10. If all the firms in an oligopoly have a constant marginal cost of $5 and produce
     homogeneous goods, the Bertrand equilibrium entails all firms to set their prices:
     A.   above $5.
     B.   at a level for which long-run profit is positive.
     C.   equal to $5.
     D.   Both A and B are correct.

11. For duopolists producing homogeneous goods with the same constant marginal cost, the
     Bertrand-Nash equilibrium outcome has the same price, output, and profit levels as the:
     A.   Cournot-Nash equilibrium.
     B.   monopoly outcome.
     C.   perfectly competitive outcome.
     D.   full cartel outcome.

12. Which of the following models is the most appropriate description of the new car industry in the United States?
    A. The Bertrand model.
    B. The Cournot model.
    C. The perfect competition model.
    D. The monopolistic competition model.

Questions 13-15 refer to the following:

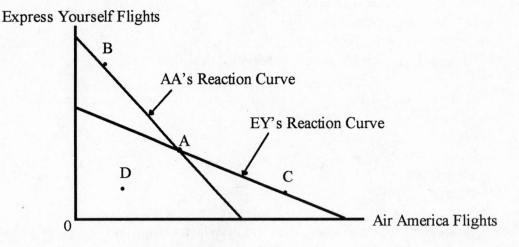

Refer to the reaction curves in the figure above.

13. On the reaction curves in the figure, the unique Cournot-Nash equilibrium is represented by:
    A. point A.
    B. point B.
    C. point C.
    D. point D.

14. According to the reaction curves in the figure, if Air America and Express Yourself want a self-enforcing agreement, then they should pick the output levels represented by:
    A. point A.
    B. point B.
    C. point C.
    D. point D.

15. Suppose Air America and Express Yourself have agreed to operate at the output levels represented by point D in the figure. If each airline believes that the other airline will stick to the agreement, then Air America will want to _____ and Express Yourself will want to _____.
    A. increase output / increase output
    B. decrease output / increase output
    C. increase output / decrease output
    D. decrease output / decrease output

Questions 16-17 refer to the following:

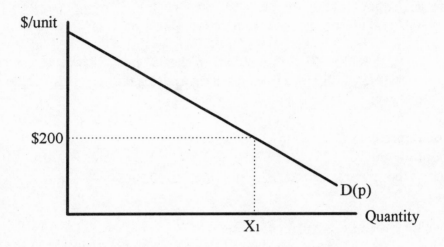

Refer to the figure above, which shows the market demand curve, D(p), for a duopoly with Firm Y and rival Firm Z. The firms are producing homogeneous goods.

Consider the market demand curve in the figure

16. If Firm AZ charges a price of $200, Firm Y sells:
    A. an output level between zero and X_1 if it also charges a price of $200.
    B. an output level between zero and X_1 if it charges a price less than $200.
    C. zero output if it also charges a price of $200.
    D. zero output if it charges a price less than $200.

17. If Firm Z charges a fixed price of $200, then Firm Y's firm specific demand curve:
    A. coincides with the vertical axis if Firm Y's price is less than $200.
    B. coincides with D(p) if Firm Y's price is greater than $200.
    C. coincides with D(p) if Firm Y's price is less than $200.
    D. never coincides with D(p).

18. In an oligopoly with repeated interaction, the incentive to cheat on a collusive agreement is lower, the:
    A. lower the probability that a cheater is caught.
    B. harsher the punishment upon being caught.
    C. longer the time lag before getting caught.
    D. All of the above are correct.

19. A cartel is less likely to be successful the:
    A. smaller are individual orders relative to the overall market.
    B. more homogeneous are the products cartel members produce.
    C. more similar are the costs of the cartel members.
    D. more stable is industry demand from period to period.

20. In an oligopoly with repeated interaction, a firm cheats on a collusive agreement if and only if the _____ value of the gains from cheating exceeds the _____ value of the losses from being punished.
    A. future / future.
    B. present / present.
    C. present / future.
    D. None of the above is correct.

Problems

1. Usually, democracy abhors government secrecy. But why would it be in the best interests of voters and taxpayers for local governments not to reveal all of the bids submitted by contractors competing for service contracts?

2. Coffee producers typically meet and set the price of coffee. While they meet, coffee prices soar. After a few weeks, prices are right back where they started. Explain this outcome using the predictions for collusion in this chapter.

3. The market for baseball players is an oligopsony (a few buyers with price-making power). How likely was such collusion, given the predictions for collusion in this chapter? What type of evidence would be needed to overcome this strong theoretical argument? [The team owners were found guilty of colluding to keep salaries down for the 1989 season.]

4. The trucking industry has never been able to maintain cartel pricing. Of all the factors that would lead to successful tacit collusion, which do you think most hindered this industries efforts to monopolize highway shipping?

5.   American Airlines announced that it was eliminating all of its "special" discount fares. Their justification was that fare structures were so complex that customers couldn't figure them out and the only people making money on them were travel agents who searched out the discounts. The result was a fare war between major carriers. What was American Airlines actually trying to do? How do you characterize the industry's response?

6.   Using the description of a market structure that would facilitate cartels, identify one or two and suggest which of the factors you have listed most contribute to their success.

CHAPTER 16. GAME THEORY

Chapter Introduction

An economic "game" is a strategic situation in which each economic actor must act based on their beliefs about what the other actors are likely to do, and vice versa. In the last chapter, we introduced Nash equilibrium which occurs in a non-cooperative game context. Decision makers each act only in their own self-interest. Equilibrium happens when all actors satisfy their self-interests, simultaneously.

But even selfish actors will cooperate when their self-interest so dictates. These situations are commonplace. Teammates pass to each other, even though individual performances typically earn them financial rewards. Soldiers cooperate even though it reduces their chance of individual survival. Individual firms that compete in the same market have agreements about supplying each other in times of down-inventory; car-swapping is very common among dealers in a particular area. A more complex type of cooperation occurs when oligopolists face the threat of entry by another firm.

But more complex situations beg more complex tools. Game theory allows us to analyze complex strategic interaction among economic agents. First, we characterize the game that is being played. Do the different actors have complete or incomplete information? What strategies might each actor may choose? What pay-offs accrue to each actor given the different strategies they might choose? Is the game played one time, or is it a repeated game? Then, we adopt a consistent concept of equilibrium: the "answer" to the game must satisfy the actors in terms of their basic economic goals.

Chapter Outline

The **game tree** provides the primary tool to analyze strategic situations. The game tree is like a rule book and map, combined: it represents who gets to make choices and when, the choices that are open at each stage of the game, the information each player has at each stage, and the pay-offs. Game trees are composed of **decision nodes** (at some point in the game, it is some actor's turn to make a choice), the **actions** available at each node (for example, raise price or don't raise price), and, eventually, the **pay-offs** at the end of the (potentially long) branches of the game tree. The series of actions that lead to a particular pay-off result for all of the players is called a **game outcome**. Clearly, given all of the possible actions and responses by all players, many possible outcomes to the game arise.

Now, consider some point on the game tree. It might be your move. But the actions you might take are influenced by the actions that you and the other players already have taken, as well as what you think the other players will do in response to the action you are about to take. Thus, the game tree represents the complete strategic situation confronting all of the players.

With the game represented completely in the game tree, players can look at all possible outcomes, reason back through the branches of that outcome, and determine the set of actions they should take. This set of actions, which dictates what each player should do every step along the way, is called the **player's strategy**. The strategy may be straight forward; in poker, many players adopt the strategy, "Call all bluffs." But a strategy may be conditional on what other players have done. A conditional version of the "call all bluffs" strategy might be, "Call all bluffs if I see the player bluff once."

With the rules and outcomes of the game in place, the next logical step is to find the result, or equilibrium. In equilibrium, the players' strategies must result in an outcome acceptable to all players, simultaneously. The simplest result is the **dominant strategy equilibrium**. A dominant strategy works at least as well as any other one, no matter what the other player does. A dominant strategy equilibrium requires that all players choose a **dominant strategy**. For example, if "Call all bluffs" provides at least as high a pay-off as any other strategy a poker player might choose, it is a dominant strategy. If it is the dominant strategy for all players at the table, then all bluffs will be called at all times; the dominant strategy equilibrium. A dominant strategy equilibrium also is a Nash equilibrium. Each player's equilibrium strategy is its best response to the equilibrium strategy chosen by the other players.

But sometimes there is no dominant strategy equilibrium. If one of the players can only determine a strategy depending on what other players choose to do, then some other equilibrium basis must be found. Here is where the fundamental belief in rational actors comes to the fore. For example, if your strategy depends on another player's choice, and you know what the other player's choices and pay-offs are, then, if all players act rationally, you know what the other person will do in the first place. This may make your strategy clear. You can use a **backward induction** method, working the game out to its conclusion, determining what is rational for the other player, and choosing among the conditional strategies that would make you as well-off as possible. You will discover the **perfect equilibrium** to this game since it is a Nash equilibrium and both players will have chosen credible strategies.

One broad application for game theory involved players precluding entry in an oligopoly market. The game theory setting involves the strategies that incumbent firms might adopt in order to convince a potential entrant that it would be unprofitable to do so. Both incumbents and entrants must form sophisticated expectations about what the state of their world will be after entry occurs. Essentially, the incumbent must create a **credible threat** to deter potential entrants. Since the stake is the incumbents' positive economic profits, they will be willing to spend up to and including the entire profit attempting to deter the entrant. For example, one strategy would be to spend some of the economic profit on expanding capacity as a real threat to the entrant. With over-capacity, incumbents could simply put it into production and drive price down. In such a case, the commitment threat to increase output and drive the entrants' profits to zero is credible. Writing a contract promising to match any other price also is a credible commitment.

Another variation on game theory concerns the amount of information available to players. **Imperfect information** means that one player does not know all of the others' previous or subsequent moves. **Incomplete information** occurs when a player is not sure about the game situation itself. For example, one player may not know the pay-offs at the end of each branch of the game tree, either for their own or for other players. In games of imperfect or incomplete information, **mixed strategies** may provide the best guidance for a player. A mixed strategy occurs when the best a player can do is to choose their strategy based on their best estimate about the missing information. To continue on with the poker example, a mixed strategy would be "Call the bluff half the time, and choose when to call by tossing a coin."

Finally, equilibrium in **repeated games** can differ dramatically from equilibrium in once-and-for-all games because of the opportunity to institute strategies that are unavailable in once-and-for-all games. The **grim-trigger** strategy punishes cheaters on collusive self-enforcing agreements. Basically, if one firm cheats, the other firms agree to drive price to marginal cost for an extended number of repeat plays as a punishment. This **credible threat** (since all the other firms are worse-off under cheating than they would be in the absence of cheating when the competitive return with price equal to marginal cost forces potential cheaters to re-evaluate the net benefits of cheating. Other variations on this theme, including **finitely-repeated games** rather than **infinitely-repeated games**, yield similar results.

A Game Theory Application

Let's think some more about Wal-Mart (success is fascinating, isn't it?). The chain has grown from less than 50 stores in a three-state region to over 2,000 stores, nation-wide at last count. But here is a unique observation: When Wal-Mart moves in, no other similar store follows.

Question 1: Design a game tree that yields the following, identical strategy for Wal-Mart and competitors: If the other firm enters, then don't enter but if the other firm does not enter, then do enter.

Question 2: Using the definitions in this chapter, completely characterize this type of game (for example, is it a game of perfect information with a perfect equilibrium, or what?).

Question 3: What sort of business strategy is suggested by your game characterization? Remember, the accepted wisdom was locate in large population areas and after establishing a going concern, think about expanding.

Question 4: At the time of his death, Sam Walton (Wal-Mart and Sam's Club founder) was one of the richest Americans. Do you think his fortune was very liquid? Why or why not?

In some small towns, regional chains are attempting to stage some competition against existing Wal-Mart stores.

Question 5: Given the game tree analysis you have just done, assess the chances for these regional chains going up against an established Wal-Mart store.

Question 6: What sort of long-run equilibrium does this analysis suggest to you?

Multiple Choice Questions

1. A decision rule:
   A. is an arbitrary guide to action.
   B. depends on the pay-offs to different actions.
   C. specifies an action, contingent on previous actions in the game.
   D. is always well-known to all players.

2. A game tree shows:
   A. the information set of all players.
   B. the actions that all players may take.
   C. the pay-offs for all players.
   D. all of the above.

3. A strategy that works at least as well as any other, no matter what the other players do is known as a:
   A. decision rule.
   B. dominant strategy.
   C. perfect strategy.
   D. non-cooperative strategy.

Questions 4-6 refer to the following:

		Publisher B	
		10	40
Publisher A	20	100, 50	40,70
	50	80, 30	30, 20

Refer to the above diagram, which illustrates the actions and pay-offs of two book publishing firms. For example, if Publisher A sticks with 20 titles and Publisher B goes with 40, Publisher A earns $40 million while Publisher B earns $70 million.

4. A decision rule for Publisher B is:
   A. always publish 40 titles.
   B. always publish 10 titles.
   C. publish 40 titles when Publisher A publishes 20 and 10 when Publisher A publishes 50 titles.
   D. all of the above.

5. Publisher A's dominant strategy is to publish:
   A. 20 titles.
   B. 40 titles.
   C. 10 titles.
   D. 50 titles.

6. Publisher A wants Publisher B to announce 10 titles so that it can publish 20 titles and earn $100 million. It threatens to produce 50 titles regardless of Publisher B's choice. This threat is:
   A. credible because Publisher A should keep its word.
   B. credible because it is always best for Publisher A to publish 50 titles.
   C. credible because 50 titles it always is best to publish more, rather than less.
   D. not credible since 20 titles is Publisher A's dominant strategy.

7. A dominant strategy equilibrium results whenever:
   A. each player has a dominant strategy.
   B. one player has a dominant strategy.
   C. both the Nash and the credibility conditions are satisfied.
   D. the game has a perfect equilibrium.

8. Someone passing a car in the oncoming lane is bearing down on you. Suppose both you and the other driver prefer to swerve if the other does not and not if the other does. This game has:
   A. a single dominant strategy of swerving.
   B. many dominant strategies.
   C. no dominant strategy.
   D. a dominant strategy of not swerving.

9. A perfect equilibrium satisfies:
   A. the Nash condition, but not the credibility condition.
   B. the credibility condition, but not the Nash condition.
   C. either the credibility condition or the Nash condition, but not both.
   D. both the credibility and Nash conditions.

Questions 10-12 refer to the following:

		Kathleen	
		Hard	Soft
Michael	Hard	0, 0	60, 40
	Soft	40, 60	50, 50

Refer to the above diagram, which illustrates the actions and pay-offs of two people involved in pre-trial divorce proceedings. For example, if Michael bargains "hard" and Kathleen bargain "soft" then Michael gets $60,000 and Kathleen $40,000 of the total $100,000 in joint assets. If they both bargain "hard" then each receives none of their total asset value, all of which ends up being paid in legal fees since they go to court.

10. The following is a Nash equilibrium for this pre-trial divorce proceeding:
    A. both bargain hard, no matter what.
    B. Kathleen bargains soft and Michael bargains hard, no matter what.
    C. Kathleen bargains hard and Michael bargains soft, no matter what.
    D. both B and C are correct.

11. According to the diagram:
    A. bargaining hard is a dominant strategy for Kathleen .
    B. bargaining soft is a dominant strategy for Kathleen.
    C. there is no dominant strategy for Kathleen.
    D. there is more than one dominant strategy for Kathleen.

12. The only perfect equilibrium in this pre-trial game is:
    A. both bargain hard, no matter what.
    B. Kathleen bargains soft and Michael bargains hard, no matter what.
    C. Kathleen bargains hard and Michael bargains soft, no matter what.
    D. Michael bargains soft if Kathleen bargains hard, but Michael bargains soft if Kathleen bargains hard.

13. Suppose a conspiracy to overthrow the government arises. The leader informs the government and then informs all of the conspirators. This action:
    A. enhanced the credibility of the groups intentions.
    B. undermined the credibility of the groups intentions.
    C. entailed engaging in a commitment.
    D. both A and C are correct.

14. When a firm irreversibly alters its pay-offs in advance so that it will be in its own interest to carry out a threatened entry deterring action, the firm:
    A.   is adopting a decision rule.
    B.   is demonstrating commitment.
    C.   has achieved a Bertrand equilibrium.
    D.   has achieved a Cournot equilibrium.

15. Which of the following are aggressive entry deterrence strategies for an oligopolist:
    A.   engaging in R&D that makes producing low output more profitable than producing high output.
    B.   building a small plant with high marginal costs.
    C.   signing contracts with existing customers that bind the firm to match any future offers by a new firm.
    D.   all of the above are correct.

16. If a player knows all of the details of the game but doesn't know some of the other player's actions, then this game is one of:
    A.   imperfect and incomplete information.
    B.   imperfect information.
    C.   incomplete information.
    D.   full information.

17. A game of imperfect information is one in which:
    A.   an incumbent firm distorts its behavior in order to conceal its true costs from a potential entrant.
    B.   a potential entrant into a market is unsure whether the incumbent firm has high or low marginal costs.
    C.   a player must make a move without being able to observe the earlier or simultaneous move of another player.
    D.   one of the players is unsure about the other player's pay-offs.

18. In a prisoner's dilemma, both players confessing forms a:
    A.   Nash equilibrium.
    B.   dominant strategy equilibrium.
    C.   perfect equilibrium.
    D.   all of the above.

19. "A house divided against itself cannot stand." Abraham Lincoln was describing a:
    A.   prisoner's dilemma.
    B.   game of entry deterrence.
    C.   game of limit pricing.
    D.   game of incomplete information.

20. A provision in a price-setting agreement where the firms commit themselves to punish a cheater by setting all future prices equal to marginal cost:

     A.   is a type of grim-trigger strategy.
     B.   is a type of Cournot strategy.
     C.   is not a credible threat.
     D.   reduces the likelihood of successful collusion.

Problems

1.   Foreign consulates are highly vulnerable to attack. Using the idea of credible commitment, explain why such consulates are so inadequately defended.

2.   A tit-for-tat strategy is "If the other player did not cheat last time, then I won't either. But if the other player cheated last time, I will cheat this time." Show that not cheating in a repeated game can dominate cheating if you believe that the other player has adopted a tit-for-tat strategy.

3.   Sometimes people play a game against themselves. Weight-loss is a good example; the thinner individual that you wish to be is choosing a strategy against the heavier individual that you are, currently. Can the "person you wish to be" make a credible threat against the "person you are?" Explain. What are the implications for successful weight loss (that is, losing weight and keeping it off)?

4.   The coffee cartel, as noted before, is a weak one. Can you imagine a credible commitment that really would keep coffee prices at the monopoly level? How could it be carried out?

5.   Use backward induction to prove that two kids who must share a popsicle will almost immediately agree to split it down the middle before it melts.

6.   The most common response among airlines to a rival dropping its price is to drop prices on competing routes only by even more. Explain this choice from the perspective of the grim-trigger strategy.

CHAPTER 17. ASYMMETRIC INFORMATION

Chapter Introduction

In many situations, people have different amounts of information about a potential transaction. The classic example concerns buying a used car. Nobody wants to get stuck with a lemon, but a seller who only cares about profits has a clear incentive to misrepresent lemons as cherries (quality used cars). As another example, employees are much more likely to know their true abilities than prospective employers are. When one side of a transaction is more well-informed than the other, the situation is characterized by asymmetric information.

In asymmetric information situations, sometimes we say that the less-informed party can learn a lot from the well-informed party by making inferences based on the actions of the other party to the transaction. Relative to a complete inability to learn anything, this inferential ability by the less-informed can dramatically alter the equilibrium in markets characterized by asymmetric information.

The basic problem in markets with asymmetric information is that one side does not trust the other and suspects that quality always will be low, given that the net return is larger if the seller peddles lemons at the cherry price. But that means that buyers will only pay the lemon price. Knowing this, sellers only will offer lemons. This market is inefficient since some customers actually are willing to pay for higher quality output but won't find any.

Two types of asymmetric information arise. A characteristic of the good in question may not be known by both sellers and buyers. The other type of information problem concerns actions that can't be observed. For example, employers want employees to work hard, but may not be able to monitor whether they really do or not. This chapter explores the logic of asymmetric information and the inefficiency that can result but, more importantly, shows how mechanisms have developed to deal with the asymmetric information problem. After all, there are both high and low quality used cars on the lot!

Chapter Outline

Asymmetric information problems occur for two reasons. First, a good's characteristics or description may remain as **hidden information** in the market. In these questions, the quality of goods is known by one side of the market only. Second, **hidden actions** by individuals may not be observable or discoverable. Insurance companies want to know if the people being insured are practicing high-risk behavior but may not be able to find out whether insureds really do indulge in high-risk actions.

Let's start with hidden information problems. We tend to think of asymmetric information problems plaguing buyers rather than sellers. But consider **price discrimination**. Here, a price-maker wishes to know which buyers are willing to pay more, rather than less, for units of output. Buyers surely know how much they are willing to pay, but also know that if they tell the seller, then the price to them will rise. If the firm can successfully price discriminate, it will find information that allows it to separate buyers by willingness to pay. The monopolist must find a **signal** of willingness to pay. The usual method is to offer a selection of prices based on a common-sense separator and let customers **self-select**, revealing their willingness to pay. Time of day pricing for phone calls, time of week ticket prices for airlines, and movie ticket prices by age all do the job of **screening** buyers based on their willingness to pay.

Certification, such as education, provides another kind of signal. Employers want to be able tell high- and low-ability workers apart. But if they just ask them, low-ability workers may misrepresent their ability and, at least for a short time, earn the return of a high-ability worker. On average, high-ability individuals will do better in school than low-ability individuals. Thus, obtaining the education signal, such as a college degree, sorts out high- and low-ability individuals as long as the cost of the signal is high enough to keep low-ability people from obtaining the signal (at much higher cost than high-ability people).

But it is difficult to tell whether or not the signaling process is socially beneficial, on net. In a competitive market, employers earn zero economic profit regardless of whether they hire high- or low-ability workers. And workers bear the cost of obtaining the signal; the higher return to high-ability workers really represents a redistribution from low-ability workers to high-ability workers. On net, society may not be better off. Other benefits to education, such as true enhancements to human capital and the satisfaction of the individual help swing the balance in the direction of making signals socially beneficial, on net.

Adverse selection represents another asymmetric information problem. If buyers can't tell lemons from cherries, dealers have the incentive to put lemons on the lot and charge the price of cherries. But if buyers know that sellers will do this, they will never pay more than the lemon price. But if they are unwilling to pay anything but the lemon price, then dealers will not put anything but lemons on the lot. The market has adversely selected only lemons due to the information asymmetry. The obvious, and pervasive response to the lemons problem is a simple **warranty**. If a car has a warranty, it isn't a lemon (since, under a warranty, a lemon must be made into a cherry at the seller's expense). Insurance markets are also plagued by adverse selection. Companies constantly try to tell high-cost from low-cost customers. Revenues rise when they can draw more customers by charging premiums that reflect coverage costs.

In a **full-information equilibrium**, high-cost customers would pay higher premiums than low-cost customers. But in an **asymmetric-information equilibrium**, if companies charge a premium that allows them to break-even on average, the high-cost customers buy more insurance than the low-cost customers, and collect more often. The insurance company can't break even until it sorts these customers out, after the fact. If low-cost customers are highly risk-averse, they may buy enough insurance so that companies break even (or earn positive profits). Note that the asymmetry of the information (the idea that one side of the market has it) drives these problems, rather than just the lack of information. Also note that correcting such problems only redistributes wealth between insurance companies and customers; no new surplus is created by overcoming adverse selection.

Markets have responded to adverse selection problems. Health insurance companies can require physical examinations. Group health plans with mandatory participation remove the adverse selection problem since all employees, high- and low-cost, must participate. Careful historical studies of different groups in the population may also identify possible candidates for adverse selection. Government information-disclosure policies also are aimed at reducing information uncertainty.

Now, let's turn to hidden action problems. These types of problems fall under the general heading of **principal-agent relationships**. These relationships are interesting because the principal and the agent may have **different objectives** and the principal can only **monitor the agent imperfectly** and at some cost. **Moral hazard** is one type of hidden action problem plaguing insurance markets. Once insured, home owners may be less careful or practice less fire prevention. This creates inefficiencies if the market values insured homes at full value. Insurance markets have responded by designing policies that make customers responsible for their actions. **Co-payments** and **deductibles** put a share of the cost of carelessness back on the customer.

The remaining area of interest is in employer-employee relations and contracting problems. If managers (the agents of the owners of the firm) are going to earn $100,000 whether or not they actually monitor their employees, or just take leisure on the job, then owners should expect them to take leisure on the job. An incentive pay structure can overcome this type of "**shirking**" of firm owner interests. If firm profits rise when the manager does not shirk, paying a bonus equal to some share of the increased profits will induce some managers to shirk less. In any event, certainly managers who do not wish to go after the bonus (and are, consequently, shirkers) can be identified. This is the logic behind **performance-based compensation** such as stock-options and profit-sharing. Similar logic holds for consulting contracts. If the quality of effort is unobservable, the only way to assure high-quality effort is to tie rewards to the final outcome. In addition, if reputation generates a return, **threats against reputation** can elicit quality effort.

An Asymmetric Information Application

Auctions pose and dispose of asymmetric information problems. On any given day, economics instructors have been known to walk into a class with a bag full of money and offer to sell it to the highest bidder, using sealed bids. Invariably, the instructor can at least make lunch money on the sale by eliciting the most optimistic bid. This outcome is commonly referred to as the "winner's curse."

Question 1: Describe the situation from an asymmetric information standpoint; is it hidden characteristics or hidden actions driving this problem?

Question 2: How can your instructor be so sure of the outcome?

Question 3: What sort of mechanism would change the outcome in favor of the bidder? [Hint: Why does the instructor use a sealed bid rather than just auctioning it off in the usual oral fashion?]

Recently, a famous 1910 baseball card came up for auction. It had fetched $451,000 at a previous auction. There are 50 cards of this variety, but only one in near mint condition. Forging a card is relatively easy with modern desk-top capabilities. Rumors flew that the card, while not a forgery, wasn't what it claimed to be; that it had been altered by cutting it from a strip, rather than being from an original tobacco pouch that had been in circulation. Cards that are in mint condition after being circulated are rarest of all.

Question 4: Again, describe this situation from an asymmetric information standpoint.

Question 5: Do you think there will be a winner's curse in this case? [Hint: Remember your answer to Question 3, above.]

The largest collector in the world did not participate in the auction. Again rumors flew that this other collector might sell his two cards of the same player and vintage (but of lower quality) at about the same time.

Question 6: What impact would the absence of the largest collector in the world, as well as the possibility that he might put his two similar cards on the market at the same time, have on the price of the card at auction? [Hint: Think both about the demand for the card, as well as the information content in the bidding process.]

By the way, eventually, the card ended up as a give-away promotion to sell other cards through the Wal-Mart chain.

Multiple Choice Questions

1. Whenever one side of the market has better information than the other side, the situation is one of:
    A. asymmetric information.
    B. moral hazard.
    C. adverse selection.
    D. screening.

2. Adverse selection occurs
   A. when information is asymmetric.
   B. when there is a hidden characteristics problem in the market.
   C. when people on the informed side of the market self-select in a way that is harmful to the uninformed side of the market.
   D. All of the above conditions are needed for adverse selection.

3. An observable indicator of a hidden characteristic is known as:
   A. asymmetric information.
   B. adverse selection.
   C. screening.
   D. a signal.

4. Which of the following is ignored in the simple signaling model of education?
   A. The consumption benefits of obtaining an MBA, such as fond memories.
   B. Productivity increases due to an MBA raising the stock of human capital.
   C. Using the MBA degree to better match individuals to jobs.
   D. All of the above are correct.

5. Market responses to adverse selection in the insurance industry include:
   A. group health plans.
   B. targeted insurance rates.
   C. mandatory physical examinations.
   D. All of the above are correct.

6. Which of the following is not a government response to the problems raised by hidden characteristics?
   A. Laws against deceptive advertising.
   B. Mandatory participation in the Social Security program.
   C. Mandatory disclosure laws.
   D. Mandatory physical examinations for life insurance buyers.

7. Which of the following is a necessary feature of a situation of hidden action?
   A. One side of an economic relationship, the agent, takes actions that cannot be observed by the other side, the principal.
   B. Both sides of an economic relationship agree on which action is best for each to take.
   C. The situation involves a hidden characteristic.
   D. All of the above are correct.

8. Blood banks that pay for donations face the problem of:
    A. adverse selection.
    B. moral hazard.
    C. second-degree price discrimination.
    D. signaling.

9. A partial remedy to the problem of moral hazard in insurance markets is the use of:
    A. deductibles.
    B. co-insurance.
    C. group health plans.
    D. Both A and B are correct.

10. Insurance in a market with moral hazard causes:
    A. the social marginal benefit of care taken by the insured to equal the private marginal benefit.
    B. an increase in total surplus above the level achieved without insurance.
    C. a reduction in the level of care taken by the insured.
    D. All of the above are correct.

11. Suppose that the board of directors of Acme Books, Inc. is thinking of giving its chief executive officer a non-tradable option to buy up to 10,000,000 shares of Acme stock at today's price anytime in the next two years. If you also own Acme stock, then you should be:
    A. indifferent to giving the CEO such an option.
    B. against giving the CEO such an option.
    C. in favor of giving the CEO such an option.
    D. either indifferent to or against giving the CEO such an option.

12. Charging different premiums depending on the size of the deductible chosen by the insured is an example of:
    A. third-degree price discrimination.
    B. second-degree price discrimination.
    C. moral hazard.
    D. co-insurance

13. In ancient China, individuals paid their doctors as long as the individuals were not ill, but withheld payment once they were sick until they had recovered. This is an example of:
    A. a response to the problem of moral hazard.
    B. a response to the problem of hidden action.
    C. a principal-agent relationship.
    D. All of the above are correct.

14. In ancient China, individuals paid their doctors as long as the individuals were not ill, but withheld payment once they were sick until they had recovered. This created a:
    A. problem of moral hazard on the part of the patients.

B. problem of moral hazard on the part of the doctors.
C. self-selection device.
D. All of the above are correct.

15. Since some people rent cars on which to learn to drive a stick shift, car rental agencies face the problem of:
A. moral hazard and co-insurance.
B. adverse selection and co-insurance.
C. moral hazard and adverse selection.
D. adverse selection only.

16. Consider an insurance company that does not know any particular individual's probability of making a claim on the insurance policy. However, each individual knows his or her probability of making a claim. If the insurance company offers the same policy to all insured parties and charges a premium that will allow the company to break even on average:
A. the insurance will be actuarially unfair for the high-risk individuals.
B. low-risk individuals will buy less than full insurance.
C. the insurance will be actuarially unfair for the low-risk individuals.
D. Both B and C are correct.

17. An insurance market is inefficient in that risk-averse individuals are forced to bear risk whenever:
A. both sides of the market are uninformed about the probabilities of each individual making a claim.
B. only the insurance company is uninformed about the probabilities of each individual making a claim.
C. both sides of the market are informed about the probabilities of each individual making a claim.
D. Both A and B are correct.

18. In an employer-employee relationship involving unobservable shirking by the employee, switching from a flat salary to a residual claimant compensation scheme:
A. is a Pareto improvement.
B. decreases the owners' income.
C. makes the employee worse off.
D. makes the employee better off.

19. Designing a compensation scheme for employees who can engage in unobservable shirking involves a trade-off between:
    A. hidden action and hidden characteristics.
    B. screening and signaling.
    C. providing incentives and sharing risk.
    D. self-selection and adverse selection.

20. The development of a firm's reputation:
    A. is a type of market response to the problem of moral hazard in product markets.
    B. is an effective response to the problem of moral hazard if a good reputation leads to zero economic profit on future sales.
    C. restores a product market with asymmetric information to a fully efficient competitive equilibrium.
    D. leads to actions by the firm that maximizes total surplus in the product market.

Problems

1. Universities want to charge different students different prices based on willingness to pay. Explain how discounts off of so-called "full tuition" accomplish this task. What information signal do students supply to universities which facilitates the university's price discrimination?

2. Why does it matter to new car buyers that the car they are considering has a high resale value. Why do sales people make such a big deal out of high resale value?

3. Blood tests are becoming increasingly sophisticated and insightful. For example, prostate cancer now can be detected by a blood test. Will this overcome some adverse selection problems in health insurance? Does blood-testing for this reason enhance efficiency? Why or why not?

4. Hazardous waste incinerators are universally despised by those who live in close proximity. Proponents argue they are perfectly safe. From a moral hazard perspective, is there any validity to the idea that they ought to be built right next to the firms that create the waste in the first place? Or right next to the individuals who use the products that leave hazardous waste as a by-product? Explain.

5. Describe how you can be sure that your economics professor isn't just making it up as they go. What sort of mechanisms has your university developed to protect you from shirking by your professor?

6. Explain why consumers would rather buy from a sales person who is on salary, but employers would rather hire sales people who only work on commission. How do markets work out this apparent conflict?

CHAPTER 18. EXTERNALITIES AND PUBLIC GOODS

Chapter Introduction

Sometimes, competitive markets produce too much or too little output, relative to the ideal where prices equal marginal costs. The activities of one person, group, or firm that directly effects the welfare of others in a way that market prices cannot capture, creates what economists refer to as an externality problem. Unlike effects that are transferred through market prices, externalities can lead to inefficiencies.

On the one hand, if firm cost structures cannot capture all of the costs that some type of production imposes on society, then the output is "too cheap" from society's perspective. Too much of it will be produced relative to the amount that would be produced at society's true cost. Oft-cited examples include noise, water, and air pollution.

On the other hand, if all of the benefits that some type of production generates for society do not get incorporated into the firm's perception of marginal revenue, then the output is in a very real sense "under-valued" from society's perspective. Since producers can't capture the full value of their production, too little of it will be produced relative to its true social value. Inoculation and neighborhood beautification are common examples. A special case is national defense.

The First Fundamental Theorem of Welfare Economics states that competitive markets satisfy consumption, production, and allocation efficiency. Does this mean that levels of pollution and national defense are efficient? If not, then what can we do to move production in these areas toward more efficient outcomes? These are the questions identified and addressed in this chapter.

Chapter Outline

Externalities are examples of **market failures**. In the case of **negative externalities**, competitive market supply functions do not include all of the costs borne by members of society. The root of the problem lies in the **definition and enforcement of property rights**. If harmed parties have no rights, or their rights are weakly enforced, then producers can make choices that are harmful to others and not bear the full costs of their actions. In the case of **positive externalities**, the competitive market demand function does not include all of the benefits of production.

This is a **missing markets** problem. If the harm done, say, to air when it is used as a waste repository, had a market, then the value in its alternate use of clean air would be determined and producers would simply include the price of air as a waste repository in their cost calculations. But the market does not exist because it is prohibitively expensive to devise and enforce air property rights. If the market for a commodity is missing, market forces will not lead to efficient production.

Exercise caution in this analysis: Economic analysis indicates that we can determine an **efficient level of harm**! After all, production is happening because there are marginal benefits associated with the good in question. However, costs also accrue to production, including costs borne by others not party to the market transaction. In this setting, producers will generate too much harm because they don't have to pay for it.

Typically, **four externality characteristics** emerge. They can be produced by individuals as well as firms. There is a reciprocal aspect to externalities; who causes the harm to whom, the firm when it creates pollution, or the people trying to force producers to higher costs (and lower return) by incorporating pollution costs into the costs of production? Externalities can be negative or positive (we'll cover positive externalities next). Finally, following usual marginal analysis, as long as it costs something to "fix" an externality (positive or negative), and as long as the marginal benefit of reducing the externality falls, the efficient level of "fixing" is less than 100%.

The analysis of negative externality in a supply and demand context must separate **private marginal costs** from **social marginal costs**. Private marginal costs are those that are generated by markets for inputs; raw material costs, rent, and the opportunity costs of the producer's own resources. **Marginal damages** exist, but because of the missing market problem, they do not get added in to the producers' cost considerations. The greater the level of output, the higher the marginal damages due to production. The vertical sum of private marginal costs and marginal damages equals social marginal costs. Here is where we find the inefficiencies of negative externalities. Producers make their output decisions based on private marginal costs. If they had to add in marginal damages, their marginal costs would shift to the left and equal the true marginal social costs. Such a shift would reduce output. Thus, if marginal damages are not added in, the competitive firm will produce an inefficiently large level of output.

The analysis of positive externalities in a supply and demand context must separate **private marginal benefits** from **social marginal benefits**. Private marginal benefits represent the ability of producers to charge for their output. An effective demand for their product exists. But additional marginal benefits exist without a market through which producers can collect them. Thus, these other benefits do not get added in to the producers' effective demand curve. The vertical sum of private marginal benefit and other marginal benefits that cannot be collected equals social marginal benefit. The inefficiency of markets with positive externalities occurs because producers make output decisions based on private marginal benefits. If they could add in the other, uncollected, marginal benefits, their marginal benefit would shift to the right and equal marginal social benefits. Such a shift would increase output. Thus, if uncollected marginal benefits are not added in, the competitive firm will produce an inefficiently small level of output.

Sometimes, **private market responses** to externality problems do occur. When this happens, market forces lead firms and consumers to "**internalize**" the externality. One way this can happen is to increase the scope of production to include those effected by the externality. If one firm is producing a negative externality that is harmful to another firm, a **merger** would force the new, combined firm to include the costs that one of its divisions is putting onto another. Research ventures often produce positive externalities after the results are released. As a result, R&D may be too small. But **joint research ventures** can help solve this problem; each firm contributes to the joint venture and the amount of R&D increases to a level closer to the true benefit produced for all firms. **Malls** also represent a response to positive externalities. Large stores are called anchor stores since they bring in most of the customers that visit small, peripheral stores. A mall internalizes the positive externality produced by the anchor stores by charging rent to the peripheral stores; the level of retailing approaches the place where social marginal benefits equal social marginal costs. **Social convention** also can help reduce externality problems: "Give a hoot, don't pollute," and "Do unto others as you would have other do unto you."

Another way to handle externalities is to simply **assign the rights** to either producers or damaged parties. **The Coase Theorem** shows that it doesn't matter which side of the externality problem gets the rights, the optimal level of output will result. For example, if producers are given rights to the air, and clean air is valuable, then if it dumps pollution into the air it forgoes the fee it could have charged to those willing to pay for clean air. This shifts the opportunity costs of production to the left, in the direction of the true social marginal costs, and output falls. Conversely, if damaged parties own rights to the air, they can charge the firm when it wants to use their air. Again, private marginal costs shift to the left in the direction of social marginal costs. For positive externalities, subsidies play the same role. If producers are subsidized, their perception of the value of production moves toward the social marginal benefit curve and output increases.

Government remedies may be justified if they are cost-effective. Governments must generate and analyze a vast amount of information in order to determine which activities are subject to externality problems, how dramatic the problems are, the value of the harm (for negative externalities) or reduced satisfaction (positive externalities). Finally, if action is indicated policy makers must arrive at some solution if the value of action is greater than zero after they include the costs of the action and its administration.

However they choose to proceed, governments really just try to create market prices that are missing in externality situations. One approach is **corrective taxes and subsidies**. A **Pigouvian tax**, equal to the amount of marginal damage that would occur at the efficient level of output, shifts private marginal costs to the left far enough to result in the optimal level of output. A **Pigouvian subsidy**, equal to the amount of uncollected benefit at the efficient level of output, will shift private marginal benefits to the right far enough to result in the optimal level of output. Another approach to negative externalities is to create a situation where individuals pay the marginal damages done at the efficient level of output in order to pollute. A competitive auction should generate the right "price" of polluting, or **effluent charge**. Even just **assigning transferable rights** to someone and allowing the rights to be sold to the highest bidder in an open market will do the same thing.

Public goods present a particularly thorny variation on the positive externality theme. Public goods are characterized by **non-rival consumption**. Once produced, one person's consumption of a public good in no way interferes with its simultaneous consumption by others. Non-rival consumption makes it difficult for any single producer to collect for the provision of a pubic good; it may not be possible to withhold consumption from non-payers and everyone has an incentive to report that the good is worth nothing to them. As a result of this **free rider** behavior, the private marginal benefit is zero and so is output. This under-spending violates allocation efficiency.

Market responses to public good problems can occur for **excludable goods**. If consumption can be withheld from any individual who does not pay a price, then output will occur. **Toll goods** (like roads and amusement parks) represent excludable goods which are also (to a greater or lesser extent) non-rival in consumption. Sometimes, even the classic public good example of the lighthouse is actually excludable. Modern sensor technology has made price excludability a much more viable option for many non-rival goods.

But, again, cost-effective government remedies may be justified. Governments will still face extraordinary costs in determining whether and how to handle public good problems. The social marginal benefit of any level of a public good, due to non-rival consumption, is the **vertical sum of all private marginal benefits**. Once this is derived, however, the impossible task is to pick a price to charge for provision. Everybody will say the good is worth nothing, and the potential supplier knows that nobody has the same willingness to pay. The practical result is the government-chosen **tax system**. In such a setting, some members of society feel that their tax bill is too high, while others know that their bill is too low, relative to the benefits they receive (but these taxpayers would be foolish to pay more). On a final note, exercise caution in analyzing public production since not all goods produced publicly are public goods. For example, consumers sometimes demand **publicly provided private goods**, like public and private golf courses and public and private universities.

An Externality Application

Socially conscious production can ameliorate negative externalities, but may create an externality situation of its own! Ben and Jerry's highly publicized "Rain Forest Crunch" ice cream is an example. It is a market-based attack on environmental destruction. The ice cream is made using non-timber rain forest produce (nuts, essentially). By making the renewable resources that derive from rain forests more valuable, it is hoped that destruction of the rain forests will be reduced.

Question 1:   Graph the rain forest timber situation before Ben and Jerry's move.

Question 2:   Graph the externality situation that Ben and Jerry's is combating. Identify the optimal level of rain forest timber activity. What is the fundamental economic factor leading to the destruction of the rain forests?

Now for the externality created by the approach. Many people receive benefits from Ben and Jerry's activity without buying the ice cream. If they are sympathetic to Ben and Jerry's cause, then they gain satisfaction from any success Ben and Jerry's may achieve without having to buy any ice cream.

Question 3:   Graph the Rain Forest Crunch ice cream market. Identify the optimal level of Rain Forest Crunch ice cream. What fundamental economic factor leads to the non-optimal result?

Question 4: In your graph, identify the Pareto subsidy that would be required to get the ice cream market to its optimal level.   What would such a subsidy do to the ice cream picture?

Question 5: Rather than a subsidy to Ben and Jerry's, is there a subsidy to buyers that would push the market to the optimal result? How could such a subsidy be issued so that people simply wouldn't keep the money and buy something else?

Question 6: If the ice cream market were pushed to its optimal level, would Ben and Jerry's impact on the rain forest situation be larger? Can you show by how much in your graph?

Multiple Choice Questions

1. Dana lives in Wisconsin and loves eating cheese. So many people move to Wisconsin and start eating cheese that the price of cheese goes up. This is an example of a:
    A.   positive externality.
    B.   negative externality.
    C.   public bad.
    D.   None of the above is correct.

2. An externality exists whenever:
    A.   the activity of one entity directly affects the welfare of another.
    B.   the direct impact of one entity's actions on the welfare of another is transmitted by market prices.
    C.   the direct impact of one entity's actions on the welfare of another is not transmitted by market prices.
    D.   economic efficiency is adversely affected.

3.   An externality's detrimental impact on economic efficiency is a consequence of:
   A.   the impact of the externality on market prices.
   B.   the failure or inability to establish ownership rights.
   C.   private ownership rights to resources.
   D.   the price system's transmission of the externality's effect on welfare.

4.   Graphically, the social marginal cost schedule for a good whose production involves a negative externality equals:
   A.   private marginal benefit minus the marginal damage schedule.
   B.   private marginal benefit minus private marginal cost.
   C.   private marginal cost plus the marginal damage schedule.
   D.   private marginal benefit plus the marginal damage schedule.

5.   Consider a good whose production involves a negative externality. The benefit of moving from the equilibrium output level in the absence of intervention to the socially efficient output level includes:
   A.   a drop in the private cost of resources used in production.
   B.   a reduction of external costs imposed upon another person or firm.
   C.   a gain in benefits to consumers of the good.
   D.   Both A and B are correct.

6.   Consider a situation involving a negative externality. According to the Coase theorem, which party receives the assignment of property rights has:
   A.   no effect on the efficiency of bargaining.
   B.   no effect on the income distribution resulting from bargaining.
   C.   no effect on the efficiency of bargaining and the resulting income distribution.
   D.   an effect both on the efficiency of bargaining and on the resulting income distribution.

7.   Private responses to externalities include:
   A.   Pigouvian taxes.
   B.   effluent fees.
   C.   direct regulation.
   D.   mergers of the affected parties.

8.   Government responses to externalities include:
   A.   direct regulation.
   B.   bargaining between the affected parties.
   C.   mergers of the affected parties.
   D.   None of the above is correct.

9. A tax levied upon each unit of a polluter's output in an amount just equal to the marginal damage it inflicts at the efficient level of output is known as:
    A.   a Pigouvian tax.
    B.   an effluent fee.
    C.   an asymmetric tax.
    D.   an efficient tax.

Questions 10-12 refer to the following:

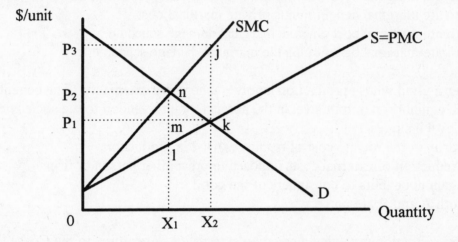

Refer to the figure above, which illustrates the supply and demand conditions for a good whose production involves negative externalities. PMC is private marginal cost; SMC is social marginal cost.

10. In the figure, the socially efficient level of output is _____, and the equilibrium output level in the absence of any intervention is _____.
    A. X_1 / X_1.
    B. X_1 / X_2.
    C. X_2 / X_2.
    D. X_2 / X_1.

11. In the figure, the net gain to moving from the equilibrium output level in the absence of intervention to the socially efficient level is represented by the area of:
    A.   region kln.
    B.   region kmn.
    C.   region jkn.
    D.   region jklm.

12.   In the figure, in order to induce the socially efficient output level, the government could impose a tax per unit equal to:
      A.   distance ln.
      B.   distance jk.
      C. P_3-P_2.
      D. P_2-P_1.

13.   A lighthouse today can be automatically turned on when a laser from the lighthouse detects a passing ship that broadcasts a special code. This means that such lighthouses are no longer:
      A.   non-excludable.
      B.   non-rival.
      C.   a negative externality.
      D.   Pigouvian.

14.   In the case of a non-excludable public good, the market without intervention is likely to produce:
      A.   the efficient amount of the good.
      B.   more than the efficient amount of the good.
      C.   less than the efficient amount of the good.
      D.   a negligible number of free riders.

15.   The total willingness-to-pay schedule for a public good is the:
      A.   vertical summation of individual demand curves.
      B.   horizontal summation of individual demand curves.
      C.   vertical difference between individual demand curves.
      D.   horizontal difference between individual demand curves.

16.   Suppose Donald and Marla move to a Caribbean island, where only two goods are in scarce supply: maple syrup (m) and fireworks displays (f). At the present quantities of these items, Donald's MRS between fireworks and maple syrup is 1/3, while Marla's is 1/2 and the marginal rate of transformation (MRT between fireworks and maple syrup) is 1. The price of maple syrup is $1 per unit. Currently, there is:
      A.   an efficient amount of fireworks displays.
      B.   an inefficiently large amount of fireworks displays.
      C.   an inefficiently small amount of fireworks displays.
      D.   an efficient amount of maple syrup.

Questions 17-19 refer to the following:

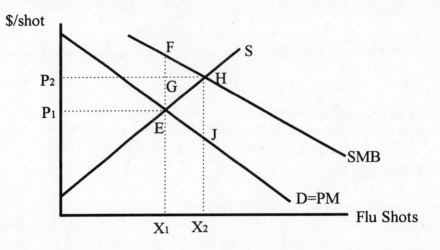

Refer to the figure above, which illustrates the supply and demand conditions for flu shots, a good whose use involves a positive externality. PMB is private marginal benefit; SMB is social marginal benefit.

17. In the figure, the socially efficient number of flu shots is represented by _____, and the equilibrium number of flu shots in the absence of any intervention is _____.
    A. X_1 / X_1.
    B. X_2 / X_1.
    C. X_1 / X_2.
    D. X_2 / X_2.

18. In the figure, the total subsidy amount that would induce people to have the socially efficient number of flu shots is represented by the area of:
    A. region O P_2 H X_2.
    B. region 0 P_1 E X_1.
    C. region P_1 P_2 H E.
    D. region X_1 X_2 H E.

19. In the figure, the net gain to moving from the equilibrium number of flu shots in the absence of intervention to the socially efficient number of flu shots is represented by the area of:
    A. region EFH.
    B. region EHJ.
    C. region EGH.
    D. region FGH.

20. Which of the following is an example of a private good that is sometimes publicly provided?
    A. Library books.
    B. Medical services.
    C. Housing.
    D. All of the above are correct.

Problems

1. Using the Coase theorem, discuss how the efficient level of noise pollution would be achieved either by penalizing the noisemakers, or by forcing those who bear the noise damage to wear earplugs.

2. Perhaps the cheapest way to reduce speeding on the highway was demonstrated in the movie, Speed; if cars go faster than the speed limit, they can simply be rigged to explode. Is this method efficient? Is it equitable? (Be careful: speeders cause accidents that kill people.)

3. As you have seen repeatedly, one value of the economic way of thinking is that it can help people think about unintended consequences. Here is an interesting one. One way to move the number of fine arts performances, a good with positive externalities, toward the optimal level is through subsidy. But even though subsidies to the performing arts have kept pace with inflation, and sometimes grown over time, the number of performances has fallen. Given that the performing arts are heavily unionized, explain how this can happen.

4. Carefully delineate the difference between a public good and a publicly provided good, since they need not be the same thing.

5. Show that the optimal level of nearly nothing is zero.

6. Explain why most major university libraries are in disrepair (litter as common as books, noisy "study" areas that actually are social gatherings). [Hint: Remember the tragedy of the commons.]

CHAPTER 1. ANSWERS TO EXERCISES

Answers to Questions in the Application

Question 1: Opportunity costs are what must be given up to get more of something else. In this case, we are asked what must be given up to get more wild bees by maintaining wild bee habitat. The answer is what destroyed the wild bee habitat - housing development. Thus, the opportunity costs of maintaining wild bee habitat is the housing that could have been developed on the sites.

Question 2: When something that is not a scarce resource it means that there is a sufficient amount available that anyone who wants it can have it without paying for it. Essentially, there is no opportunity cost for the good. That means the price of the service wild bees provided when they were not a scarce resource was zero.

Question 3: As shown to the right, the demand curve must have intercepted the horizontal axis somewhere to the left of the (vertical) supply curve of wild bees.

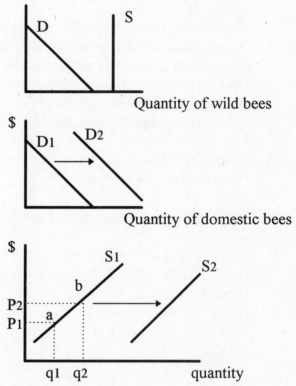

Question 4: As shown in the graph to the right, the disappearance of wild bees will shift the demand curve for domestic bees to the right.

Question 5: Any change in quantity supplied in response to *price* is a change in the quantity supplied. As shown in the graph to the right, a change in supply would be a shift of the supply curve from S1 to S2. A change in the quantity supplied is move along the supply curve from point a to point b so quantity supplied changes from q1 to q2 as the price goes up from P1 to P2.

Question 6: The supply (curve) of domestic bees depends on the cost of producing them. As costs increase, the *quantity supplied* at any particular price goes down, which means the supply curve shifting inward. It is a shift of the curve, not a move along the curve.

Question 7: As shown at the right, as demand for domestic bees increases (shifts to the right) and the costs increase (so the supply shifts to the left) the equilibrium price will go up. Equilibrium quantity can go up or down, depending on whether the demand or supply shifts the most.

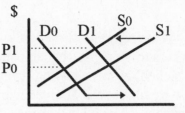

Quantity of domestic bees

Answers to Multiple Choice Questions

1. B	6. D	11. D	16. B
2. A	7. B	12. B	17. C
3. B	8. C	13. C	18. B
4. B	9. D	14. B	19. B
5. D	10. C	15. A	20. C

Answers to Problems

1. The easiest way to check this is with graphs. To the right are two graphs starting with the same price and quantity, one with steep demand and one with flat demand. The supply curve is the same for both. The mite infestation shifts the supply curve to the left. As we can see, the effect on the price (rental rate of hives) is larger when the demand curve is steep. The effect on the equilibrium quantity is larger when the demand curve is flat.

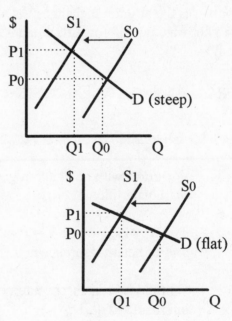

2. As plastics replace chromium the demand for chromium will shift to the left. With a steep supply curve, the equilibrium price should fall sharply.

3. Economics argues that actions should be taken only as long as the marginal benefit of the action exceeds its marginal cost. Right now the evidence is that mammograms for women between the ages of 40 and 50 have only a small marginal benefit. Since it is costly to provide the mammograms to women in this age group, the marginal benefit does not exceed the marginal cost, and thus we should not give them.

4. Whether mammograms should be given is a normative question. Studying whether or not women will seek mammograms is a positive question.

5. This is simply a question of allowing markets to work, so that an equilibrium is reached, or not allowing the market price to adjust so that an equilibrium is reached. The oil embargoes shifted the supply curve to the left. During the first embargo, price was kept low, at the original price, P_0. At that price, after the supply curve shifted to the left, there was a shortage of Q_1-Q_2. During the second embargo, price was allowed to go up, until a new equilibrium was reached at a price of P_3 and a quantity of Q_3.

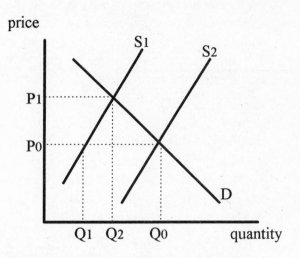

6. As women found increasing opportunities the supply of nurses decreased - meaning the supply curve shifted to the left, causing a shortage of nurses at the old wage. So this part was the structural change. As wages increased in response to the shortage, the market was moving towards equilibrium (a movement along the demand curve for nurses).

CHAPTER 2. ANSWERS TO EXERCISES

Answers to Questions in the Application

Question 1: A worker with no children gets no value from subsidized child care so the marginal utility is zero.

Question 2: $T = W + P_H H$ where T = total compensation, W = wages, P_H = price per unit of health insurance and H = units of health insurance offered.

Question 3: On the wages axis, the intercept = T. On the health insurance axis the intercept = T/P_H.

Question 4: The slope of the budget constraint equals $1/P_H$. By default, the "price" of a unit of wages is $1.

Question 5: The MRS_{WH} is less than the price ratio.

Question 6: We know that $MU_H/MU_W > P_H/P_W$. Thus $MU_H/P_H > MU_W/P_W$.

Question 7: If the employer switched to flexible benefits, the worker illustrated would decrease the amount of health insurance he bought, and increase other goods (his wages).

Question 8:   The MRS$_{WH}$ would increase as the worker moved up the budget constraint and found a point where the indifference curve is tangent to it. Total utility would increase.

Question 9: The MRS$_{WH}$ exceeds the price ratio at point b.

Question 10: The worker shown maximizes her utility at point c, where the indifference curve U2 is tangent to her budget constraint. Her fixed benefit package puts her at point b. which gives her W2 in wages and H2 in health insurance. She gets more utility with W3 in wages and H3 in health insurance, so she would spend W2-W3 of her wages to buy H3-H2 more health insurance. This assumes she can buy the additional health insurance at the same price her employer can.

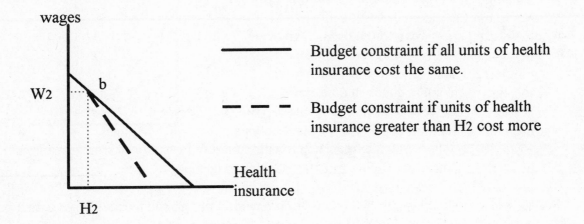

Question 11:   Since the price per unit of health insurance increases for units greater than H2, the budget constraint gets steeper to the right of that amount, as shown below.

―――――― Budget constraint if all units of health insurance cost the same.

― ― ― Budget constraint if units of health insurance greater than H2 cost more

Answers to Multiple Choice Questions

1. D	6. B	11. C	16. B
2. C	7. C	12. B	17. C
3. B	8. C	13. B	18. A
4. D	9. C	14. D	19. C
5. C	10. A	15. C	20. B

Answers to Problems

1. No. This student's preferences violate transitivity.

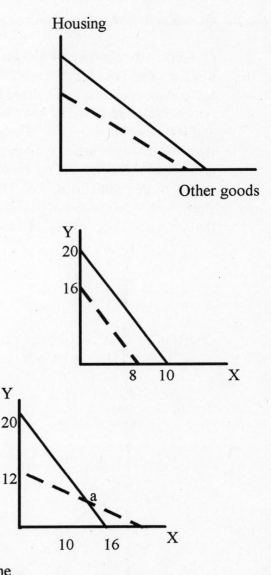

2. Two changes that must be considered. First, the price of housing relative to both income and other goods has increased. Second, the price of other goods relative to income has increased, while relative to the price of housing it has fallen. Thus, the budget constraint will shift towards the origin and become flatter (with housing on the vertical axis). It shifts from the solid line to the dotted line.

3. This requires putting both constraints on the same graph, and taking the lower boundary. In this case $20 can buy 20 Y type rides or 10 X type rides, or something in between. The solid line in the money budget constraint. The dotted line is the time budget constraint. This person will go home with $4.

4. The money budget constraint stays the same, but the time constraint shifts to the dotted line shown to the right. The new feasible consumption set connects points 12, a and 10. We may be tempted to say that the individual will consume at point a, but we cannot tell. She may have preferences that put her on the segment between 12 and a (in which case she goes home with money) or on the segment between a and 10 (in which case she leaves before 4 hours are up).

5. This is a tricky question. Make sure you pay attention to the facts. Candy bars are clearly $1 each, but how much is popcorn? If we measure it in "small bags" then 1 unit of popcorn (1 small bag) costs $2 since the large bag is twice as large the small bag, and costs twice as much. The sisters face the same prices for popcorn and candy, and both spend their entire budgets, so their MRS's must be equal. We cannot say which sister has a larger marginal utility of popcorn. All we can say is that the ratio of the marginal utility of popcorn to the marginal utility of candy is the same, since the MRS equals the ratio of the marginal utilities.

6. The MRS_{CP} tells how much candy the sister will give up to get 1 more unit of popcorn. Since she spends all her money on candy, she must be *willing* to give up less candy for a unit of popcorn than it would cost. That is, the price of popcorn in terms of candy must exceed her MRS_{CP}. Thus, $MRS_{CP}<P_P/P_C$.

7. This is a simple application of consumer choice to wages and benefits like Social Security. Consider the situation shown to the right. The government forces people to put more of their compensation to Social Security than they would on their own. That means they are at some point like a, where the slope of the budget constraint ($-P_S/1$ since the price per unit of wage equals one) exceeds the slope of the indifference curve (the negative of MRS_{WS}).

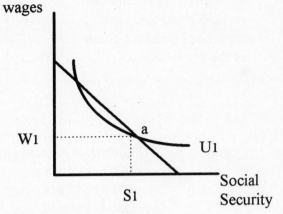

CHAPTER 3. ANSWERS TO EXERCISES

Answers to Questions in the Application

Question 1: As the price of caviar goes up and consumption of caviar falls to 1 ounce from 2, the amount spent falls from $60 per year to $45 per year. Since income has not changed, the amount spent on other goods goes up by $15, and since those prices have not changed, the consumption of other goods must increase, to G_2 from G_1.

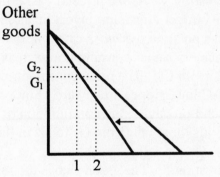

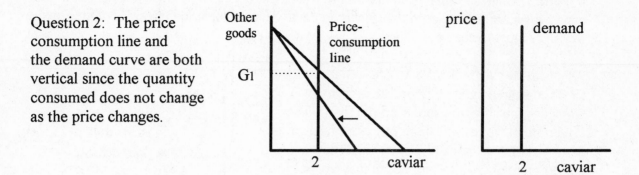

Question 2: The price consumption line and the demand curve are both vertical since the quantity consumed does not change as the price changes.

Question 3: Unit elasticity means that the percentage change in quantity demanded will exactly equal the percentage change in price. An increase from $30 per ounce to $45 per ounce is a 50 percent increase in price. Thus, quantity demanded would need to *decrease* by 50 percent. Since you were consuming 2 ounces per year, your consumption would fall to 1 ounce per year.

Question 4: As the price of caviar goes up the budget constraint pivots in, as shown. This person buys *more* caviar at the higher price, so caviar consumption increases to C2 from C1. The price-consumption line (P-C line) slopes downward. Since more is spend on caviar, the consumption of other goods must fall (from G1 to G2 in this case).

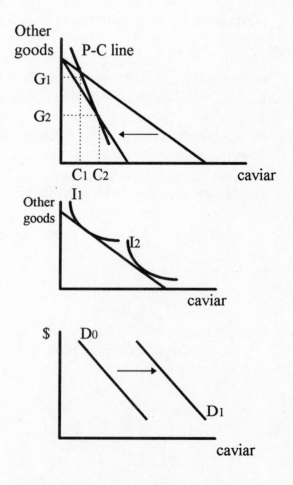

Question 5: The graph shows the same budget constraint, indicating prices and incomes have remained the same. Indifference curves must have moved to favor caviar over other goods, to I2 from I1.

Question 6: Mr. Gilbert likes his caviar with champagne, so we can take them to be complements. Champagne is a normal good. If the price of champagne goes down, his consumption of it goes up, and, since caviar is a complement to champagne, a decrease in the price of champagne shifts the demand curve for caviar outward, from D0 to D1.

Question 7: The cross-price elasticity of demand for caviar with respect to the price of vodka is negative, since they are complements. An increase in the price of vodka will cause the quantity demanded of caviar to fall.

Questions 8: An increase in income causes a parallel shift in the budget constraint. Since the demand has grown faster than income, people are devoting a greater share of their income to caviar, leaving less for other goods. So the consumption of other goods must go down, meaning the income-consumption line (I-C line) must have a negative slope. Caviar consumption goes from C_1 to C_2 while the consumption of other goods goes from G_1 to G_2.

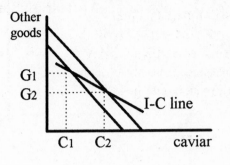

Question 9: The slope of the Engel curve would have a positive slope. As income goes up, the quantity demanded of caviar goes up. Because caviar demand has grown faster than incomes, the percentage change in caviar exceeds the percentage change in income, so the income elasticity of demand for caviar must be greater than 1.

Question 10: No. We can not say the price elasticity of demand for caviar = -0.8 because we cannot apply *ceteris paribus*. It is possible that income, tastes or the prices of complements and substitutes have changed.

Answers to Multiple Choice Questions

1. B	6. D	11. D	16. B
2. B	7. B	12. C	17. C
3. D	8. B	13. B	18. B
4. B	9. B	14. B	19. B
5. D	10. A	15. D	20. A

Answers to Problems

1. The cross-price elasticity equals the percentage change in quantity demanded of hot dogs divided by the percentage change in the price of beer. Thus, $-0.15 = \%\Delta Q_H/25$. So $\%\Delta Q_H = -0.15 \times 25 = -3.75$. Hot dog sales should decrease by 3.75%.

2. The three graphs below address each situation: a) The 10% decrease in the price of beer pivots the budget constraint outward. b) The coupon lowers the price only of the first 4 bottles, then the slope of the budget constraint returns to the original price level. c)A coupon causes a parallel shift outward of the budget constraint.

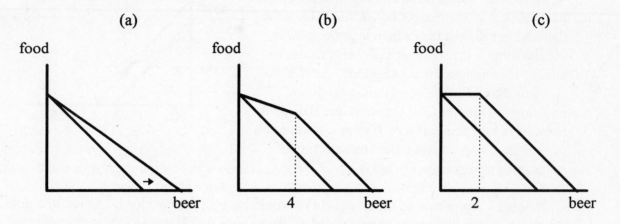

3. You would need to make some rather severe assumptions that would be difficult to defend to do comparative statics between the two communities. Although the effect of taxes on the relative prices of food and other goods is clear, we have no individual whom we can observe under both sets of prices. We would need to assume individuals in Washington and Idaho have the same incomes, which is questionable, and that all other taxes were the same. Additionally, we would have to assume that individuals in the two states have the same tastes. In effect, comparative statics would require we make interpersonal comparisons of utility, something that we really cannot do as economists.

4. We know from the point elasticity of demand has the formula $o_p = -(1/s) \cdot (p/X)$ where s is the slope of the inverse demand curve, p is the price and X is the quantity. Since the demand curve is linear, $1/s = -20$ so applying the formula, $o_p = -(-(20)) \cdot (p/X) = 20(p/X)$. From the demand curve, when $P = 10$, $X = 800$; when $P = 20$, $X = 600$; and when $P = 30$, $X = 400$. So applying the formula, the answers are a) $20(10/800) = 0.25$, b) $20(20/600) = 0.67$, and c) $20(30/400) = 1.5$.

5. These two plans shift the budget constraint differently. The first causes a parallel shift in the budget constraint, the second causes pivot outward. If education is a normal good both plans would increase the demand.

    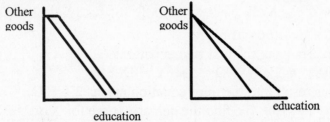

6. Since the first plan gives a parallel shift out in the budget constraint, it is equivalent to increasing income (by the $500 that is available for free education). If education per employee went down, that means overall, an increase in income decreased the demand for education, indicating that education was an inferior good.

7. When Ann's income is $100 she consumes 10 units of food. When her income is $140 she consumes 13 units of food. The graph shows this relationship.

    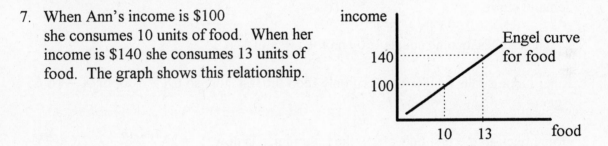

8. Housing is obviously a luxury good for this person. The income-consumption line must have a negative slope, and the Engel curves must have a positive slope.

    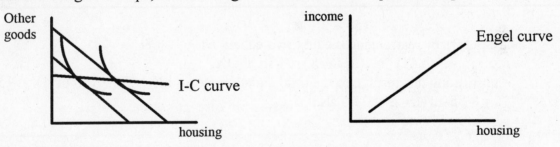

9. Using the numbers given, the price elasticity of demand equals -25/20=1.25 which is elastic. When demand is elastic, an increase in price lowers total expenditure on the good. Thus, raising the price would make the total revenue coming into the public transit system go down. But since demand is elastic, lowering price increases total spending on the good. So by lowering the price of a ride, the transit system would increase its revenue.

10. The Lagrangian expression is $L = 2X^{1/2}Y^{1/2} - \lambda(2X + Y - 150)$. The first-order necessary conditions are:

$$X^{-1/2} - 2\lambda = 0$$
$$Y^{-1/2} - \lambda = 0$$
$$2X + Y - 150 = 0$$

Therefore by rearranging the first two equations

$$(Y/X)^{1/2} = 2 \text{ or } (Y/X) = 4 \text{ so } Y = 4X.$$

Substituting this result into the third equation means $2X + 4X = 150$ or $6X = 150$ so $X = 25$. Thus, $Y = 100$. To find the demand curve for X, at the first-order necessary conditions substitute P_X for 2, so

$$X^{-1/2} - P_X\lambda = 0$$
$$Y^{-1/2} - \lambda = 0$$
$$P_XX + Y - 150 = 0$$

From the first two equations, $(Y/X)^{1/2} = P_X$ or $(Y/X) = P_X^2$ so $Y = P_X^2X$. Substituting this into the third equation gives $P_XX + P_X^2X - 150 = 0$. Solving for X gives the demand curve

$$X = 150/(P_X + P_X^2)$$

which assumes income equals 150 and the price of Y is 1.

11. If her income falls to 100, we need only redo the last step, so $6X = 100$, or $X = 16.66$. Again, $Y = 4X$, so $Y = 66.67$.

12. Going back to the first part of 10, the Lagrangian is now $L = 2X^{1/2}Y^{1/2} - \lambda(2X + 2Y - 150)$ and the first order necessary conditions are

$$X^{-1/2} - 2\lambda = 0$$
$$Y^{-1/2} - 2\lambda = 0$$
$$2X + 2Y - 150 = 0$$

Therefore by rearranging the first two equations

$$(Y/X)^{1/2} = 1 \text{ or } (Y/X) = 1 \text{ so } Y = X.$$

Substituting this result into the third equation means $2X + 2X = 150$ or $4X = 150$ so $X = 37.5$. Thus, $Y = 37.5$ also.

CHAPTER **4.** ANSWERS TO EXERCISES

Answers to Questions in the Application

The following graph is used to answer questions 1 of the application.

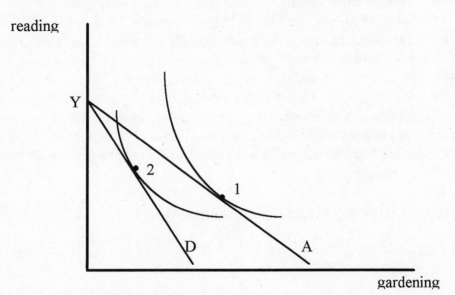

Question 1:   The graph shows the budget constraint moving from line A (pre-injury) to line D (post-injury). Consumption moved from point 1 to point 2.

Question 2:   The CV is X-Y (line D to line C). The EV is Y-Z (line A to line B). The CV is larger than the EV.

Question 3:   The proper compensation is the CV which allows her to achieve the same utility level, at the new prices, as she could before the injury.

The following graph is used for question 4.

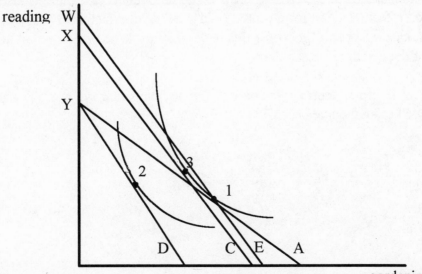

Question 4:   The Fort and Rosenman compensation allows the injured party to consume at point 1 with the new price ratio. It is necessary to move the individual to line E from line D. Thus, the compensation needed is W-Y which is larger than X-Y. This is overcompensation in the sense that theoretically this person could achieve a higher utility level than was originally enjoyed.

Question 5:   The overcompensation comes about because we ignore that the substitution effect mitigates to some extent the utility loss. As the price of gardening increases, the injured person substitutes reading for gardening, at least somewhat. Compensating the individual so she can consume her old levels of gardening and reading ignores that she has this ability. A more severe injury, with the larger amount of time it takes to do the old level of gardening, carries with it more of a substitution effect. Thus, we are ignoring more of a utility compensating change in behavior, and thus the individual with the more severe injury will enjoy a greater level of overcompensation.

Answers to Multiple Choice Questions

1. A	6. D	11. B	16. B
2. C	7. C	12. D	17. C
3. C	8. A	13. B	18. C
4. B	9. B	14. A	19. C
5. A	10. C	15. A	20. D

Answers to Problems

1. The son is right that it would be easier, but it would not be as effective in cutting his consumption of comic books. Recall that the Slutsky equation is
$$\Delta x/\Delta p = (\Delta x/\Delta p)_{comp} - x_1 \times \Delta x/\Delta I$$
where the second term on the right hand side is the income effect. Without the tax there is only that part of the change. But with the 25 cents tax, there is also the substitution effect (the first term on the right hand side) which is always negative. Comic books are a normal good for this boy, making $\Delta x/\Delta I$ positive, and hence, because of the negative sign
$$(\Delta x/\Delta p)_{comp} - x_1 \times \Delta x/\Delta I < -x_1 \times \Delta x/\Delta I$$
which means the total decrease in comic book buying is larger if there is a substitution effect as well as an income effect.

2. As shown in the graph, the ability to substitute away from comic books allows the son to avoid some of the burden of the tax. The father's plan shifts the budget constraint from line 1 to line 2, the son's from 1 to 3. Line 2 allows the son to achieve a higher level of utility than does line 3. He actually pays less than a dollar to his Dad, since fewer than 4 comics will be bought with the tax.

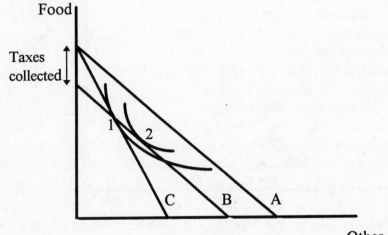

3. No, this is exactly Carter's gasoline tax plan discussed in the textbook. The rebate is less than the CV, and so utility is lower.

4. Look at the following graph:

The graph is constructed so under either scheme the same amount of tax is collected from the person shown. The Washington tax, which does not tax food, shifts the individual's budget constraint from line A to line C. Utility is maximized at point 1. The amount of tax collected is the vertical distance from point 1 to line A. A sales tax on all goods (which does not change relative prices) that would collect the same amount of tax would shift the budget constraint from line A to line B. Utility is maximized at point 2, indicating that the Idaho plan has less of a welfare loss when an equivalent amount of tax revenue is raised from any particular person.

5. The Slutsky equation is $\Delta x/\Delta p = (\Delta x/\Delta p)_{comp} - x_1 \times \Delta x/\Delta I$ where the left hand side determines the observed demand curve, while the first term on the right hand side shows the compensated demand curve. Because the ordinary demand curve includes the income effect, for normal goods it is flatter than the compensated demand curve. The small substitution effect means the compensated demand curve is very steep, while the large income effect makes the ordinary demand curve flat. Thus, we have the relationship shown to the right. If a subsidy lowers the price from P_1 to P_2, the gain in exact consumer surplus is area A (using the compensated demand curve) but the gain in Marshallian consumer surplus is areas A + B (using the ordinary demand curve).

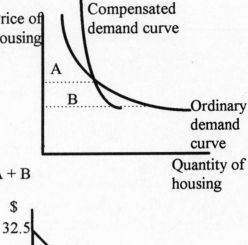

6. This information provides some information about Marshallian consumer surplus. Travel costs make the price of a Spokane Indians game $15 more expensive for residents of Colfax than for residents of Cheney. Thus, we can measure approximately how much consumer surplus the residents of Cheney are gaining by the difference in average attendance from the two town.

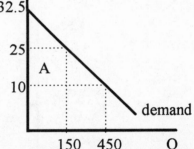

    The graph shows the story. Consumer surplus is the area under the demand curve and over the price. The two points of observation provide a way to approximate a linear demand curve. The slope of the demand curve is $\Delta P/\Delta Q$. We have that $\Delta P = 15$ and $\Delta Q = 300$ so the slope is approximately $-15/300 = -0.05$. Additionally, we know that $25 = a - 0.05 \bullet 150$ so the intercept of the approximate demand curve is 32.5. Thus the consumer surplus enjoyed by residents of these two towns from attending Spokane Indians baseball games is $\frac{1}{2}(32.5 - 10) \bullet 450 - (15 \bullet 150)$ where the first term $(\frac{1}{2}(32.5 - 10) \bullet 450)$ is the area under the demand curve and the second term $(15 \bullet 150)$ is area A that residents of Colfax pay in extra travel costs. This value equals $2182.50.

7. The answer is obvious. The gain in consumer surplus from getting the lower price must be greater than the fee for membership.

The graph at the right shows the demand curve for the typical coop member. The normal price per unit of food is P_1, and membership lowers the price to P_2. The gain in consumer surplus is A, which must exceed the membership fee.

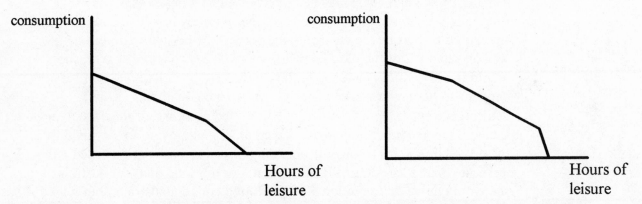

CHAPTER 5. ANSWERS TO EXERCISES

Answers to Questions in the Application

Question 1:   This graph really requires knowing the individual's hourly wage rate. The graph below on the left assumes that the hourly wage is only sufficient to get the individual to the lowest marginal tax rate above the standard deduction. The graph on the right is for a high wage person who surmounts two thresholds as she works more and more hours.

Question 2:   As you can see from the graph, the work disincentive is not great for low wage individuals since they rarely move to high marginal tax rates. Higher wage individuals may see some disincentive for working longer hours, because they may keep only 67 cents for every additional dollar earned. However, it depends on the income effect. Anecdotal evidence shows most highly paid individuals working long hours, indicating the work disincentive is not great, although we cannot say for certain.

Question 3:   Work incentives will differ depending on the individual. Below we've gone from 2 tax rates to one, and suppressed the standard deduction. So, for example, we have an initial tax system of 10% up to income (consumption) c_1, then a tax rate of 30%. Superimposed on that system is a straight 20% tax (dotted line).

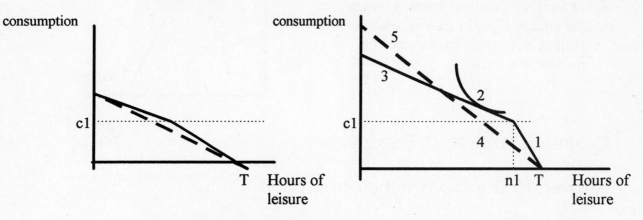

The low wage individual is clearly hurt by this change. His new budget constraint is everywhere below his old one, so he achieves a lower level of utility than under the old tax law. Whether he will work more or less will depend on the income effect.

The high wage individual may be helped or hurt by this change. If she originally was on section 1 of the solid line (working less than $T-n_1$ hours) she would be hurt by the change in the tax law. If her old optimum point was on section 2 of the solid line with the indifference curve shown, she would lower her utility and move to section 4 of the dotted line . What happens to her hours worked depends on the income effect. If the indifference curve were flatter, so it intersected section 5 of the dotted line, she could increase her utility by working more and moving to section 5 of the dotted line. This is the *only* unambiguous case that hours worked will increase. If she was originally on section 3 of the solid budget constraint she would move up to section 5 of the dotted budget constraint, but whether hours worked increases or decreases depends on the income effect.

Study Guide Answers to Exercises

Question 4: This is an important point that is often missed in debate about a flat tax.

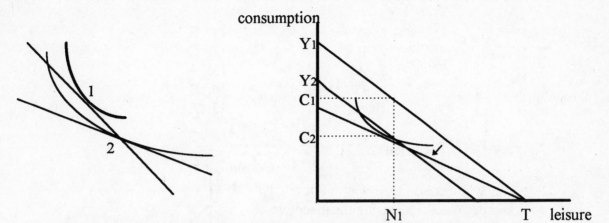

The graph on the right shows the entire picture, while the left is a blow up of the relevant portion. With this flat tax the budget constraint pivots down as shown. N_1 hours are devoted to leisure, $T - N_1$ hours are worked, and C_1-C_2 dollars are paid in taxes. This is just equal to Y_1-Y_2, which is found by taking a line parallel to the original budget constraint but intersecting the tangent at N_1 hours of leisure. This is shown clearly on the left, at point 2. Notice that if this person were assessed a lump sum tax of Y_1-Y_2, he could get a higher utility (by working more) as shown by point 1 on the left graph.

Question 5: The current tax system penalizes saving by taxing interest and capital gains.

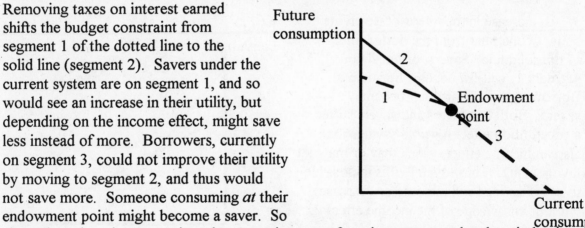

Removing taxes on interest earned shifts the budget constraint from segment 1 of the dotted line to the solid line (segment 2). Savers under the current system are on segment 1, and so would see an increase in their utility, but depending on the income effect, might save less instead of more. Borrowers, currently on segment 3, could not improve their utility by moving to segment 2, and thus would not save more. Someone consuming *at* their endowment point might become a saver. So altogether, there is no certainty that removing taxes from interest earned and capital gains will increase savings. In fact, many empirical studies have indicated that the biggest change from exempting interest from taxes is to change where people save their money. The same amount is saved, it is just put in IRAs instead of regular savings.

197

Answers to Multiple Choice Questions

1. C	6. A	11. B	16. B
2. B	7. B	12. C	17. C
3. C	8. A	13. A	18. B
4. A	9. D	14. B	19. C
5. B	10. A	15. A	20. D

Answers to Problems

1.   This will increase their wages after 40 hours per week, increasing the incentive to work more. The individual shown would rather work (T-N) hours than (T-40) hours.

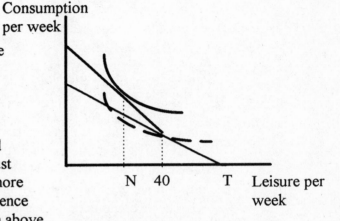

2. Using the same graph, the heavy dotted indifference curve shows a person who must work 40 hours a week, but would prefer more hours per week. Alternatively, the indifference curve could cut the budget constraint from above, showing that the person would prefer to work fewer than 40 hours per week. If these people could find jobs with more flexibility to the hours, they would be happier.

3. An increase in the interest rate pivots the budget constraint from the dotted line to the solid line. Savers, originally on segment 1, will *not* become borrowers. Borrowers may or may not become savers. Both borrowers and savers suffer a substitution effect *towards* savings, but also an income effect, which may or may not favor saving. Thus, overall, it is impossible to say if savings will increase or decrease without knowledge of the income effect.

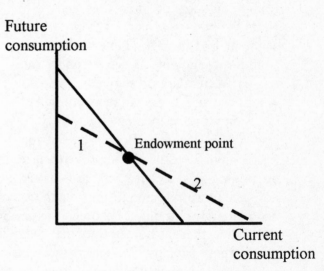

4. The Social Security program minimizes the work incentive impact by allowing workers to keep most of their earnings. As shown, only at earnings above $9000 is there a penalty for earnings, and then only at 33 percent tax. S is the amount of the Social Security payment made to this person, so the labor-leisure budget constraint moves from that minimum level of income. The earnings tax shifts the budget constraint from the solid line to the heavy dotted line. As always, the substitution effect is to work less since the after tax wage is lower, but the income effect is uncertain.

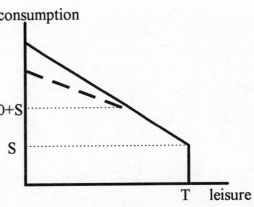

5. If you look back to the answer to question 4 of the application, a lump-sum tax which is payable whether or not a person has any income will not have any excess burden (excess welfare loss). In the past such taxes were called "poll" taxes but were ruled illegal because they violated the right to vote. However, some artifacts of the head tax remain. For example in New Hampshire, residents need pay no tax to vote, but to get a drivers license and other benefits of living in the state, a form of resident's tax must be paid.

6. The graph shows that until the tax law changed the intertemporal budget constraint was a straight line with slope $-(1+(1-t)i)$ where t is the tax rate and i is the interest rate. When interest paid was no longer deductible on taxes, the slope for borrowers shifted to the solid line with slope $-(1+i)$. Savers (on segment 1 originally) were unaffected. Borrowers, at 2 originally, saw their feasible set diminish. Whether their borrowing increased or decreased depended on the income effect, although the substitution effect was toward less borrowing.

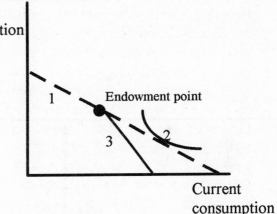

7. We use the formula $PV = 100 + 100/(1+r) + 100/(1+r)^2 + 100/(1+r)^3$ where r is the interest rate. When $r = 10$ percent, $PV = \$348.65$. When $r = 5$ percent, $PV = \$372.32$.

199

8. Given that investment in human capital has increased, we have a good idea of how individuals' consumption decisions reacted to the ability to borrow money. Without the student loans, the utility value of the endowment was maximized at point 1, and human capital investment was a0-a1. Consumption was also at point 1. With the availability of student loans, the utility value of the endowment is maximized at point 2, with consumption at point 3. Human capital investment equals a0-a2, which is larger.

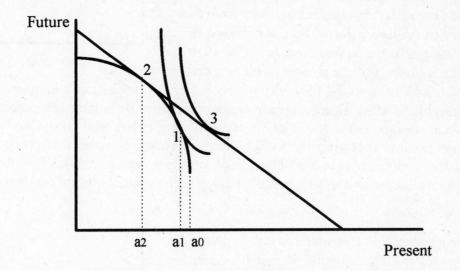

9. The graph shows the labor supply curve, which is backward bending.

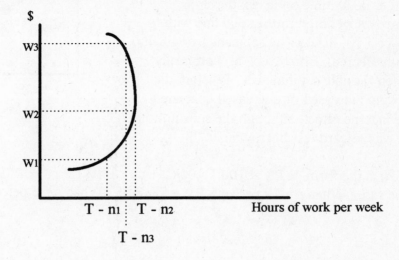

CHAPTER 6. ANSWERS TO EXERCISES

Answers to Questions in the Application

Question 1: The graph to the right shows the game with the odds of 25 cents for a win against minus one dollar for a loss.

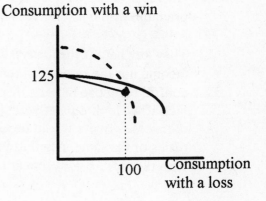

Question 2: The same graph applies to this game. The gambler cares only about the amount she will win against the amount she will lose - not the fair odds. How she cares about the relationship of the fair odds to the actual odds could be reflected in the level of risk loving. The dotted indifference curve Shows a risk lover who would turn down both of these bets because of the poor odds.

Question 3: Facing both games, this player would prefer the table that pays 30 cents for a win - it yields a higher level of utility. In fact, as drawn, this person would decide not to gamble if the only choice was the table than pays 25 cents for a win.

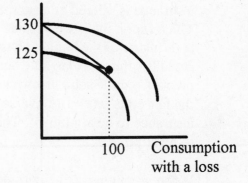

Question 4: To get this person to play the bet would require a payment of at least 60 cents for a win, which is found by the intersection of her indifference curve and the vertical axis.

Question 5: The highest utility is achieved with a $200 bet.

Question 6: This person would pay the $100 bet with the lower payment for a win only if she could not afford the $200 bet.

Answers to Multiple Choice Questions

1. A	6. C	11. A	16. B
2. D	7. D	12. D	17. B
3. A	8. B	13. C	18. B
4. A	9. B	14. D	19. A
5. A	10. D	15. C	20. B

Answers to Problems

1. When there is a deductible on an insurance policy, the person is not fully insured. However, a risk averse person will buy a policy with a deductible if there is a risk premium or the insurance is not actuarially fair.

2. They key here is the *ceteris paribus* requirement. Young males have neither the same income nor the same preferences, including risk attitude, as other people. *If* we could control for those factors, then young males would be more likely to buy insurance. In fact, if we look only at young males, of those with the same income and risk attitude, the worse drivers would be most likely to buy insurance. Similarly, among young males of the same income and with similar driving records, we would expect those with the more risk averse attitudes to more likely be insured

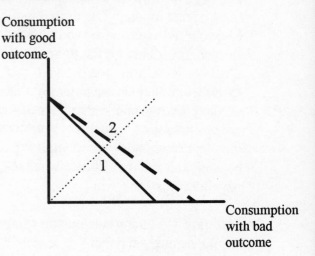

Consumption with good outcome

Consumption with bad outcome

3. When $p<\rho$ then $p/(1-p) < \rho/(1-\rho)$. The term of the right hand side is the slope of the budget constraint when the insurance is insurance is offered at an actuarially fair rate. The term on the left hand side of the inequality is the slope of the budget constraint at the rate actually offered. Thus, the budget constraint pivots from the solid line to the dotted line. At the fair odds rate a risk averse person would buy insurance to be at point 1. This person will buy to be at point 2.

When premiums are actuarially fair risk averse people buy insurance until they are fully insured. With a 1/10 probability of getting sick, Jim can buy insurance at the rate of 10 cents per $1 of insurance. Jim has an expected loss of $0\times.9 + 10000\times.1 = 1000$ so he can buy $10,000 of insurance for $1000. Jim would buy this amount of insurance, thus having $29,000 of consumption whether he gets sick or not.

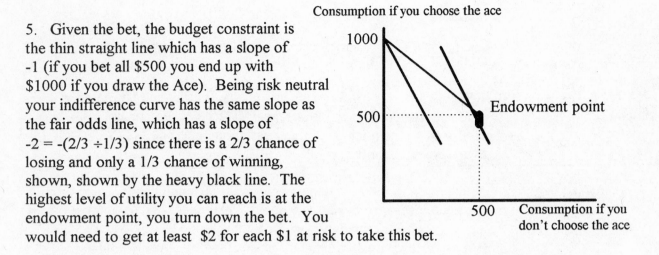

Consumption if you choose the ace

5. Given the bet, the budget constraint is the thin straight line which has a slope of -1 (if you bet all $500 you end up with $1000 if you draw the Ace). Being risk neutral your indifference curve has the same slope as the fair odds line, which has a slope of -2 = -(2/3 ÷1/3) since there is a 2/3 chance of losing and only a 1/3 chance of winning, shown, shown by the heavy black line. The highest level of utility you can reach is at the endowment point, you turn down the bet. You would need to get at least $2 for each $1 at risk to take this bet.

6. Definitely. When you make your first choice there is only a 1/3 chance that you chose the Ace. That means there is a 2/3 chance that the winning card is one of the other two. Revealing one of those cards after the fact doesn't change that probability. Since there was only a 1/3 chance the card you chose is the Ace, there is a 2/3 chance that the remaining card of the other two is the Ace. So by switching, you increase the probability of winning $1000 from 1/3 to 2/3. You can see this intuitively by supposing there was 100 cards to start, 1 Ace and 99 jokers. If after you indicate your card of choice, 98 of the other cards are revealed to be jokers, would you switch? Of course!

7. We can build decision trees, as shown below. Without the advice the expected return for stocks is 1/5 × 0 + 3/5 × 400 + 1/5 × 1500 = 540, so the T-bill return is better. With the advice, after paying the $100 the expected return on stocks is -100 × 1/4 + 1100 × ¾ = 725. Thus, your best choice is to buy the advice and invest in stocks.

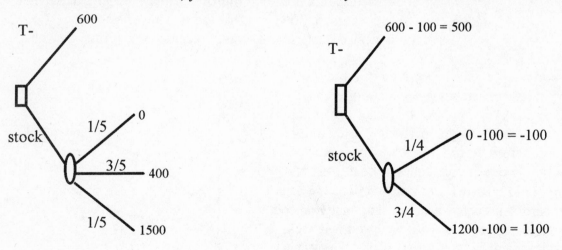

CHAPTER 7. ANSWERS TO EXERCISES

Answers to Questions in the Application

Question 1:   By tying the 55 cents price to also buying a soft drink and fry, McDonald's was defining the product as a (full) meal. Thus, consumers had to make a choice based on the price of all three parts together, not simply that a sandwich costs 55 cents.

Question 2:   McDonald's expected the quantity sold to go up significantly, since total sales were expected to increase by about $50,000 at a typical restaurant. If the price goes down, the only way for total revenue to go up is for the quantity sold to go up as well. This means the firm specific demand curve must have a negative slope.

Question 3:   McDonald's Corporation plays the role of an agent for the principals who are the franchises owners. The owners of the franchises expect McDonald's Corporation to structure programs to make them money - that is, to maximize the profits of the franchise. Additionally, many of the owners of McDonald's franchises may also manage them, and work in them. Although the McDonald's Corporation managers probably own stock in the company, they are principally managers, not owners. Their job is to make money for the stockholders, not for themselves.

Question 4:   McDonald's Corporation managers must have their first allegiance to the stockholders of the corporation, not the franchisees. Thus, if long term profits for the corporation are maximized by making a move that is at the expense of the franchisees, a profit maximizing manager should make that move. McDonald's argued, however, that the move was also in the interest of the franchise owners, and would increase their profits as well.

Question 5: When McDonald's lowered the price of its sandwiches (when bought with a fry and drink) it expected total sales (revenue) at its restaurants to go up $50,000 as quantity increased from Q_1 to Q_2. However, as quantity goes up, so does total economic cost. As shown, profit could go down from π_1 to π_2 which means that marginal revenue was less than marginal cost. We might expect that profit will go down because a profit maximizing manager-owner at a franchise would have tried lower prices for sandwiches earlier if it would increase profit.

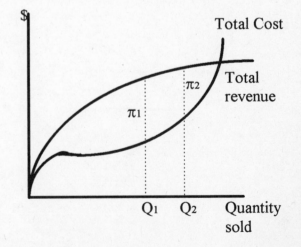

Question 6:   Yes, particularly from the corporation's point of view. Even risk averse managers are pushed into risky projects with high expected value by internal and external controls. The fact that Burger King went through four CEOs showed that within the industry there was precedence for replacing nonperforming management. Since stockholders can diversify away the risk, they should want McDonald's to take a risky path that promised a high expected return.

Question 7:   Clearly, investors believed that McDonald's strategy would hurt the future profits of the entire industry, thus decreasing the present value of expected future dividends.

Answers to Multiple Choice Questions

1. B	6. A	11. D	16. C
2. C	7. A	12. A	17. D
3. A	8. D	13. B	18. A
4. B	9. C	14. B	19. A
5. C	10. B	15. A	20. D

Answers to Problems

1. Helen's imputed cost for her own labor equals the opportunity cost of the next best alternative use of her time. We can infer that the job she left was the best use of her time, otherwise she would have done something else. Thus, the imputed cost of her own labor is $50,000. Her total economic costs include the opportunity cost of her labor, the direct expenses for paper and utilities, and the lost interest on the $10,000 investment, thus $55,500. The $10,000 investment itself is not an economic cost, because the opportunity lost by investing it in the economic consulting firm is the lost interest, which we counted already.

2. If Helen provides 1,000 hours of consulting at $100 per hour, she earns a total revenue of $100,000. Economic profit equals total revenue minus total economic cost, or $100,000-$55,500=$45,500. Accounting profit would likely include the $10,000 investment as a cost but not the lost $500 of interest, so an accounting measure of profit would equal $35,000.

3. The graph to the right helps us see the alternatives. The raise in wages increases total cost, causing it to pivot from TC₁ to TC₂. a) Profit maximizing output would shift from π_1 to π_2. b) If the firm has as its goal zero economic profit, output would fall from n_1 to n_2.

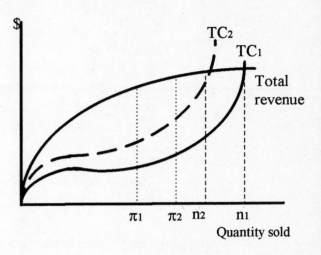

4. At a price of $60 per share and earnings of 60 cents, American was earning about 1 percent return per year. The opportunity cost of having $60 invested in American Airlines was about 7 percent, using to the return on government bonds. Seven percent of $60 is $4.20. Subtracting the 60 cents earned, American Airlines has economic losses of about $3.60 per share.

5. According to the shut down rule, these banks should not have been closed. The shut down rule says to shut down production when the average economic cost curve lies above the demand curve everywhere . Clearly, since economic costs were being covered, the banks were making positive economic profits.

6. Not necessarily. The principal-agent relationship between a firm's owners and managers is often structured so that the agents maximize expected profit. If the bank managers took the risky investments because the expected profit from those investments was high, they were doing what the market for investment said they should.

7. Assuming the hockey season extends about 35 weeks from October to May Weinberg and Finch have total revenue of $79,800. Their total accounting costs were $1200 × 35 plus the $12,000 initial investment or costs of $52,000 leaving an accounting profit of about $27,800. This would be an astounding return of about 232 percent for the year. However, this both over counts and under counts costs. The $12,000 is a sunk cost, and the only opportunity cost related to it is the lost interest earning, about $840 per year at 7 percent. So that would lower the costs by $11,160. But costs were underestimated by the $100,000 opportunity costs of wages they lost by leaving the other jobs. Thus, economic profits were actually *losses* of $61,040.

8. The graphs below tell the story. A profits tax affects both the total revenue and total economic costs curves proportionately (left panel). Thus, marginal revenue and marginal cost shift but since marginal profit is zero, output is unchanged, although owners make lower profits. With a lower Social Security tax, only cost is affected, so

marginal cost falls while marginal revenue is unchanged (right panel). Output increases. The curve pivot because both taxes are percentages of the base.

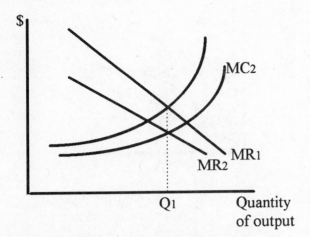

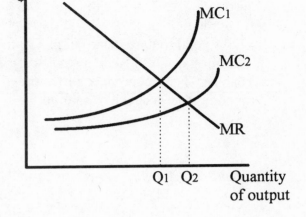

CHAPTER 8. ANSWERS TO EXERCISES

Answers to Questions in the Application

Question 1: The isoquants shift in towards the origin. For the same amount of seeds and other inputs, total output has increased. Thus, to get an output of 100 bushels previously required S_1 units of seed and I_1 units of other inputs. Now the same output requires only S_2 units of seed and I_2 units of other inputs. The isoquant shifts from the solid line to the dotted line.

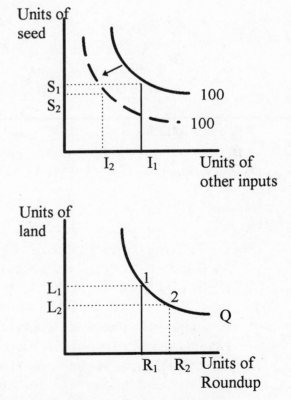

Question 2: The isoquant to the right shows the tradeoff between Roundup and land holding all else constant. After the change by using more Roundup farmers can get the same number of bushels with less land. Thus, they move from point 1 to point 2 on the isoquant, using more Roundup and less land.

Question 3: For the same output, less land was used and more Roundup. The MPP_{land} increased and the $MPP_{Roundup}$ went down. As we can see on the graph above, the MRTS, which is the negative of the slope of the isoquant, got smaller.

207

Question 4:   The graph is the same as the one used for Question 2, but label the horizontal axis units of other inputs instead of Roundup.

Question 5: As shown to the right, the total product of labor curve will shift up from the solid to dotted line (from TP1 to TP2) after genetically altered seed becomes available. The total product curve for farm equipment would also shift up.

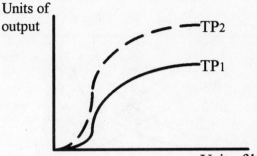

Question 6:   There is no information that should lead us to believe that the change in MPPs and MRTS has changed the returns to scale. We would need information about how the new technology changed output when there is a proportionate increase in all inputs to know the answer to this question.

Question 7:   Mr. Greiner is making a long run decision when he decides to plant more acres in genetically altered seed, because land (and seed in farming) is not immediately changeable. Once he decides how much land to plant, it is fixed for that season. Holding output constant, Mr. Greiner is moving towards other inputs and away from land if he plants more of his acreage with genetically altered seeds. He will need fewer acres of land, because each acre has a higher yield.

Answers to Multiple Choice Questions

1. D	6. B	11. B	16. D
2. C	7. A	12. A	17. B
3. A	8. B	13. D	18. B
4. B	9. D	14. C	19. D
5. C	10. C	15. A	20. B

Answers to Problems

1. When there is 1 worker the machine operates for 8 hours straight, so total product is 80 units and the marginal product of the first worker is also 80. Adding a second worker means that before he can work the machine shuts down for 1 hour to refill with gasoline. That makes only 7 hours available for this worker to use the machine. The oil is scheduled for the third shift, to avoid losing the machine time. Thus, his MPP is 70. The third worker loses 1 hour for gasoline refilling, and one-half an hour for adding the oil, leaving only 6.5 hours of production, or an MPP of 65. Thus, we have the following table of MPP and TP curves:

Worker	TP	MPP
1	80	80
2	150	70
3	215	65

2. When refilling is done automatically and we increase the workers and machines proportionately, output will go up proportionately as well. Thus there is constant returns to scale. But suppose manual refilling is necessary. Then at least one refill worker is needed if one machine is in place. Increasing all inputs, including this refill worker, proportionately will still increase the output proportionately. Thus, there is no change in the returns to scale. (As we shall see in the next chapter, however, there is what is called economies of scale.)

3. Since the machines need an operator and operators without machines can't produce anything, the isoquants are right angles at ratios of 3 workers to 1 machine for an output of 215 per machine. Theoretically, if only 1 worker were hired, only 1/3 of a machine would be used, or 2 workers and 2/3 of a machine. This answer ignores the lumpiness of machines and workers.

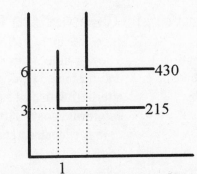

4. This is a multiplicative production function where each unit of output requires that $N \times H = 3$ where N is the number of nurses and H is the number of hours. Thus, the number of procedures, Q, is given by the formula $Q = (N \times H)/3$. There are increasing returns to scale. To see this, suppose $N = 1$ and $H = 3$. Then $Q = 1$. But if $N = 2$ and $H = 6$, $Q = 1\ 2/3 = 4$. It has increased more than proportionately.

5. The four month training requirement sets the lower bound for having more nurses able to do the procedure in the hospital. (The requirement for on-sight training makes it impossible to just hire new nurses ready to do the procedure.) Thus, the short run is four months based on the information we have. The long run is anything longer than that. To increases production of the procedure in the short run, the hospital would have to convince already trained nurses to work longer hours. In the long run, it can do either that, or hire and train new people.

6. Yes, this production function shows diminishing MPPs. As L and K get larger, 2/L and 1/K get respectively smaller. The $MRTS = MPP_L/MPP_K = (2/L)/(1/K) = 2K/L$. Substituting when $K = 10$ and $L = 30$, we have the $MRTS = 2/3$. When $K = 45$ and $L = 60$ the $MRTS = 1.5$. There is diminishing MRTS as well. We know this because diminishing marginal products implies diminishing MRTS.

7. Suppose we double the amount of inputs. If there are constant returns to scale, output will double as well. If we let $K^* = 2K'$ and $L^* = 2L'$ where K' and L' are the original levels of inputs used so $Q' = aK' + bL'$, then $Q^* = aK^* + bL^* = a2K' + b2L' = 2(aK' + bL') = 2Q'$. Doubling the level of inputs doubled output. Similarly, $Q' = K'^a L'^b$ so $Q^* = K^{*a}L^{*b} = (2K')^a(2L')^b = 2^{a+b} K'^a L'^b = 2^{a+b}Q'$. If $a + b = 1$ then $2^{a+b} = 2$, and there are constant returns to scale. Similarly, if $a + b < 1$ then $2^{a+b} < 2$ and there are decreasing returns to scale, and if $a + b > 1$ then $2^{a+b} > 2$ and there are increasing returns to scale.

8. We can substitute 800 pounds of grain for 150 pounds of young cattle weight, so the MRTS is approximately $800/150 = 5.33$.

CHAPTER 9. ANSWERS TO EXERCISES

Answers to Questions in the Application

Question 1:   The variable input would be the amount of Roundup used, and the labor and fuel used to apply the Roundup. However, if the farmer has no other alternative use of his time, including no leisure activities, his time carries no economic cost. However, if he can sell it in the marketplace, or use the time for leisure activities he values, the time has an economic (opportunity) cost.

Question 2:   Now, since spraying will definitely take place, the only variable input is the Roundup used. And in fact, since not spraying is not an option, Roundup is variable only to the extent of using the extra 2 gallons per acre. The farmer should ignore the fact that genetically altered seed was planted since it has no opportunity cost anymore. We call it a sunk cost.

Question 3:   By spraying one acre more intensively, output can be increased by 7 bushels. The cost of the extra spray is $10, so the short run marginal cost is approximately the change in cost divided by the change in output, or $10/7 or just under about $1.43 per bushel.

Question 4:   Mr. Greneir's minimum output (ignoring the not spraying at all option) is to do less intensive spraying of all 200 acres, getting a yield of 45 bushels per acre at a cost of $15 per acre. After than he can pick 20 acre parcels and spray more intensively, at an additional cost of $10 per acre, and getting an additional yield of 140 bushels. The following table lays out the possibilities from not spraying or spraying.

Acres With Extra Spray	SR Variable Cost	Total Output	SR Marginal Cost
0	$3000	9000	-
20	$3200	9140	$1.43
40	$3400	9280	$1.43
60	$3600	9420	$1.43
80	$3800	9560	$1.43
100	$4000	9700	$1.43
120	$4200	9840	$1.43
140	$4400	9980	$1.43
160	$4600	10120	$1.43
180	$4800	10260	$1.43
200	$5000	10400	$1.43

Notice that when no acres get the extra spray, short run average variable cost = $3000/9000 or about 33 cents per bushel. Short run marginal cost is above this amount, so short run average variable cost must be increasing. If all 200 acres are sprayed intensively short run average variable cost = $5000/10400 = 48 cents, approximately. So we see that the short run average variable cost is everywhere increasing.

Question 5: This is similar to question 4, except now there is an extra cost of $25 per acre to use the altered seed.

Acres With Altered Seed	SR Variable Cost	Total Output	SR Marginal Cost
0	$3000	9000	-
20	$3500	9140	$3.57
40	$4000	9280	$3.57
60	$4500	9420	$3.57
80	$5000	9560	$3.57
100	$5500	9700	$3.57
120	$6000	9840	$3.57
140	$6500	9980	$3.57
160	$7000	10120	$3.57
180	$7500	10260	$3.57
200	$8000	10400	$3.57

Notice how the variable cost and marginal cost are lower once the seed cost becomes sunk.

Question 6: We need to understand the production function a little more. Each time we use a unit of "innovative technology" we get 7 units more of output per acre. Since each acre without the innovative technology produces 45 units of output, we need 45/7=6.43 units of innovative technology to offset one acre of land. Thus, every 10 units of technology offsets about 1.56 acres of land. We can get the desired bushels of soybeans by the following combinations. (NOTE: To calculate each cell, multiply the number of units of technology times 7, subtract it from the quantity, and divide the remainder by 45. That plus the number of units of technology tells the total number of acres of land needed.)

Isoquants for various output levels

2000 bushels		5000 bushels		9000 bushels	
land (acres)	technology	land (acres)	technology	land (acres)	technology
44.44	0	111.11	0	200	0
42.88	10	109.55	10	198.44	10
41.33	20	108.00	20	196.88	20
31.28	30	106.44	30	195.32	30
38.46	38.46	104.88	40	125.20	40
-	-	103.32	50	123.65	50
-	-	…	…	…	…
-	-	96.15	96.15	173.07	173.07

The MRTS is constant. Each 10 units of technology can replace 1.56 acres of land no matter what the desired output is.

Question 7: Ten units of technology costs $250. Each acre of land costs $200 so cost of technology/cost of land = 25/200 = ¼. Another way to look at it is that 10 units of technology (costing $250 replaces 1.56 acres of land (costing $312). The optimal combination of land and technology is to use the maximum technology possible. The graph below show the isoquants as dotted lines and the isocost lines as solid line. The expansion path is shown by the ray.

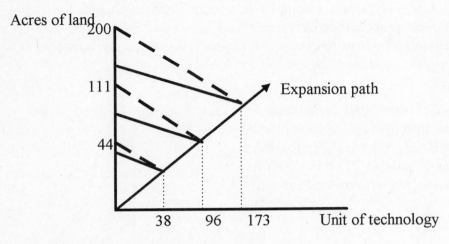

Acres of land

200

111

44

38   96   173   Unit of technology

Expansion path

Question 8:   This is an example of economies of scope.

Answers to Multiple Choice Questions

1. A	6. B	11. C	16. B
2. D	7. D	12. B	17. D
3. B	8. A	13. C	18. B
4. A	9. D	14. C	19. B
5. A	10. A	15. A	20. C

Answers to Problems

1. We know that short run marginal cost equals the marginal factor cost divided by the marginal physical product of labor. Thus, the marginal cost of the first 80 units is about $80/80 or $1, for the next 70 units is $80/70 or $1.14, and for the next 65 units it is about $80/65 or $1.23. Average cost is total cost divided by total product. With one worker, average cost is thus $1. With two workers, average cost is $160/150 or $1.06, and with three workers average cost is $240/215 or $1.16.

2. For the sake of argument, suppose the refiller also makes $10 per hour, and works 8 hour days. (we don't need this assumption, but it makes things clearer.) Without the refiller, there are constant returns to scale, so doubling inputs doubles output, and thus long run average cost is constant. But with the refiller able to be scheduled to handle more than one machine per day, we can double machines, double machine workers, but keep only 1 refiller. Thus, we can lower the average cost (output doubled, but costs didn't since there is only 1 refiller's salary). The refiller in this case plays a similar role to large set up costs for production: we have economies of scale.

3. The comparable worth plan increased the wages of female dominated jobs relative to the wages of male dominated jobs. Denote female dominated jobs as F and male dominated jobs as M. The input combination that minimizes cost requires that $MPP_F/MPP_M=W_F/W_M$ where the W's represent the wage rates for each group. If W_F/W_M increased, then MPP_F/MPP_M needs to increase as well if cost is to be

minimized. Generally, this is accomplished by substituting male jobs for female jobs because of diminishing marginal returns. Since the average wage rate went up overall, a similar argument leads us to expect that production of state government in Washington state used more capital and less labor after comparable worth was implemented.

4. The graph shows that after comparable worth, the expansion path should have pivoted towards male dominated jobs, shifting from the solid ray to the dotted ray. Both the short run and long run average cost curves shifted up.

"female" jobs

"male" jobs

5. The graph to the right shows the isoquants. If there is increasing returns to scale, $Q_2 > 2Q_1$ but since inputs have doubled, $C_1 = C_2$. This is true for increasing or decreasing returns to scale. However, average cost, C_2/Q_2 is smaller than C_1/Q_1 if there is increasing returns to scale and larger if there are decreasing returns to scale.

6. Using calculus, the Lagrangian function is given by
$$L = 15L + 5K + \mu(100 - 5L^{3/4}K^{1/4})$$
The first order necessary conditions are given by
$$\partial L/\partial L = 15 - \mu 15/4 L^{-1/4}K^{1/4} = 0$$
$$\partial L/\partial K = 5 - \mu 5/4 L^{3/4}K^{-3/4} = 0$$
$$\partial L/\partial \mu = 100 - 5L^{3/4}K^{1/4} = 0$$

Solving the first two equations together gives $L = K$. Using this equality in the third equation tells us that $100 = 5L$ or $L = 20 = K$. To increase output to 200 in the short run, L must be higher since K is fixed at 20. The production function becomes $200 = 5L^{3/4}20^{1/4} = 5L^{3/4}2.114 = 10.573L^{3/4}$ so $L^{3/4} = 18.92$ and $L = 50.42$ approximately. L has gone up 30.42 so total cost increased by $15 \times 30.42 = 456.3$ dollars. So the marginal cost for 100 new units out output is 456.3 dollars, or about \$4.56 per unit. In the long run, we would still have $K = L$ and $200 = 5L$ so $L = 40 = K$. In this case, total cost has gone up to $15 \times 40 + 5 \times 40 = 20 \times 40 = 800$. Previous cost (for 100 units) was $20 \times 20 = 400$, so long run marginal cost for 100 units is about 400 or \$4 per unit.

7. Isoquants are right angles, and so the long run expansion path goes has a slope of ½ as shown. In the short run, if capital is fixed at 100, adding more labor will not increase output, so there is no way to get more output, thus no short run expansion path. Since there is no substitution between inputs, the input prices don't matter for optimal input combination.

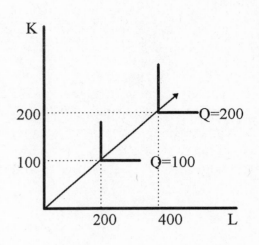

CHAPTER 10. ANSWERS TO EXERCISES

Answers to Questions in the Application

Question 1: Profit maximization dictates economizing on inputs. If the firm can pay inputs less, it earns more (a share of labor's marginal revenue product, plus the profits from output). A player's salary would have been just enough to bid them away from their next best opportunity outside of baseball.

Question 2: The graph should show a shortage at the price prior to free agency. Then, owners bid up the price of players.

Question 3: Now, instead of their next best choice outside of baseball, players will earn just enough more than their next best baseball alternative to keep them with their current team.

Question 4: Firms would try to reduce output in the short-run. But if output is fixed, such as with sports schedules, the only thing that can happen is for firms to suffer reduced profits. It is entirely possible that, in the short-run, team owners lost money just after free agency occurred.

Question 5: In the long-run, changes in demand make it tough to sort out the responses by individual team owners. Without any change in demand, teams would have been forced to leave the industry. But, in the early 1980s just after free agency occurred, there was a tremendous boom in fan interest in professional baseball.

Question 6: Draw a supply and demand diagram that starts with a price below the competitive equilibrium. Then, move the wage toward the intersection of supply and demand. The surplus analysis should show a loss of surplus to team owners (labor buyers) and a gain in surplus to sellers of labor.

Question 7: Marginal revenue product equals marginal physical product multiplied by output price; if output price is rising, willingness to pay for players increases. If the market is competitive, then salaries will rise. Ticket prices rise first, raising marginal revenue product, and then payment to players rises due to competition.

Answers to Multiple Choice Questions

1.	C.	6.	D.	11.	B.	16.	D.
2.	D.	7.	B.	12.	A.	17.	A.
3.	D.	8.	A.	13.	A.	18.	D.
4.	B.	9.	D.	14.	A.	19.	C.
5.	D.	10.	D.	15.	B.	20.	C.

Answers to Problems

1. To an outside observer, a change in price happens simultaneously for all sellers under pure competition. Without explicit evidence of collusion (witnesses, recorded phone conversations), one cannot distinguish between responding to the market and setting the market price.

2. In the short-run graph, firms suffer losses in the short-run. In the long-run, exit happens, and price rises back up again. Thus, the distinguishing idea is that a low price results in fewer firms participating in the market in the long-run, but in the new short-run situation, some firms remain even though they lose money for a while.

3. Every point along the long-run supply pertains to some short-run supply curve. Indeed, the way one derives the long-run supply is to map out all of the short-run supply shifts that occurred as firms adjusted to profit or loss situations and summing them.

4. Under the competitive theory, inputs are paid according to the marginal revenue product of the last unit hired. Thus, one would have to look at how extremely well-paid individuals contribute to the value of their firms. For example, millions may ride on a single decision made by top-level execs; their marginal revenue product is high. The only way these individuals can be over-paid, under the competitive theory, is if their wage exceeds their marginal revenue product. One would expect this to be a short-run problem. Of course, if the market for these top-level executives is not competitive, then a non-competitive theory may generate more precise, and different, insights.

5. In the short-run, firms decrease output and hiring. In the long-run, the firm will find ways to substitute away from the input if it can. Thus, the short-run picture is a movement along the demand function, while the long-run picture will shift the

demand for labor as changes in the use of other inputs alters labor's marginal physical product.

6. The graph shows the following. In the short-run, input use declines since the output effect is negative (movement along the demand curve). In the long-run, substitution among inputs shifts demand, left or right, depending on production relationships. Further, in the long-run, the firm must choose its scale; output may increase or decrease.

CHAPTER 11. ANSWERS TO EXERCISES

Answers to Questions in the Application

Question 1: Draw a downward sloping demand curve. The graph should show a shortage at a price equals zero. The quantity supplied is all from charity (horizontal, along the x-axis, but short of the quantity demanded at price equals zero).

Question 2: Shortage equals quantity demanded minus charity giving quantity supplied, at price equals zero. Consumers' surpluses are the area under the demand, out to the quantity charitably supplied. No producers' surpluses exist since price equals zero!

Question 3: If selling, per se, is repugnant to demanders, the demand function will shift to the left. On the other hand, if "legalization" lends legitimacy to the market, then demand may actually shift to the right.

Question 4: The new supply function should slope upward out of the *new* charitable level of kidneys; some giving at price equals zero may still occur, but probably less since there now is a positive return to selling a kidney. The equilibrium is at the intersection of the new supply and demand curves. The shortage is eliminated by definition.

Question 5: Fewer kidneys under a competitive equilibrium can occur if there is a large enough decrease in charitable giving and the supply function is steep enough. If enough people who would have given their kidneys for free change their mind, this could happen.

Question 6: Surpluses follow the usual idea. But now, there *are* consumers' surpluses. Sellers with the highest opportunity cost will drive the price at the margin. Sellers with the lowest opportunity costs will earn the larger surplus. This low-cost type of provider would have no qualms about supplying a kidney and probably would be a low-income individual (be careful about how you describe charitable givers).

Question 7: Efficiency certainly favors such a market. But "should we" questions always depend on definitions of fairness. Thus, the more important parts of this answer depend on your definition of fairness, containing many personal considerations which all should be included in your answer.

Answers to Multiple Choice Questions

1.	D.	6.	A.	11.	B.	16.	C.
2.	A.	7.	C.	12.	D.	17.	B.
3.	D.	8.	D.	13.	A.	18.	B.
4.	D.	9.	C.	14.	C.	19.	A.
5.	C.	10.	A.	15.	B.	20.	C.

Answers to Problems

1. No, this does not mean that opportunity costs are falling. What it means is that the entire cost structure of all firms in the industry fall as the industry grows.

2. Rent control and economic rent are related. The idea of rent is payment over and above what it takes to keep the resources employed in a given endeavor. If the possible rent is reduced, then the economic rent earned also falls. But if there is a higher alternative rent that can be earned, apartment buildings will be demolished in favor of the new higher-valued uses for the land on which the building sat.

3. Interfering with the market will reduce the amount of necessities supplied and may just encourage a black market. Now, since the risk of getting caught must enter into the price, prices actually rise! Whether or not you think gouging should go on depends on who you think should receive the necessities and whether or not government can bring some other aid to the process.

4. The analysis here is the same as in the market for kidneys. The price of housing will rise but, in this case, so will the quantity (unless housing was originally offered on a charitable basis that dries up when competition takes over). Efficiency will reign; total surpluses will be maximized. Fairness is in the eye of the beholder.

5. Liability ceilings reduce the amount that lawyers can earn in such cases and the quantity of lawyers' time supplied will be reduced. Since lawyers will seek the next highest valued uses of their time, they will begin to compete with other types of legal cases, such as divorce. The supply of those services shifts to the right and prices fall.

6. Windfall profit taxes will not change the allocation of resources because the windfall profits earned were pure economic rent. If the resources were being put to their highest valued use before the profit increase, they remain in their highest valued use

after the tax. Fairness is in the eye of the beholder. If the producer should not get these rents, then who should and why?

CHAPTER 12. ANSWERS TO EXERCISES

Answers to Questions in the Application

Question 1: At price equals marginal cost, the only way a firm can respond to CAFE is to *reduce* the number of large cars and increase the number of small cars. But this created a surplus of smaller cars and a shortage larger cars, relative to demand.

Question 2: Neither consumption efficiency nor production efficiency are satisfied. At price equals marginal cost, but under the incentives of CAFE, there is a surplus of small cars and a shortage of large cars results.

Question 3: The only way to remove the surplus is to alter prices; smaller car prices must be *lowered* and larger car prices *increased*. Only in this way can the consumers' budget constraints be flattened so that the surplus of small cars and shortage of larger cars is eliminated.

Question 4: Now, consumption and production efficiency would be restored since price equals marginal cost but, remember, the marginal cost firms face has been imposed upon them by CAFE requirements and do not necessarily reflect true marginal production costs.

Question 5: Allocation efficiency cannot be satisfied; total surpluses would be higher if CAFE were removed and the economy could move to a higher point on its production possibilities.

Question 6: Political outcomes are driven by political incentives; apparently, lawmakers found CAFE to be most politically profitable in terms of reelection. Another way would simply be to tax cars for fuel efficiency violation, shift the supply function to the left, and obtain the efficient level of mileage by making the market reflect true social marginal costs.

Answers to Multiple Choice Questions

1.	D.	6.	B.	11.	C.	16.	B.
2.	D.	7.	C.	12.	D.	17.	B.
3.	B.	8.	D.	13.	A.	18.	C.
4.	D.	9.	C.	14.	D.	19.	A.
5.	B.	10.	B.	15.	B.	20.	B.

Answers to Problems

1. Clearly not. A quantity restriction is imposed that leads to nearly the same problems described in the CAFE example. Marginal rates of substitution cannot equal the marginal rate of transformation. The combination of French versus other music may not be on the production possibilities curve.

2. While the chance for one farmer to lose their crop rises, the total output of the economy will be larger with this cooperative act than without it. Thus, a careful comparison of the likely outcomes shows that this cooperative act puts society on a higher expected production possibilities curve.

3. With a negative externality of this sort (individual firewood consumers are not responsible for the costs of the reduced forest), there is a missing market. Since the existence of a complete set of markets is one of the requirements for the First Fundamental Theorem, the situation cannot be Pareto optimal.

4. Crop insurance: As long as its priced correctly, it fixes a missing market problem and represents an improvement. First-time buyer subsidies: This is primarily a poverty problem, but poverty can be Pareto optimal. Environmental restrictions: It depends on how the policy formulates restrictions to fix a missing market problem. While standards probably won't be a Pareto improvement, incentive approaches can be.

5. The use of currently illegal drugs often is characterized as a "victimless" crime. Legalization would be a Pareto improvement if some are better off without anybody else being hurt. Economics can take you no farther than this. Fairness is in the eye of the beholder.

6. No individual opinion can be right or wrong on this issue. But social welfare theory takes as given that society confronts satisfaction trade-offs among its members even while it recognizes that these choices are difficult. With such a starting place, economists can make very careful statements about how such trade-offs will effect individual happiness. However, economists have no special status concerning just how the social welfare function looks, or should look.

CHAPTER 13. ANSWERS TO EXERCISES.

Answers to Questions in the Application

Question 1: High fixed costs are an entry barrier: airlines must be of a large scale in order to cover high fixed costs. Artificially scarce airport space, due to limited government spending, also makes for specialized inputs that are used by current airlines to exclude others. Eventually, at their hub cities, a given airline can become the only game in town, or one of a very few producers.

Question 2: The shut-down rule applies to price-makers, too. If an airline can't cover the variable costs of a given flight, then it will cancel it. Often, excuses to customers have something to do with vague reference to mechanical difficulties, but the logic follows the shut-down rule.

Question 3: Airlines practice third-degree price discrimination, since they charge different prices to different groups of fliers (week-end versus week day, for example).

Question 4: Just cast this example as serving two types of demanders. Then, follow the dictates of profit-maximization and equate MR1=MR2 and insert the definitions. After a little arithmetic, you'll see that the lower price goes to consumers in the market with the highest elasticity of demand.

Question 5: The expected costs to the airline of reserving seats for "same day" travelers are larger since not all will show up. As a result, airlines run the risk of having some empty seats just before take-off and the average cost rises. These will be expensive seats if there are no stand-by customers. Spreading these costs over expected users results in a higher price. In this case, the higher price to "same day" fliers is not price discrimination.

Question 6: If you really need "same day" service, then your elasticity of demand is very low; you do not have many substitutes because you waited so long to get your ticket.

Question 7: Successful price discrimination requires that implementation be worth it. One problem to overcome is resale; as a producer, if you sell to a low-price buyer they could simply go into competition with you by reselling to higher-price buyers. Restrictions stop frequent-fliers from competing with the airline by selling their frequent-flier miles.

Answers to Multiple Choice Questions

1.	C.	6.	C.	11.	C.	16.	C.
2.	C.	7.	A.	12.	D.	17.	C.
3.	C.	8.	D.	13.	C.	18.	B.
4.	A.	9.	B.	14.	A.	19.	C.
5.	D.	10.	A.	15.	B.	20.	B.

Answers to Problems

1. You'd pay up to and including the discounted present value of future profits. In turn, you'd sell it for a different amount, but based upon the same idea– the discounted present value of future profits. No monopoly profits are earned after the firm changes hands since the profits all were extracted in the first sale. After that,

the owner must charge the monopoly price in order to maintain zero economic profits.

2.   The price of soda rises since the bidder will bid under the assumption that they will become the short-term monopolist. The variety falls: any given seller only sells their own brands. Letting competition determine the result has its good side since price should fall and variety increase. But the university will forgo the monopoly profits that it can extract from the pop bidders.

3.   One would expect the power in this market to swing away from monopoly teams and leagues in the direction of local government and fans (buyers). Instead of being constantly asked to subsidize a given team, many teams would be bidding for a stadium in a given city. The price of games would fall and the number of games (with the increased number of teams and competition) would rise. The impact on the quality of games isn't clear. Wal-Mart leagues (low quality, low price) might arise but other competitive sports providers, like colleges, generate a variety of quality. Whether or not it would be desirable depends on who you are. Teams and leagues will be against it. State and local governments and fans should, for the most part, be for it.

4.   In order to sell beer, the establishment must have a government-issued tavern license. The result is a restricted number of firms and less competition. Prices rise and the quantity of beer available is lower relative to a more competitive result. The impacts of instilling competition would be to lower price and increase quantity. But externalities arise associated with this increase in alcohol consumption.

5.   The conventional wisdom applied to a fairly competitive situation in large population areas. Sam Walton, founder of Wal-Mart, realized that the conventional wisdom could be beat if Wal-Mart was the only game in town. He took low-price items to rural areas, became the only game in town, and earned the monopoly return. By quickly plowing profits back into expansion, Wal-Mart grew to its current empire status.

6.   The university should extract the monopoly profits from its student union building renters. Given their high rent, businesses in the student union building must be able to charge the higher monopoly price. Any competition that forces it to lower its price, even a little, results in losses for the renter.

CHAPTER 14. ANSWERS TO EXERCISES

Answers to Questions in the Application

Question 1:   Minimum wage markets may not be very competitive if there are not many buyers. Youth and young adult labor markets are one example. These type of workers typically work in some sort of fast service firm. Just review the market setting that is most likely to generate price-making buyers and you'll see that many of the criteria characterize minimum wage markets, especially for young adults. The graph should be the standard one from the text (see Figures 14.18 and 14.19).

Question 2: The marginal factor cost function is horizontal at the minimum wage out to the supply function; the extra costs of hiring at a wage floor is the floor on all units hired under the floor. Then, the extra costs of hiring jumps up and follows the usual marginal factor cost. Marginal factor cost equals demand at the point of discontinuity. For a minimum wage in the range described, both employment and the wage rise. Thus, in this range, if the market is not competitive, employment does not decrease. Under this analysis, the classical theory is not wrong, it's irrelevant. One should not use a model based on competition to analyze a non-competitive situation.

Question 3: The approach is similar. Marginal factor cost is horizontal out to the supply function, then jumps up and follows the usual marginal factor cost. Marginal factor cost intersects the demand function at the point of discontinuity.

Question 4: For minimum wages in this range, again, both employment and wage rise. But now there is a surplus of labor, drawn from other employment. At the going rate quantity supplied exceeds quantity demanded. This excess supply is unemployed in the true sense of looking for work and not finding it.

Question 5: Follow the same steps and you'll see that the "classical" sort of result occurs. The wage rises, employment falls, and workers are drawn from other employment who never will find a job in this market.

Question 6: The policy advice is clear. If you are going to set a minimum wage, don't set it too high.

Answers to Multiple Choice Questions

1.	D.	6.	B.	11.	D.	16.	B.
2.	D.	7.	A.	12.	C.	17.	A.
3.	D.	8.	B.	13.	B.	18.	B.
4.	C.	9.	B.	14.	B.	19.	D.
5.	D.	10.	B.	15.	A.	20.	C.

Answers to Problems

1. All that has to happen is for students to realize that they will get a better grade than all their fellow conspirators without much additional strain by answering just a few more questions. Even if a few of them don't cheat the first time, they will see the variation in scores early on and be forced to adopt the cheating approach.

2. Accreditation is just an entry barrier, operating under the disguise of quality control. As a result, accreditation should raise the value of degrees by reducing competition from other, non-accredited schools. Review must occur, periodically, in order to make sure that schools maintain the barriers to entry. This is equivalent to investigating schools for cheating on the maintenance of the barrier.

3. Just follow the description in your text of the criteria that most likely will generate a monopolistic competitive result. The beer industry matches all of them.

4. Product differentiation is essential to *maintaining* share, but not to getting *additional* market share, since other firms simply respond and expenditures on differentiation offset. Business people really mean one of two things. Either they mistake innovation for differentiation, or they mean that they are trying to hold on (for dear life) to their current zero profit market share so they don't lose money.

5. The theory in this chapter gives little insight into this question. Nothing about monopolistic competition theory suggests the "correct" number of firms. The only generality that holds is that there is an optimal amount of variety, and as a society we must consider both the costs and benefits of variety.

6. Employers state that salary discussion just creates disharmony; some employees are disheartened to know that they are less valued than their co-workers. Another explanation is that employers are trying not to raise the salary of infra-marginal workers when the marginal worker is hired. This is a wage discrimination idea. If employers can pay just the marginal worker the increased wage, and not raise the wage to all workers, then the marginal factor cost function becomes the supply function and the employer keeps all of the surpluses generated in this market. If all workers knew each others' wages, it would be much more difficult for employers to extract surplus from workers.

CHAPTER 15. ANSWERS TO EXERCISES

Answers to Questions in the Application

Question 1: The requirements are in the text. Think these through and you will see that the Burger King-McDonald's battle fits the duopoly requirements.

Question 2: The text suggests that the limiting factor, price or quantity, dictates which model is likely to carry more explanatory power. In this case, with quantity so easy to vary, the limiting factor seems to be price. This suggests a Bertrand-Nash model.

Question 3: There are two barriers to self-enforcing agreement. First, it's easy to differentiate products. Second, it's unlikely that companies' cost functions are the same. In this case, very small changes can be very rewarding. But once firms start down the slippery slope, small levels of cheating on self-enforcing agreements can accumulate and end up in a price war.

Question 4: Somehow, these factors would have to be ameliorated. If differentiation were reduced and/or if costs became more equal, tacit agreement would be more likely. Perhaps, with Burger King's move into the "sandwich plus feature film memento" mode, the gap is closing.

Question 5: If Burger King costs are higher than McDonald's, pushing price to marginal cost would cost them more than the punishment strategy is worth. Further, as suggested in the next question, a low-price action might never have worked in the first place since the price of burgers already is so low.

Question 6: Remember that both the Nash and credibility conditions must hold. McDonald's price reduction move is not credible. It didn't help that consumers didn't respond, or were confused by the cost of extras like fries and drinks. In this situation, Burger King will not respond.

Answers to Multiple Choice Questions

1.	C.	6.	B.	11.	C.	16.	B.
2.	A.	7.	D.	12.	B.	17.	C.
3.	C.	8.	C.	13.	A.	18.	D.
4.	D.	9.	C.	14.	A.	19.	A.
5.	B.	10.	C.	15.	A.	20.	C.

Answers to Problems

1. Bidders cannot reach a tacit agreement if they don't know each other's bids. Voters and taxpayers should get "honest," low bids if they remain secret.

2. It's worth trying to collude in the coffee market. But once the cartel output level is set, each producer finds it worth cheating. It has been estimated that, with a price elasticity around 0.5, a 20% reduction in output would generate 40% price increases. The prize for cheating is nearly a 40% increase in the price of each unit sold. Markets just respond first to the price-setting information and, then, to the discovery that the cartel cannot hold its members in line.

3. Such collusion is very likely given the arguments in this chapter. Since the costs of getting caught are small relative to the penalty, enforcement by other members of the oligopsony is highly likely, and punishment by the input cartel expensive. Since already it is legal for them to meet and discuss the economic situation of the game, very overt evidence of collusion would be required.

4. Cartelization of the trucking market ran afoul of the basics: share of the market by many firms was small, monitoring was expensive, and products– for example, routes– were quite different.

5. American Airlines actually was trying to *raise* price. Its average price with discounts was lower than the everyday "low" price when discounts were removed. The industry's response was to punish American by driving price to marginal cost in order to gain larger market share at American's expense.

6. Once you have reviewed all of the elements for a successful cartel, detailed in the text, many examples should occur to you. Here are a few you might choose between: the NCAA, the American Medical Association, the American Hospital Association, government-sponsored marketing boards (hops in the west and oranges in the southeast and west), real estate developers and real estate agents in smaller towns.

CHAPTER 16. ANSWERS TO EXERCISES

Answers to Question in the Application

Question 1: This is just like Figure 16.5 in the text, with Wal-Mart and Other Firms as the actors and enter or stay out as each firm's actions. Essentially, the Nash response is "enter if the other firm does not, and not if the other firm does enter."

Question 2: This is a non-cooperative game of complete information, with multiple Nash equilibria, but no perfect equilibrium.

Question 3: This suggests a preemptive strategy: get there first or don't go at all. Further, this strategy can be profitable in smaller population areas since, once in, you are the only game in town.

Question 4: One would expect that nearly all of his wealth was tied up in his stores, given this strategy. In order to win, Walton would have to constantly plow-back profits in order to be first in all geographic areas that are amenable to entry.

Question 5: Their chances are negligible, at best. Their only hope is some sort of sub-market, either by product niche, some curious geographic anomaly which allows for entry, or growth in an area that previously could support one but now supports two stores.

Question 6: This suggests that price-making will occur in output in the long-run. Be first or be gone and the result is one store in a given area, a sure prescription for market power.

Answers to Multiple Choice Questions

1.	C.	6.	D.	11.	D.	16.	B.
2.	D.	7.	A.	12.	D.	17.	C.
3.	B.	8.	C.	13.	D.	18.	D.
4.	D.	9.	D.	14.	B.	19.	A.
5.	A.	10.	D.	15.	C.	20.	A.

Answers to Problems

1. Leaving an important strategic site under-protected guarantees that you will fulfill on a commitment to send a large force. If your threat is credible, you don't have to post the large force in order to protect the consulate!

2. Use the "prisoners' dilemma" pay-off structure in the book (Figure 16.7), and choose the pay-offs according to a tit-for-tat assumption about the other player. For example, choose a series of actions where first you cheat and then don't. After you write down how the flow of pay-offs will follow, you will find that a non-cheating result can have higher pay-offs in a repeated game.

3. Yes. For example, the thinner person you wish you were can throw all the food in the garbage, or wire your jaw shut. But the real problem here is credibility; the heavier you can always undo any action taken by the thinner person you wish you were. The current heavier you can always go buy more food, or go to the dentist and end the wired-jaw approach. It's tough to lose weight, isn't it.

4. A credible commitment would be the destruction of stored coffee stocks, or existing coffee production capacity. It would have to be monitored, though, wouldn't it?

5. At the end of this game, if no agreement is reached, the popsicle will just be a melted puddle. One step before this total melt-down, Child A (who is offering the deal) knows there is nothing left if Child B says no. So, A can essentially offer B nothing and get that tiny morsel just before total melt-down. Moving back one more step, there is twice as much popsicle left on the stick. In order for A to say yes, half must be offered by B and it is the best that B can hope to get. From here on, the game is pretty well-determined. Child B knows they will always be stuck offering Child A half of the popsicle. Work your way back a few more steps for Child A and you'll see that the closer Child A gets to the beginning of the game, the closer the offer gets to 50-50.

6. Pulling the grim-trigger means dropping price toward marginal cost once another player drops price. That the firm should pull the grim-trigger only on competing routes happens for two reasons. First, pulling the grim-trigger in any other market would not be a credible response since the firm would lose more profits without any

pay-off in terms of disciplining the other firm and, second, the other firm may pull the grim-trigger, itself, on the other routes!

CHAPTER 17. ANSWERS TO EXERCISES

Answers to Questions in the Application

Question 1: This asymmetric information problem is driven by hidden characteristics. Nobody knows how much money is in the bag except the seller, and students have only limited ability to ascertain the amount (weight, visual inspection of the exterior of the bag).

Question 2: Any given sample from the population will not be able to solve the hidden characteristics problem. While some very good guessers appear out of the over-all population, the chances that they will be in any given class of students is small.

Question 3: If this were an oral auction, all bidders could observe who bid and how much. The amount of information now includes the distribution of expected value in the bidding population, as well as the bids of what may be acknowledged as more-informed bidders. With all of this added information, the tide may well turn toward bidders and away from those selling items at auction.

Question 4: Once again, this is a hidden characteristic problem. Rumors fly but only the seller really might know the status of this particular baseball card.

Question 5: A winner's curse seems less likely. This will not be a sealed auction and the type of individuals drawn to the auction of this special type of product will all be very knowledgeable about the card, and about each other.

Question 6: There will be two impacts. First, it is highly likely that the largest collector in the world will be more likely to know the status of the card at auction. This person's bid is much more likely to reveal the card's true worth. The effect of selling his own two cards should reduce the price of the card at auction if there is any substitutability between them. But a new information problem now becomes one of hidden action. This particular seller may be claiming that he will sell his two cards in order to drive the price down so that someone else can buy it for him.

Answers to Multiple Choice Questions

1.	A.	6.	D.	11.	C.	16.	D.
2.	D.	7.	A.	12.	B.	17.	B.
3.	D.	8.	A.	13.	D.	18.	D.

4.	D.	9.	D.	14.	A.	19.	C.
5.	D.	10.	C.	15.	C.	20.	B.

Answers to Problems

1. If the university can determine individual willingness to pay by offering discounts below the "full tuition" rate, then it can practice close to first-degree price discrimination. But the university needs an information signal in order to tell demanders apart. Fortunately, since buyers are the less-informed party, they happily provide the signal to the university on their financial aid forms.

2. Even new cars can have hidden characteristics. Resale value reduces the risk from information asymmetry that might exist, even in new cars. High resale value also reduces other types of more expensive "guarantees" that the dealer may have to offer.

3. Blood tests are a very cost-effective screening device so they should help reduce adverse selection problems. Efficiency is not enhanced by screening devices. All they do is redistribute income.

4. Yes. When an action makes some types of action cheaper than it used to be, then moral hazard can lead to more of that behavior. If the consequence of firm or individual behavior was brought to bear back on them, then actions that increase the amount and nastiness of hazardous waste should be reduced. It's a type of co-insurance.

5. Professors are paid *after* they perform and on the basis of the quantity and quality of their output (typically, teaching, research, and service to the state and nation). In addition, a very rigorous signaling process (getting their education and passing review by their professors during that process, plus continuous review by their peers during the tenure process, both professionally and by administrators) governs their success. Finally, reputation provides another market test.

6. Customers like salaries sales persons because there is no incentive for the sales person to reduce the time spent with them. Employers want total sales maximized while the employee would rather do less. The market works this out mostly in the direction of commission sales with close monitoring of how sales persons treat customers.

CHAPTER 18. ANSWERS TO EXERCISES

Answers to Questions in the Application

Question 1: This graph simply shows the negative externality result; PMC and SMC and damages, along with the demand curve.

Question 2:   Use the previous graph to identify the over-production relative to SMC. Be sure to show the level of losses associated with this over-production. The fundamental factor here is government policy that leads to under-priced forests.

Question 3:   Now, the graph shows a positive externality problem. Many get benefits without paying so PMB and SMB diverge. Be sure to identify the losses that occur due to under-production. The fundamental problem here is enforcing B&J's rights to collect, that is, non-excludability.

Question 4:   The subsidy must be equal to the total costs (area under the supply curve) of moving from the private to the socially optimal level of output. The result would be an increase in ice cream sales and more good done by B&J's crusade.

Question 5:   Yes. In fact, if you gave a subsidy to buyers just enough to cover the losses to sellers, then it would work. But you'd have to direct that spending somehow, perhaps through a voucher good only for B&J's ice cream (the horror).

Question 6:   Pushing the ice cream market to its optimal level would increase the amount of profitability from non-extractive uses. You can't find it in your picture; the benefits ice cream buyers receive from saving the forests is clouded by the consumption benefits of the ice cream. You'd need to see the returns to the input markets that happen in order to see the impact on the rain forest situation.

Answers to Multiple Choice Questions

1.	D.	6.	A.	11.	C.	16.	C.
2.	C.	7.	D.	12.	A.	17.	B.
3.	B.	8.	A.	13.	A.	18.	D.
4.	C.	9.	A.	14.	C.	19.	A.
5.	B.	10.	B.	15.	A.	20.	D.

Answers to Problems

1. Assign the rights and the optimal result happens. Here, penalizing noise-makers makes them reduce their noise-making activity. This is an assignment of rights to the peace-and-quiet lovers. An opposite assignment would force those bearing the costs to pay the noise-makers to stop. Earplugs might be cheaper.

2. It is efficient if it is least cost to get to the same end. Equity, or fairness, is in the eye of the beholder. Sometimes, you might wish rude people would just blow up but, since it might be us one day, few would go for it. So we penalize them, instead.

3. Unions simply extract the subsidy. If the "show can't go on" without them, and the union knows that the value of what they do is going up, then there will be no increase in performances and the rents will simply accrue to the fixed factor. In this case, union musicians.

4. A public good is non-rival in consumption and usually non-excludable. But many publicly-provided goods do not meet these criteria. Freeways are not always non-rival and they surely are excludable. Toll roads do exist.

5. Just do the extra benefits and extra costs of stopping some bad thing, since this is what must be under discussion. The only way the result is zero is if extra costs don't increase, or extra benefits increase. Neither of these seem particularly likely.

6. The tragedy of the commons is driven by the idea that each individual captures the private benefit fully but only bears part of the cost. All acting together bring ruin, even in the library. This is even worse if someone else cleans up after them.